FORENSIC ACCOUNTING

FORENSIC ACCOUNTING
HOW TO INVESTIGATE
FINANCIAL FRAUD

William T. Thornhill

IRWIN
Professional Publishing
Burr Ridge, Illinois
New York, New York

Senior sponsoring editor:	Amy Hollands Gaber
Project editor:	Jean Lou Hess
Production manager:	Laurie Kersch
Designer:	Mercedes Santos
Art studio:	TCSystems, Inc.
Compositor:	TCSystems, Inc.
Typeface:	10/12 Times Roman
Printer:	Quebecor Book Group

Library of Congress Cataloging-in-Publication Data

Thornhill, William T.
   Forensic accounting : how to investigate financial fraud / William T. Thornhill.
     p.   cm.
   Includes index.
   ISBN 1-55623-733-2
   1. Forensic accounting—United States. 2. Evidence, Expert—United States. I. Title.
KF8968.15.T48 1995
363.2'5963—dc20   94–25000

Printed in the United States of America
1 2 3 4 5 6 7 8 9 0 Q–K 1 0 9 8 7 6 5 4

PREFACE

Forensic and investigative accounting is a relatively new discipline. Its roots, however, are based on principles, practices, and approaches that have been in place for some time. As an evolving new discipline, there is still flexibility as to the final make-up of the principles, practices, and approaches that will ultimately define the profession. Further, there is still flexibility as to the application of the various principles, practices, and approaches that will ultimately define the profession. This is a challenge to the imagination and creativity of the forensic accounting practitioner. The profession is still seeking out its final breadth and depth of utility to management, in government, industry, and commerce; to law-enforcement authorities; and to the legal profession, including the courts. On the basis of the past, it can be projected that the profession, over time, will probably be used wherever it has the potential of making a meaningful contribution, relative to any specific scenario.

Some purists will, no doubt, contend that the scope of involvement of practitioners of the profession should be limited only to fraud matters (e.g., possible, probable, or known fraud scenarios). Why? Because those are the areas where the profession began to evolve. I disagree! Why? Because that perspective, in my opinion, is too narrow a utilization of a profession that has more to offer.

In my perspective, fraud is the "cornerstone" of the profession but, in the final analysis, it is "alpha" (the beginning) and not "omega" (the end). We are still attempting to determine to what limits the forensic accountant can be utilized, relative to any "risk scenario." Therefore, "omega" has yet to be defined. Consider that once the profession expanded its activities to deal with possible, not only known, fraud, it established the precedence that the forensic accountant can be involved in a variety of scenarios where the perceived risks warrant further review by qualified personnel. Those reviews, when completed, may not have resulted in the discovery of an actual fraud. Such efforts, however, should, at a minimum, identify and evaluate the "three musketeers of fraud exposure": risks, threats, and vulnerabilities, in the subject environment. I refer to these three as the "risk scenario." In using them, the forensic accountant would examine and evaluate whatever factors should be so analyzed to draw the appropriate conclusions. This book is designed for three distinct audiences:

1. Those of you who are forensic accountants. The objective is to indicate how the discipline has evolved to this point in time and to identify how the profession can be expected to expand, as to value-worth relative to a variety of differing scenarios.
2. Those of you are considering the possibility of attempting to become qualified to practice as a forensic accountant. The objective is to indicate what is expected of the practitioners of the profession. It focuses on the need for both (i) extensive training in the field of accounting and (ii) broad experience in either or both the fields of accounting and auditing. It emphasizes the need for
   a. Broad understanding of all management disciplines. This includes knowledge of accounting, administration, finance, internal controls, operations, organization, personnel management, planning (strategic and budgeting), risk management (insurance), security, and systems—computer and noncomputer.
   b. Strong interpersonal skills, which will be used in interviewing (data development) and, if appropriate, interrogation (accusatory) efforts.
   c. Ability to work with professionals in other disciplines, as part of a review team, on fraud-related or other scenarios.
   d. Highly developed analytical skills, so information developed during the reviews can be put into proper perspective, enabling the drawing of sound conclusions based on those findings.
3. Members of management, law-enforcement authorities, and the legal profession, including the courts (judges), so they can determine how they might effectively utilize the services of the forensic accountant, relative to any specific scenario in which they are involved.

In summary, the objective of the book is to show how the discipline of forensic accounting has evolved, over recent decades, to become an important tool for management and the legal profession. The focus, overall, is to indicate where the profession is today and how its importance can be projected to grow in the future.

William T. Thornhill

June 1994

CONTENTS

PART 1

PERSPECTIVE OF FORENSIC ACCOUNTING

CHAPTER 1

OVERVIEW OF ACCOUNTING—FORENSIC AND GENERAL

Facts mean nothing unless they are rightly understood, rightly related and rightly interpreted

R. L. Long

INTRODUCTION

The discipline of **forensic accounting** is relatively new. It has come into its own in this century, with its primary growth in the last two to three decades. Why is it needed now? Primarily because of the proliferation of regulatory and criminal statutes and laws to deal with real problems in government, business, and society. Since these regulations and laws are on the books, it is necessary to ascertain the level of compliance or identify situations of partial compliance or noncompliance. Some of the regulatory statutes that must be reviewed for compliance are (dates shown for oldest only)

1. The Sherman Antitrust Act (1890).
2. The Internal Revenue Act (1913).
3. Securities Act (1933).
4. Securities & Exchange Act (1934).
   a. The Trust Indenture Act.
   b. The Investment Company Act.
   c. The Investment Advisors Act.
   d. Public Utility Holding Company Act.
5. Federal Trade Commission Act.
6. The Robinson-Patman Amendment.
7. The Clayton Act.
8. The Davis-Bacon Federal Contracts Act.
9. Labor-Management Reporting and Disclosure Act.
10. The Welfare-Pension Fund Act.
11. Employee Retirement Income Security Act (ERISA).
12. Tax Equity and Fiscal Responsibility Act (TEFRA).

Some of the criminal statutes are (Title 18, U.S. Code, unless otherwise indicated)

1. Mail Fraud.
2. Wire Fraud.
3. Interstate Transportation of Stolen Property.
4. Racketeer Influenced and Corrupt Organizations (RICO).
5. Conspiracy.
6. Aiding/Abetting.
7. Obstruction of Justice/Perjury.
8. Tax Evasion, False Returns, and Failure to File.
9. Federal Corruption Statutes.
10. Money Laundering Act of 1986.
11. Fraud in Connection with Federal Interest Computers.
12. The Electronic Funds Transfer Act.
13. Computer Security Act of 1987 (Public Law 100-235).
14. False Claims Act (Title 31, Money and Finance, Sections 3721 to end).
15. Anti-Kickback Act (Title 41, Public Contracts, Sections 51 through 58).
16. Bank Secrecy Act of 1970.

Where the initial forensic accounting reviews, relative to determining levels of compliance or noncompliance regarding either regulatory or criminal statutes, identify less than full compliance, then the original planned review scope would have to be broadened in an effort to determine the full range of noncompliance. Such expansion of scope would, as deemed appropriate, involve

1. Organizational appraisals.
2. Review of lines of authority and responsibility, relative to any activity/function/product/service/facility/entity.
3. Competency of personnel in sensitive positions (e.g., specific jobs and/or managerial/supervisory responsibilities).
4. Procedural adequacy and compliance.
5. Internal control evaluations and tests to confirm compliance.
6. Interviews (data gathering) and, if applicable, interrogations (accusatory).

When performing such reviews, either to prove level of compliance or to determine level and areas of noncompliance, it is necessary for the forensic accountant to always keep in mind that the evidence developed must be oriented for a court of law, regardless of whether the court will be criminal or civil. The orientation of evidence for a court of law forces the forensic accountant to continually strive to maintain the highest quality of work possible, by recognizing that their findings will be subject to public scrutiny should the matter at issue go to trial. Such potential public scrutiny of their efforts is one of the factors making forensic accounting unique. It is a discipline on which others rely because of the high visibility of the efforts undertaken.

While the indicated areas represent the genesis of forensic accounting, the need for the discipline is not limited to compliance with new governmental regulations. The potential values in the private sector are described later in this chapter in the section on "Perspective of 'Forensic Accounting.'"

In this book, the terms *forensic accountant* and *forensic auditor* will mean the same. This is also true of forensic accounting and forensic auditing.

A PERSPECTIVE OF "FORENSIC"

When you see or hear the word *forensic*, do you immediately think of forensic medicine? This is logical, because it is a discipline that has been used for some time. *Forensic medicine* is defined as

> The application of medical knowledge to questions of civil and criminal law, esp. in court proceedings.[1]

> A science that deals with the relation and application of medical facts to legal problems.[2]

The word *forensic*, by itself, is defined in part as

> 1. pertaining to, connected with, or used in courts of law or public discussion and debate.[3]

You may remember Quincy on television. He was a medical examiner involved with the science of forensic medicine. He used his medical knowledge to seek out answers to the questions of civil or criminal law on cases on which he worked as a medical examiner. The medical facts he developed were important to the legal problems in those cases.

The forensic accountant, in his new discipline, applies the art of forensic accounting. To most people, forensic indicates a criminal reference. This is probably due to the fact that the press tends to report criminal cases more than civil matters. In fact, as indicated by the definition, the reference to courts of law means both civil and criminal matters.

A PERSPECTIVE OF "ACCOUNTING"

Accounting and accountancy are often synonymous terms. The latter term is used less frequently, but it can be viewed as possibly referring to the entire body of theory and practice, while *accounting* is usually perceived as an all-inclusive term. As far back as 1941, the AICPA committee on terminology proposed that accounting be defined as "the art of recording, classifying, and summarizing in a significant manner and in terms of money, transactions and events which are, in part at least, of a financial character, and interpreting the results thereof." This definition has withstood the test of time. It is still applicable.

For some years, there has been an ongoing discussion as to whether accounting is an art or a science. In fact, it has aspects of both. In *The Basic Postulates of Accounting* (1962),[4] Maurice Moonitz indicated that the function of accounting is to measure the resources of entities, reflect claims against them, and measure changes in both, all with reference to periods (and points) of time and all expressed in terms of money. But accounting has a number of other functions besides providing the components of financial statements. Among these are the contributions it has made to the development of practical ideas of shared management, such as better operating-policy formation and the improvement of controls at top levels of management; clearer delegations of management authority; operable budgets, from inception to their administration and enforcement at all management levels; cost consciousness at all levels of management; and establishment of improved conduits for intraorganizational information. Some contend that, without the techniques supplied by accounting in the orderly direction and coordination of the complex and intricate affairs of today's commercial enterprises and governmental activities, successful administration in those areas would not be possible.

An AICPA study group on "Objectives of Financial Statements" determined that

> To serve users' needs, the accounting process should consist of an interrelated and compatible system of objectives, standards or principles, and practices or procedures. Objectives should identify the goals and purposes of accounting. Standards should follow logically from objectives, and should provide guidelines for the formulation of accounting practices compatible with the desirable goals. All three levels of the system should be linked rationally to the needs of users.

The Financial Accounting Services Board (FASB) has adopted the preceding AICPA definition for its conceptual framework (see Exhibit 1–1).

EXHIBIT 1–1
The FASB Conceptual Framework for Financial Accounting and Reporting

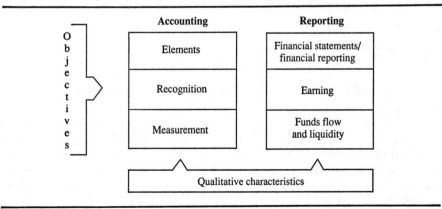

1. *Objectives:* They will underlie the other phases of the conceptual framework.
2. *Qualitative characteristics:* They are the criteria that will be used in selecting and evaluating accounting and reporting policies.
3. *Elements:* The eight elements of financial statements are assets, liabilities, owner's equity, revenues, expenses, gains, losses, and comprehensive income.
4. *Recognition and measurement:* An item, to be formally incorporated in a set of financial statements, must not only qualify as one of the eight elements (refer to 3) but must also meet criteria for recognition and have a relevant attribute that is capable of providing reliable measurement or estimate.
5. *Reporting or display:* The display of information provided by financial reports depends on elements (refer to 3) and recognition and measurement (refer to 4) and is closely related to other aspects on display (e.g., displays of comprehensive income and its components and displays showing funds flows, as well as liquidity information). The focus is on what information should be provided; who should provide it; and both how and where should it be displayed.

To date, Statements of Financial Accounting Concepts issued include

- Objectives of Financial Reporting by Business Enterprises (No. 1).
- Qualitative Characteristics of Accounting Information (No. 2).
- Elements of Financial Statements of Business Enterprises (No. 3).
- Objectives of Financial Reporting by Nonbusiness Organizations (No. 4).
- Recognition and Measurement in Financial Statements of Business Enterprises (No. 5).
- Elements of Financial Statements (No. 6).

Elements of Accounting

The American Accounting Association (AAA) committee describes the elements as[5]

1. *Accounting activities:* "These represent selected points in the flow of socioeconomic activities such as transactions and other identifiable points in the flow of activity accounted for."
2. *Accounting entities:* "This includes any organizational unit such as business enterprises, governmental units, nations, or individuals."
3. *Accounting methods:* "This includes such techniques as the computer, statistical analysis, and a variety of other measurement and communication methods."

Categories of Accounting

Financial Accounting

Financial accounting is essentially the area of general purpose external financial reporting by business enterprises. It is the primary area of concern of the FASB and is the area of accounting where most of the research and other efforts relative to the development of accounting theory have been focused.

Management Accounting

Management accounting is concerned with satisfying the needs of internal management for planning and control. Often, the same accounting system provides the basis for financial accounting and management accounting, even though the information needs of management are normally more extensive and detailed (e.g., by department, division, group, cost-center, facility, and so on). Cost accounting and cost analysis are two disciplines of management accounting.

Social Accounting

Social accounting has been defined as

> . . . the modification and application, by accountants, of the skills, techniques, and discipline of convention . . . accounting, to the analysis and solution of problems of a social nature. This concept views social accounting as essentially an extension of the principles, practices, and particularly the skills, of conventional accounting and accountants.[6]

Until recently, economists did most of the useful work in social accounting. Since the social audit has become more fashionable, accountants, who work more effectively with the auditors, have been more involved in the administration of the social accounting problems.

Tax Accounting

This discipline is concerned with

1. Setting up and maintaining the books of account where the tax approaches differ from the general books approaches (e.g., double-declining depreciation for tax purposes and straight-line depreciation for general book purposes).
2. Preparation of the various returns and reports required for compliance with tax laws and regulations, with emphasis on the federal income tax code.
3. Effective administration in the planning and control of taxes.

Other classifications of accounting that are commonly used are business accounting, nonbusiness accounting, national income accounting, specialized industry or entity accounting, and international accounting. For our purposes, we will focus only on the four primary classifications as indicated.

PERSPECTIVE OF "FORENSIC ACCOUNTING"

We have considered the basics of *forensic* and *accounting*. Now, let us consider the discipline of *forensic accounting*. A real constraint as to how rapidly this discipline will grow is the reality that there are few public accountants, internal auditors, or accountants in the private sector who have been trained in or are experienced in the discipline of forensic accounting. At the present time, the largest body of trained and experienced forensic accountants come from U.S. governmental audit and investigatory agencies, such as the Internal Revenue Service (IRS); Federal Bureau of Investigation (FBI); General Accounting Office (GAO), the audit arm of the U.S. Congress; Securities and Exchange Commission (SEC), and the U.S. Department of Defense (DOD). It is interesting to note that police authorities at the state and local levels (e.g., county, city, township) have very few such resources available to them. As a consequence, they do not perform the level of investigation on white-collar crimes that the indicated U.S. government agencies would do. Why? They recognize that commercial crime, or such type, has little so-called jury appeal, generally not creating the positive image they want for the law enforcement or governmental management authorities. They get more such visibility and publicity from "street crimes" (e.g., armed robbery, burglary, and so on).

Some contend that this attitude toward white-collar crimes is really due to their lack of knowledge, skills, and training relative to investigating such matters. Further, local prosecuting authorities and judges are quite often unfamiliar with accounting principles and audit techniques. With the publicity of white-collar crimes, particularly those involving commercial banks, savings and loans, and stock market failures and manipulations, it is hoped that, over time, the local law-enforcement prosecuting authorities will deem it in the best interest of the public they serve to react more forceably to white-collar crime. Should this occur, they will need to draw on outside forensic accountants' expertise to help them in developing their cases.

The same is true of management in the private sector. They can utilize the forensic accountant not only for fraud, but also as a management tool to

1. Review data accumulated for budgetary and strategic planning purposes.
2. Evaluate data relative to a possible acquisition or merger.
3. Evaluate data relative to actual performance.
4. Evaluate data on a product or service, relative to continuing to offer same or introducing same.

An interesting aspect of forensic accounting is that it is almost always reactive. In the preceding scenarios it can also be used in a proactive mode (e.g., budget or strategic plan development, product or service evaluation—introduction) or active mode (e.g., product or service evaluation—continuation or not, evaluation of data relative to possible acquisition or merger).

The reactive nature of the discipline is indicated by the normal areas of review work:

1. Complaints that arise relative to criminal matters.

2. Claims arising from civil litigation.
3. Inquiries relative to corporate or governmental investigations.

The investigative findings of the forensic accountant will potentially have an impact on the people and organizational entity—business or government—involved with the subject situation, possibly with respect to freedom, or loss of same, or financial gain or loss. The forensic accountant, in performing a review, will draw on various resources available to develop, interpret, and present this evidence in a logical and appropriate manner. If used properly, forensic accounting can assist involved parties to move quickly to resolve a complaint, claim, inquiry, or disagreeement. At a minimum, it can develop a foundation of financial fact(s), reducing problems and misunderstanding in the accounting or finance areas.

Forensic and Investigative Accounting Defined

The discipline is so relatively new that, up to now, there has been no formal definition accepted as the standard. The best definition that I have seen is

> Forensic and investigative accounting is the application of financial skills and an investigative mentality to unresolved issues, conducted within the context of the rules of evidence. As a discipline, it encompasses financial expertise, fraud knowledge, and a strong knowledge and understanding of business reality and the working of the legal system. Its development has been primarily achieved through on-the-job training, as well as experience with investigating officers and legal counsel.[7]

NOTES

1. *The Random House College Dictionary,* rev. ed. (New York: Random House, 1975), p. 517.

2. Webster's Ninth New Collegiate Dictionary (Springfield, MA: Merriam-Webster, 1986), p. 483.

3. *Random House College Dictionary,* p. 517.

4. Lee J. Seidler and D. R. Carmichael, eds., *Accountants' Handbook,* 6th ed., Vol. 1 (New York: The Ronald Press Company, 1981) p. 1–5. Reprinted by permission of John Wiley & Sons, Inc.

5. Ibid., p. 1–6.

6. Ibid., p. 1–8.

7. G. Jack Bologna, Robert J. Linquist, and Joseph T. Wells, *The Accountant's Handbook of Fraud & Commercial Crime* (New York: John Wiley & Sons, Inc., 1993), p. 232.

CHAPTER 2

SERVICES THAT CAN BE PROVIDED BY FORENSIC ACCOUNTANTS

Only those who have the patience to do simple things perfectly will acquire the skills to do difficult things easily

Johann Schiller

PRESENT

The variety of forensic accounting assignments is varied. Their work is increasingly relied on because of the professionalism, independence, and objectivity of the practitioners. Let us consider the three primary areas of their current activities.

Management Support

The forensic accountant can be of assistance to management by performing reviews relative to a possible or actual fraud. This can be done with the forensic accountant either

1. Working alone, or with other qualified accounting personnel, who may or may not also be forensic accountants. The assignments would normally be accounting only or accounting, administrative, or operational fraud matters.
2. Working with qualified personnel from other disciplines on possible or actual fraud situations that are not exclusively accounting related. The other disciplines will vary according to the nature of assignment. The review team may include other accounting personnel who may or may not be qualified as forensic accountants.

Where multiple disciplines are involved in a specific fraud review, the forensic accountant will often head up such "team" undertaking. Why? Because accounting is the primary managerial information function within an organization that interfaces with every other function. This interface experience enables the forensic accountant to both effectively coordinate the various disciplines and communicate with all team members. In some situations, the forensic accountant will not be designated the "team leader" of the fraud review team because of the specific focus of its efforts.

The evidence developed from such individual or "team" effort should be in form and substance acceptable for use by an attorney for a criminal or civil court action that results from the fraud review findings. The forensic accountant should have a broad understanding of the federal evidence and related state guidelines. That knowledge, with appropriate guidance from the attorney(s) with whom he or she is working, will maximize the probability of it being acceptable to the court(s).

Litigation Support

The forensic accountant can provide similar review expertise and, if appropriate, fraud review "team" direction to all members of the legal profession. In a criminal or civil legal action, they can work for the prosecution, defense, and even the court (e.g., the judge, who is an attorney, may have little or no knowledge of the accounting aspects of a case he or she is hearing). When working for the prosecution, the efforts of the forensic accountant will normally be to prove fraudulent activities relative to accounting transactions or records. To develop the desired information, the scope of such reviews will often extend into matters of

1. Organization, including job descriptions, with focus on assignments of authority and responsibilities.
2. Administration, including credit, collection, customer services, and records retention.
3. Operations.
4. Policies, practices, procedures, and standards.
5. Systems, both EDP and non-EDP.
6. Laws and regulations to determine compliance or noncompliance.
7. Adequacy or inadequacy of internal controls with respect to each of the indicated review environments.

The work of the forensic accountant has been used in a variety of situations. It has even been used in homicide cases.[1] Illogical? No! The forensic accountant could, through diligent effort, possibly identify a motive for a homicide through examination of accounting records to determine if they had been manipulated to try and hide fraudulent activity.

Forensic accounting services can also be used with equal value and effectiveness on behalf of the defense. In most such situations, the objective will be for the forensic accountant to disprove or neutralize a scenario presented or expected to be presented by the prosecution. The defense may have the forensic accountant develop an opposing scenario to that of the prosecution, to raise "reasonable doubt" in the eyes of the court. Obviously, such scenarios are always based on facts developed during a proper forensic accounting examination.

Expert Witness

As a general statement, witnesses are restricted from testifying in the form of opinions, conclusions, and characterizations. They can testify only as to the six senses (see, hear, feel, smell, taste, or touch) and what they know as fact. The exceptions to this rule are generally in reference to their perception (e.g., estimating a person's age, height, or weight; estimating speed of a moving vehicle; and so on). But qualified experts, in a given profession or discipline, may give their professional opinions in any area or discipline in which they have appropriate expertise. It is relatively routine for forensic accountants to be called upon to testify in criminal and civil prosecutions. They may be an expert for either the prosecution or defense.

The scope of such testimony can be broad. Usually, they will testify relative to reviews in which they were involved. Their testimony can cover such matters as accounting, administration, or operational fraud; theft of assets; misapplication of funds; arson for profit or other insurance scams; false claims; acceptance of kickbacks; bankruptcy fraud; tax evasion; and other identified situations of fraudulent activity.

Qualifying forensic accountants as technical experts generally is not a difficult task. When being qualified by a court, they can anticipate questions relative to their professional credentials (i.e., education; licensing or certifications; technical training taken; technical books, monographs, and articles written; teaching assignments they have undertaken to professionals in their field; awards and other recognition they have received).

The reliance on forensic accountants is increasing in each of the indicated areas. Why? Because the practicing professionals have established their value in a variety of scenarios. They have earned their reputations by practicing the Jack Webb syndrome, he of *Dragnet* fame. This is simply to "get the facts" relative to any scenario in which they are functioning as forensic accountants. In this time of reduced ethics and increased white-collar, management, and corporate fraud, as well as criminal activities of outsiders, the efforts of forensic accountants are increasingly needed. Users of their services recognize the importance of reliable facts and evidence being developed without prejudice in any scenario (e.g., possible or actual fraud, gross negligence, or mismanagement).

We will review on an expanded basis each of the three areas briefly covered in this segment of the text.

FUTURE

Obviously, because of the growing awareness of the profession, the forensic accountant will be increasingly called upon to provide management and litigation support and to function as an expert witness. These assignments will involve possible or actual fraud, negligence, gross negligence, or mismanagement. The latter two are akin to fraud in that someone was paid to do something and failed to perform properly or fulfill some responsibility assigned to them. Is this the full extent of the utility of the forensic accountant as a profession? I do not think so! While I do not have a crystal ball, it would seem that the time is ripe for forensic accountants to expand their horizons. To put that into perspective, who would have thought a decade or so ago that the forensic accountant would ever be involved in murder cases? While it seems so logical now for them to seek out financial motive for a crime, it did not seem so a decade or so ago.

The strong points of the forensic accountant are that

1. They have the education and training to enable them to effectively perform reviews in a variety of differing scenarios.
2. They are skilled at searching out facts relative to any given scenario, in their area(s) of expertise.
3. They can work alone or with other forensic accountants, as well as with practitioners of other disciplines, as part of a team of investigators in a variety of differing scenarios.
4. They are experienced at working for management, providing management support services, and they are experienced in working with attorneys, providing litigation support and functioning as expert witnesses.

Let us consider some possible areas where the forensic accountant's skills can be utilized to develop facts.

Bankruptcy Accounting

Based on information from the administrative office of the U.S. courts, the number of business bankruptcies has increased from 5,300 cases in the 1940s to 64,500 cases in the 1980s. The business bankruptcies in the 1980s roughly tripled from the average of the 1970s. They are expected to increase, possible double, in the 1990s over the 1980s.

> Since the early 1980s, the number of accountants specializing in the bankruptcy accounting field has increased significantly, and the accountant's role has changed dramatically. Organizations, such as the Association of Insolvency Accountants (AIA) have been formed to serve the needs of these accounting practitioners. In fact, the AIA has created a separate professional certification—the Certified Insolvency and Reorganization Accountant.

> Accountants working in the bankruptcy field are retained to provide advice to debtors, lenders, creditors, and other parties-in-interest in bankruptcy proceedings. Anyone interested in this area of practice must expand his or her role beyond the traditional accounting and auditing services, which focus on analyses of historical results and the related books and records.

> In a bankruptcy proceeding, services may include reconstructing the debtor's accounting records, reviewing cash balances, analyzing related party transactions, and identifying potential preferential transfers or fraudulent conveyances.[2]

The bankruptcy accountant, who could be a Certified Insolvency and Reorganization Accountant (CIRA) or Certified Management Accountant (CMA), may provide financial advisory services (e.g., assessment of the debtor's viability) and specialized bankruptcy advice (e.g., strategies to be used prior to and during the bankruptcy filing).

Why can't the forensic accountant perform such work if he or she has had proper training and/or experience in bankruptcy matters? Forensic accountants have already expanded their skills beyond traditional accounting and auditing services to be involved in the work they now perform. Therefore, it would seem relatively simple for them to have a foundation in bankruptcy matters, qualifying them to perform such reviews. Would they have any advantage over other accountants performing bankruptcy review work? I think so? Why? Because they are more conscious and aware of how wrongdoers can "cook the books" as well as manipulate the records of a company, which, in full or in part, could provide needed information relative to the cause-and-effect of any identified fraud, gross negligence, or mismanagement.

By adding bankruptcy skills, if they do not already possess them, to their other skills, the forensic accountant would appear to be a natural to either work as a subordinate to a CIRA and/or CMA who is managing the bankruptcy review team, using his or her special skills to seek out fraud, gross negligence, or mismanagement, or function as the sole or lead accountant of a bankruptcy review team. The other disciplines that may initially be involved in such reviews could include appraisers of real estate and equipment, engineers, computer analysts, and human resources experts.

The experience in working with management should make it easier for forensic accountants to find their way around any company in bankruptcy by effectively evaluating practices, procedures, records, and all internal control systems. Their experience in working with attorneys should make it easy for them to develop evidence acceptable to a court, that should show what actually occurred at the subject firm, relative to fraud, negligence, gross negligence, and mismanagement.

Internal Control Evaluation

First, with the Foreign Corrupt Practices Act (FCPA), and then with the Treadway Commission, the importance of internal control built into procedures, practices, and standards has finally been properly recognized. As a result of those broadened requirements, the public accountants, regulatory examiners, and internal auditors now devote more time to reviewing and evaluating internal control systems and the internal check requirements built into them. However, the question must remain as to whether those reviews are enough. Remember the old saying about "who audits the auditors?" In my opinion, the forensic accountant is in a position to perform supplemental reviews of the internal control systems with several objectives:

1. How good in theory are the systems of internal control as established in procedures and standards?

2. Are the personnel working in any activity or function properly trained relative to the internal control requirements, including the specific objectives of such systems relative to their work environment?
3. Are the personnel working in any activity or function properly fulfilling their specific internal control requirements?
4. Do the systems of internal control in fact, not theory, hold the perceived risks in any work environment to the levels considered acceptable to management?
5. Are the levels of acceptable risk in line with reasonable objectives or are they found, on the basis of risk assessment, to be excessively loose in any specific work environment? If so, determine what internal control enhancements are necessary to bring risks down to acceptable levels in those work environments.
6. Are the controls in place excessive and, therefore, too costly relative to the risks, as determined from the reviews in any work environment? If so, determine what revisions to the internal control systems are warranted to reduce those costs and bring them in line with an appropriate level of risk control.

Such review evaluates not only the systems of internal control but also the effectiveness of the periodic reviews performed by the external auditors, regulatory examiners, and internal auditors. Based on my observations and evaluations of such reviews, it is my opinion that they focus too much on the theoretical systems and not enough on the true effectiveness of the systems, particularly internal check requirements, or how well the personnel having primary responsibility for both performing the internal control systems steps, including internal checks, and supervising those with such responsibilities know what their efforts are intended to accomplish. To understand the *total* internal control objectives, in any procedure or standard, it is necessary for the reviewer to put specific responsibilities into proper perspective, relative to the total procedure. Since "internal check is a deterrent to fraud,"[3] it should logically follow that the forensic accountant perform the reviews described in the preceding text. The forensic accountant providing management support of this nature should provide them with a degree of understanding as to either how well or how poorly business risks are being controlled in any organization on a day-to-day basis.

Potentially, the profession of forensic accounting will evolve to the point that it can be utilized by management, law-enforcement authorities, and the legal profession, including the courts, as an important tool. How broad will its utilization be? I cannot answer that question but envision it as being able to deal with any "risk" scenario. While it starts with a foundation of accounting, that is "alpha" (the beginning), not "omega" (the end). Within the next decade, the profession of forensic accounting should evolve to the point where its potential utility is far better defined than at present.

NOTES

1. The services of Lindquest & Holmes (now Lindquest Avey MacDonald and Baskerville, Chartered Accountants) were utilized by Canadian law-enforcement authorities in several homicide cases. Two such cases were *Regina v. Serplus* and *Regina v. Kelley*. See Jack Bologna and Paul Shaw, *Forensic Accounting Handbook* (Madison, WI: Asset Protection Publishing, 1993), p. 1.

2. Frank Zolfo, Stephen F. Cooper, and Paul Dzera, "The Management Accountant as Bankruptcy Specialist," *Management Accounting*, June 1993, p. 48.

3. Eric L. Kohler, *A Dictionary for Accountants*, 4th ed. (Englwood Cliffs, NJ: Prentice Hall, 1970), p. 240.

CHAPTER 3

SKILLS REQUIRED OF THE FORENSIC ACCOUNTANT

Men must be honest with themselves before they can be honest with others. A man who is not honest with himself presents a hopeless case.

William J. H. Boetcker

WHO NEEDS FORENSIC ACCOUNTING?

It would be easy to respond to the above question by stating that potentially every governmental or business organization can utilize the discipline of forensic accounting. However, the question warrants a more focused answer. Some of the areas where the discipline has proven its value are government, corporate investigations, criminal matters, litigation support, insurance claims, and government entitlement programs.

Government

The forensic accountant can assist with regulatory compliance at all levels, not just the federal level, by assuring that government units, businesses and, in some instances, individuals are complying with applicable legislation. The same type of reviews would be applicable to grants and subsidy investigations, public inquiries relative to governmental assistance, and entitlement programs.

Corporate Investigations

The forensic accountant can assist executive management with concerns that arise in connection with possible internal or external wrongdoing with respect to any transactions, dealings, or records of the corporation. The board of directors may utilize the discipline when fines could be levied against the firm by government organizations for violation of laws and regulations or when determining if there is possible managerial wrongdoing relative to stockholder class-action lawsuits or general lawsuits where negligence, gross negligence, mismanagement, or duplicity with others (e.g., price-fixing) is indicated.

Executive management may utilize the skills of a forensic accountant for follow-up on such matters as "fraud hot-line" tips and leads, anonymous letters or telephone calls from outsiders, indicating possible wrongdoing by insiders, alone or in collusion with outsiders (e.g., duplicate payments for refund misappropriation, kickbacks, and so on); regulatory compliance (e.g., violations of social audit requirements, environmental violations, and so on); falsified accounting entries and/or records; evidence of false claims being honored, with kickbacks to approving persons; abnormal inventory shortages; questions as to integrity of accounting records and transactions; or purchasing fraud.

The forensic accountant can provide assistance as well as independence and objectivity in meeting with those persons, internally or externally, who are involved with or affected by inference, allegations, rumors, or inquiries relative to such matters.

Criminal Matters

The forensic accountant can assist the law-enforcement, prosecuting, and, in some instances, even the judicial authorities (e.g., charges of wrongdoing by other jurists or lawyers operating in their courts) with respect to civil and/or criminal wrongdoing, in particular as the courts give increasing, and appropriate, attention to white-collar criminal matters, whether they be individuals or businesses involved. This could include the full range of white-collar crime (e.g., arson for profit, violations of trust, kickbacks, theft, and other types of fraud). (Note: For a broad list of types of fraud, it is suggested that the reader obtain for his or her library the *Fraud Terminology Reference Guide,* published by the Association of Certified Fraud Examiners in Austin, Texas.) The utilization of the forensic accountant in criminal matters can be expected to grow rapidly in the coming years, especially in two separate and important ways:

1. They perform the reviews in any given situation, providing litigation support as a forensic accountant, and then testify as to their findings as an expert witness.
2. They provide litigation support as forensic accountants when they review and evaluate the work done by others, whether related to auditing, evaluations, or any aspect of forensic accounting, and then testify, as an expert witness, as to the acceptability or unacceptability of same, both as to the work done and conclusions reached in any given situation.

Litigation Support

The forensic accountant can provide litigation support in the form of assistance to counsel in any investigation, as well as in assessing the integrity of issues relating to areas involving possible or actual fraud.

Insurance Claims

The forensic accountant can be involved in both the preparation and assessment of insurance claims on behalf of the insured or insurers. The forensic accountant can assess the integrity and completeness of the information provided for any claim. Such efforts could involve either medical insurance or other insurance.

Medical Insurance

Forensic accountants can evaluate correctness of billing procedures by service providers and then determine by consultation with qualified medical personnel whether any questionable services are identified or if the amounts billed appear to be out of line. Forensic accountants can determine if co-insurance features, if applicable, are applied properly if shared-insurance risk with other carriers is properly prorated.

Insurance Other than Medical

Forensic accountants can calculate claimed loss relative to various types of insurance loss (e.g., business interruption, fidelity bond, personal injury, arson, robbery, and so on). Some of these cases may require financial analysis and projections. This can require a beginning point of historical analysis relative to the subject matter under review.

Government Entitlement Programs

The forensic accountant should be actively involved in reviewing any government program where material aggregate dollars are involved. Such reviews can involve examining overall program controls or verifying the legitimacy of individual claims and claimants. The risks to be dealt with cover the possibility of false claims. These may be fraudulently initiated solely by the beneficiary of the claim or may involve collusive action between the claimant and an internal person(s) of the administrative and paying governmental unit. Such false claims and kickbacks are a reality in many such programs.

The preceding text indicated just some instances where forensic accountants can be used. In point-of-fact, they can be utilized where there is a potential or real financial loss or risk of loss. The forensic accountant, in such circumstances, is a potential problem solver!

WHAT A FORENSIC ACCOUNTANT SHOULD KNOW

Obviously, a broad knowledge of the principles, practices, and standards of the accounting profession is required of the forensic accountant. In this regard, the forensic accountant should have accredited schooling in the field (e.g., university level), a solid base of experience (e.g., management or general accounting, public accountant, internal auditor, cost accountant, or tax accountant), with continuing professional education (on-going training) to keep abreast of the principles, practices, and standards of the profession. The forensic accountant should also have knowledge of problems encountered in mismanagement and/or fraudulent manipulations of accounting transactions, records, and reports.

It should be recognized just how important audit skills are as a foundation of review activities for a forensic accountant. Document management, as for workpapers on an audit, is an important aspect of a properly managed review of a forensic accountant. The combination of both accounting and audit skills gives the forensic accountant the ability to determine desired review scope and approaches, to accomplish desired objectives, and then to perform those reviews utilizing those skills effectively to make a final determination as to whether things are correct and controlled properly or whether problems exist and, if so, how to identify the full extent of the problems.

Other desired skills and attributes of a forensic accountant fall into the following categories: fraud knowledge, knowledge of law, rules of evidence, investigative competency, interpersonal skills, understanding of psychological theories, other important theories relative to criminal behavior, communications skills, information technology skills, PIO formula, utilization of other expert skills, and rights of persons under review.

Fraud Knowledge

Next to accounting and audit skills and experience, this is probably the most important aspect of the required skills of the forensic accountant. The broader the exposure to and knowledge of fraud, particularly in the subject industry (e.g., retailing), program (e.g., medical claims), or function (e.g., purchasing), the more competent the approach to a potential or known problem. This broad general knowledge base will enable the forensic accountant to better identify "red flags" and effectively piece together historical problems, patterns, and theories to determine "risks," "threats," and "vulnerabilities" and to put them into proper perspective.

It is important to recognize, relative to the preceding, that the forensic accountant analyzes data. The analytical process is not an easy one. It requires knowledge, skill, and experience. The objectives of such analysis are to prioritize actual problems or potential "risks," as appropriate to the situation, and define the focus of the investigation. This includes redefining the focus when the facts developed indicate that it is warranted. To identify the need for course change and to make such change promptly and effectively has proven very important when providing assistance to the courts.

The importance of experience for the forensic accountant cannot be overly emphasized. That experience is invaluable for financial analysis; evaluation of procedures, practices, and controls; determination of "risks"; adequacy of documentation supporting transactions (Note: This includes partial paper–partial computer paperless systems or total paperless computer systems, but in both instances with the ability to capture in the computer records documents relative to a transaction and to retrieve any of the documents from the computer); and the ability to assess the overall or specific situation properly.

The more fraud situations in which the forensic accountant has been involved, the broader his knowledge base. Knowledge of various types of fraud provides the forensic accountant with the experience to develop a more effective plan of investigation. Side benefits of such planning will better identify

1. Where to review procedures, practices, records, and controls.
2. When to cut off specific reviews.
3. When to expand and/or broaden the scope of specific reviews.
4. Who to interview and at what point in the overall review.
5. How to communicate findings to client and/or court.

Knowledge of Law

The forensic accountant should have a reasonable knowledge base in both civil and criminal law. Why? For the simple reason that many of these laws will have an impact on the work to be done by the forensic accountant. The forensic accountant should have a broad understanding of both criminal and other statutes. Only by such understanding will forensic accountants know when any aspect of the statutes has been contravened so they can identify possible issues for investigation.

To provide appropriate accounting support to the courts in any matter involving fraud, the forensic accountant must be able to comprehend the concerns of the court as to the issues on which a judge in the courts of law has deemed an act to be fraudulent or potentially fraudulent. This requires a knowledge base of the courts' tests for fraud (e.g., dishonest intent or state of mind of the fraud perpetrator).

Rules of Evidence

It is very important for the forensic accountant to have a broad knowledge base of the rules of evidence. Such knowledge is essential to ensure that all reported review findings will be admissible in court when such acceptance is important to any specific case situation. Following are some definitions of evidence and rules of evidence.

1. Evidence is defined as

    Any species of proof, or probative matter, legally presented at the trial of an issue, by the act of the parties and through the medium of witnesses, records, documents, exhibits, concrete objectives, etc. for the purpose of inducing belief in the minds of the court or jury as to their contention.[1]

2. Rules of Evidence are defined as

    Rules of court which govern the admissibility of evidence at trials and hearings; e.g., Federal Rules of Evidence (applicable in U.S. district courts and federal bankruptcy courts); Uniform Rules of Evidence; Maine Rules of Evidence; California Evidence Code.[2]

3. Federal Rules of Evidence are defined as

> Rules which govern the admissibility of evidence at trials in the Federal District Courts and before U.S. Magistrates. Many states have adopted Evidence Rules patterned on these federal rules.[3]

All of the following criteria are important for the forensic accountant:

- What evidence is?
- How evidence is obtained?
- Importance of original documents as evidence.
- How evidence is preserved?
- How evidence is to be presented to the courts?
- How the work of the forensic accountant(s) can become part of the evidence package presented to the court(s)?

As mentioned previously, the forensic accountant must be knowledgeable as to the various court tests of fraud. This would include, but is not limited to, the dishonest intent or state of mind of the fraud perpetrator.

Investigative Competency

Most fraud situations are well hidden under a veneer of apparent compliance with procedures and adherence to controls. The forensic accountant, however, must be fully aware that procedures can be breached and controls are vulnerable to human ingenuity. Therefore, the forensic accountant must be able to review each scenario with a level of investigative curiosity that, if a wrongdoing has occurred, may disclose indicators of fraud. This investigative curiosity must be applied with due diligence to select the "red flag" indicators of possible or actual fraud and interface them in such a way as to put potential fraud risk into perspective. Using that foundation, the forensic accountant must exercise maximum investigative competency with the tenacity of a security investigator or detective. "These attributes could be termed investigative mentality. This mentality encourages the forensic accountant to seek substance over form—to identify and analyze data and to conduct interviews in order to determine what has actually occurred in a business transaction, rather than what simply appears to have occurred."[4]

While it is important to keep the big picture in focus, the investigative mentality required of the forensic accountant necessitates that sufficient procedures and related controls be reviewed and transactions tested to enable determination of whether the conditions found warrant expanding the initial tests. The expanded tests can be supplemented, as deemed appropriate, either in a single or in multiple stages of review efforts and as broadly and for whatever time period the forensic accountant determines appropriate to any scenario. The review effort should not be concluded while any real concern exists as to the possibility of fraud. Each phase of the testing must be interfaced with all preceding review phases so that the forensic accountant can view the totality of the review efforts to determine whether each area, or even item, reviewed is or is not relevant to the subject risk scenario under review and, further, whether or not the review efforts relative to any phase of that scenario should be aborted or expanded into a full fraud review.

Remember that regular auditors have the objective of providing reasonable assurance that, based on their limited reviews, things are, in fact, as they are supposed to be. Questionable conditions are found when conducting reviews with the indicated objective. Any such situations may or may not be acted upon properly (e.g., followed up to determine if the condition identified is unique or to determine the standard for how a transaction is processed or a procedure is implemented). Remember that the regular auditor is usually under severe time pressures to complete a specific review. Accordingly, unless a questionable situation is so obviously an attempt to deceive, by breaching a fundamental monetary control procedure or practice, it may merely be documented in the workpapers for the review then being performed. Restated, it is simply one exception found in the total test performed. This is partly due to the fact that regular auditors only discover 25 percent of frauds, as indicated below.

Distribution of Fraud Discovery, Based on Available Statistics

1. Identified by auditors	25% (+ or − 4%)
2. Determined from identified breakdowns in policies, procedures, practices, and the internal control requirements relative thereto	25 (+ or − 2%)
3. Tips, leads, and accidental discovery	50 (+ or − 6%)

The disciplined approach of the forensic accountant is designed to maximize fraud discovery. The primary objective is to identify whether or not fraud exists and, if so, who is involved. As a result, the success rate of the forensic accountant in discovering fraud is substantially higher than that of any other discipline.

Interpersonal Skills

In addition to their investigative competency, the forensic accountant must have sound interpersonal skills. Such skills may be utilized at any or all of the following three levels:

1. *General:* Creating a friendly and cooperative attitude among those with whom contact is made during any part of the investigation. This is true whether the contact is with a clerk, getting a document out of file or returning it to file, or a manager you are meeting for the first time and

to whom you will explain the extent of work to be performed in his or her area of responsibility.

2. *Interviewing:* Communicating to the interviewee that the meeting is a "data-gathering exercise" and establishing a rapport so that maximum results will be accomplished in the minimum time.

3. *Interrogation:* It should be noted that many attorneys prefer to use the term *accusatory interview* rather than interrogation. Many police, security, and other law-enforcement types, however, use the term *interrogation,* as do most accountants and auditors. It is an accusatory undertaking and, accordingly, the stress level in the person being interrogated should be increased to the desired level from the beginning.

It is unacceptable for the forensic accountant not to be appropriately skilled at all three levels of interpersonal skills. At the general level, all that is required is civility. At the other two levels, however, the forensic accountant must be alert to all the responses given by the subject: that is, vocal, both what is said and how it is said; eyes; and body language. The importance of each is summarized below.

Information Source	Interview	Interrogation
1. Vocal response	60%	40%
2. Eyes	20	30
3. Body language	20	30

During these undertakings, the breakdown of who does the speaking is as follows:

	Interview*	Interrogation†
Interviewer/interrogator:		
Beginning	15%	70–85%
End	25	25–35
Interviewee/interrogated person:		
Beginning	85%	15–30%
End	75	65–75

* Start in general questioning mode. More focused questions at end.

† Start is accusatory, wanting closed answers from person being interrogated. At end, objective is to obtain confession from guilty party or revert to general questioning, as in interview, if subject is no longer considered guilty.

While these are fundamentals, they are important errors that often occur in the interview and interrogation mode. The forensic accountant should always be aware of these human frailities:

1. Not waiting for a complete response from the interviewee before asking the next question.

2. Permitting the interviewee to ramble without really responding to the specific question given him or her.

3. Unfocused questioning; that is, the interviewer/interrogator is jumping back and forth between topics without getting any substantive answers and failing to pursue any point in depth.
4. Ineffective listening, resulting in "red flags" and "clues," worthy of follow-up, not being picked up by the interviewer/interrogator.
5. Failing to give eyes and body language their proper importance when monitoring responses from the person being interviewed or interrogated.

Remember that Vince Lombardi is supposed to have said that "you win games on fundamentals." The forensic accountant will be more effective if the indicated fundamentals are always kept in mind.

Understanding of Psychological Theories

The forensic accountant must have a broad knowledge of why people act as they do with respect to wrongdoing. An understanding of psychological theories is important to having such understanding. It is a general premise of many psychologists that early personality development and personality are the greatest single influence of criminality. Based on studies, it is thought that criminals have an unbalanced id. The id, which is considered to be present at birth, is defined as "the one of the three divisions of the psyche in psychoanalytic theory that is completely unconscious and is the source of psychic energy derived from instinctual needs and drives."[5] The other two divisions of the psyche are ego and superego.

Two mental conditions are thought to be associated with antisocial activity, including crime: neurosis and psychosis, which are defined as

1. *Neurosis:* "A mental and emotional disorder that affects only part of the personality, is accompanied by a less distorted perception of reality than in a psychosis, does not result in disturbance of the use of language, and is accompanied by various physical, physiological, and mental disturbances (as visceral symptoms, anxieties, or phobias)."[6]
2. *Psychosis:* "Fundamental mental derangement (as paranoia) characterized by defective or lost contact with reality."[7]

Other Important Theories Relative to Criminal Behavior

Social Learning Theories
Some theorists have concluded that people are not actually born with violent or criminal traits but, in fact, learn these behaviors through life experiences. They believe the following factors are important with respect to violence and aggression:

1. An event that heightens arousal. Examples would be physical or verbal abuse.
2. Aggressive skills that are learned from other people showing similar traits or from the media.

3. The belief that aggression will be rewarded through either financial gain or increased respect from peers, or both.
4. The belief that aggression is justifiable.

Social Process Theories

Under such theories, criminality is viewed as a function of individual experience with other people or organizations. They hold that people from all social levels have the potential to be criminals. Ultimately, their fate may be determined by their past social learning experiences. The important factors, under these theories, are peers, family, educational institutions, and the criminal justice system. My personal experience would add the civil justice system as well. A person feeling he, his family, or his friends have been wronged by the civil justice system may turn against the entire legal system. The primary social process theories are discussed below.

Differential Association.   This theory begins by asserting that criminal behavior is learned in interaction with other persons in a process of communication. It is also learned through participation in intimate personal groups (e.g., gangs). This process includes learning techniques of committing crimes as well as related motives, rationalizations, and attitudes. Under "differential association," it is believed that a person becomes a criminal because of an excess of definitions favorable to violation of the law over those definitions unfavorable to violation of the law. It is deemed that criminal and delinquent behavior involves all the mechanisms that are considered to be applicable to any other learning. Finally, both criminal and noncriminal behaviors are expressions of general needs and values. Criminals and noncriminals react differently to fundamentally the same needs and values.

The theory of "differential association" first appeared in 1939 in the third edition of Edwin H. Sutherland's *Principles of Criminology*. The preceding paragraph summarizes his ten principles of "differential association." Mr. Sutherland is also the man who coined the term "white-collar crime" and first wrote on the subject.

Control Theory.   This theory emphasizes that the social system strives to bring all into a pattern of conformity. It indicates that the less a person becomes attached to the control agencies of society, the greater are his or her chances of violating the law.

Four aspects of affiliation are addressed by the theory:

1. *Attachment:* Refers primarily to an individual's attachment with persons such as parents, teachers, and peers.
2. *Commitment:* Refers to cost factors involved in criminal activity. What would be lost by any individual if he or she were found to be involved in criminal activity? How do the losses compare to the benefits, if any?
3. *Involvement:* Refers to participation in activities that are related to future goals and objectives.

4. *Belief:* Refers to confidence in conventional values. This would include things such as the criminal justice system.

The more an individual is concerned about the negative reaction of others should they be involved in a wrongdoing, the more of a deterrent that is against that person being involved in any criminal act.

Some Other Theories of Importance.   The forensic accountant should have some understanding of the following social process theories in connection with why some people are involved in criminal activities: labeling theory; shaming; conditioning theory; differential reinforcement; operant-utilitarianism; and techniques of neutralization. This listing is not all-inclusive but indicates some of the most commonly used or considered theories relative to evaluating causes for criminal behavior.

The objective is not for the forensic accountant to become a social scientist but to have the ability to communicate with them and understand their position relative to the action(s) of any person or group of persons with respect to some criminal wrongdoing.

Communications Skills

Forensic accountants, as part of their regular activities, will serve as expert witnesses in courts to both present and explain their findings and, as appropriate, conclusions. The forensic accountant must be able to clearly and effectively communicate that information. It is essential that no bias, in any degree or form, be indicated either in the spoken word, workpapers, or report of the forensic accountant. It is important that forensic accountants effectively communicate to all others with whom they have dealings on the subject under review the extent of the work undertaken and the findings resulting from those efforts. This is true both in a court of law and in other venues. Forensic accountants, when testifying as an expert witness, must be able to explain the accounting schedules, charts, and exhibits developed during the review efforts and, from them, be able to effectively explain their procedures, analyses, and review findings in such a way that the basis for their expert testimony is understood. This deals with both facts and, if necessary, opinion they render. It is essential that the forensic accountant have broad knowledge of the evidence developed and the primary implications thereof, as well as alternate explanations of the events and facts. This will ensure they, the facts, and the testimony given are not compromised during cross-examination.

Information Technology Skills

In today's environment, the forensic accountant must have a sound foundation in computers and all other information technology. While it is not necessary that they qualify as experts in these environments, they cannot function properly if they must seek guidance and instruction in the simple fundamentals of such equipment and technology. Below are some of the technology skills required in any ongoing fraud, mismanagement, or negligence investigation by the forensic accountant, where part or all of the accounting data and/or documents are processed through or recorded on, or reports are prepared by, computer or other technology systems:

1. A thorough awareness of the accounting system, as operated through the computer system.
2. A detailed knowledge of the documents maintained in the computer system, in general format or specific copy (e.g., image systems technology).
3. An understanding of how systems interface, one with another, and the plus factors (e.g., values and benefits) and minus factors (e.g., risks, threats, and vulnerabilities). An example of this would be an E-mail system that can be used to enter the computer system and then get into the PBX, enabling unauthorized telephone calls to be made and billed to the telephone line(s) used.
4. The use of systems for wire/money transfer transactions (e.g., SWIFT, CHIPS, etc.)
5. The interface of firm (or governmental unit) systems with general use systems (e.g., those involving people, firms, or governmental units outside the firm) and the purpose for such connection. This would include systems such as INTERNET.
6. The determination of whether data encryption is used, and, if so, for what purpose, and the level of control over that information.
7. The determination of languages used for general and restricted, or special, purposes. Ascertain what such purposes are and the level of control over the subject information.
8. A knowledge of computer graphics.
9. Use of the computer to develop appropriate analysis and to prepare graphs and charts that depict and summarize the information developed.
10. Determination of historical problems with computers and related technology within the firm. Have identified fraud situations been reported to law-enforcement authorities (e.g., any of the computer fraud laws relative to government interest computers) or fraud and/or regulatory authorities? The latter is required by laws (e.g., FDIC, comptroller of the currency for bank fraud, money laundering, wire fraud, and so on).

(Note: The FBI has indicated that, in their opinion, as little as 1 percent of actual computer/technology fraud is discovered. Other sources put that number somewhat higher, but no one thinks it is over 15 percent. There is general agreement that no more than 20 percent of discovered computer/technology fraud is ever reported outside the subject firm or organization. This is low and, in my opinion, unsatisfactory. Such reporting will probably not improve except under penalty of law. While teaching a computer fraud course in Europe, a senior official of an international law-enforcement agency indicated that, in their jurisdiction, no more than 4 percent of discovered computer fraud is being reported to them, based on information from their network of informants).

The preceding list could be substantially expanded, but it makes the intended point that the forensic accountant must have reasonable competency in the computer and other information technology areas even if only to communicate with and understand experts in the area(s) working with him or her in any ongoing investigation.

PIO Formula

All professional accountants are aware of the need for

- *P:* Professionalism
- *I:* Independence
- *O:* Objectivity

These are equally important to the forensic accountant, who has been engaged to provide the skills and input of an expert witness. Bias in any way, for or against an issue or individual, can jeopardize the value of the work performed or conclusions reached by the forensic accountant.

Utilization of Other Expert Skills

A critical part of the work of a forensic accountant with primary responsibility in any ongoing review is to know when to bring in other expert skills and how to use such person(s) effectively. It is essential to integrate the efforts of all team participants effectively and to control what information of the team efforts is communicated to other participants, and when such information is only given out on a need-to-know basis.

Rights of Persons under Review

The forensic accountant must be aware of the ethical and legal manner in which information must be gathered. In this regard, the subject's constitutional rights, particularly under the Fourth, Fifth, and Fourteenth Ammendments, must be honored. If appropriate, subjects should be "mirandized," such as just before an interrogation when the information that it is thought will be developed may be used in court against them. Relative to all of these matters, the forensic accountant should seek out the advice of the lead attorney with whom he or she is working on a particular matter. Why? There will be differences in approaches from attorney to attorney. For example, the forensic accountant may be told that it is not necessary to "mirandize" before an interrogation. In a similar situation, another attorney may feel that such action is necessary. Don't guess! Ask!

The forensic accountant cannot misrepresent himself or herself when gathering information. The forensic accountant cannot abuse the rights of others when collecting information. The rights of an individual must never be abused by the forensic accountant. The ethics of the forensic accountant must never be compromised. Any negative fact would have a negative impact on the work he or she has done on any matter before a court or where legal action is pending.

Summary

Some of the things a forensic accountant should know, as discussed previously, in addition to their accounting and auditing skills, are fraud knowledge, knowledge of law, rules of evidence, investigative competency, interpersonal skills, understanding of psychological theories, other important theories relative to criminal behavior, communications skills, information technology skills, PIO formula, utilization of other expert skills, and rights of persons under review. This listing is not all-inclusive but clearly indicates how broad the knowledge base of forensic accountants must be so they can fulfill their duties properly.

Perspective

Forensic accountants must have a broad range of skills, extending well beyond the limits of an accountant in a normal environment. They must be able to comprehend the "total picture" of any matter on which they are working. They must be able to determine initial scope and approaches. They must be prepared to change them when data developed so dictate. They must be prepared to use others, with different skills, to supplement their efforts. They must use computers and technology to maximize the productivity of their efforts. They must know how to document findings and communicate facts and conclusions, both verbally and in writing.

NOTES

1. *Taylor v. Howard*, 111 R.I. 527, 304 A.2d 891, 893.

2. *Black's Law Dictionary*, 6th ed. (St. Paul, MN: West Publishing, 1990), p. 1333.

3. Ibid., p. 613.

4. G. Jack Bologna, Robert J. Linquist, and Joseph T. Wells, *The Accountant's Handbook of Fraud & Commercial Crime* (New York: John Wiley & Sons, 1993), pp. 236–37. Copyright © 1993 by John Wiley & Sons. Reprinted by permission of John Wiley & Sons, Inc.

5. *Webster's Ninth New Collegiate Dictionary* (Springfield, MA: Merriam-Webster, 1986), p. 596.

6. Ibid., p. 795.

7. Ibid., p. 951.

CHAPTER 4

FOUR PHASES OF A FORENSIC ACCOUNTING REVIEW

Accuracy is the twin brother of honesty; inaccuracy is a near kin to falsehood.

Tryon Edwards

INTRODUCTION

Forensic accounting is also called fraud auditing or investigative accounting. By any name, it is a discipline that goes far beyond the realm of corporate and management fraud or the traditional business risks of theft, filing of false claims, or kickbacks. The discipline goes beyond the traditional definition limitations of white-collar crime. Its range of use has extended as far as involvement in homicide investigations in Canada (e.g., Lindquest & Holmes, now Lindquest Avey MacDonald and Baskerville, Chartered Accountants, in such cases as *Regina* v. *Serplus* and *Regina* v. *Kelley*). In those cases, the forensic accountant was asked to

1. Perform analysis in an effort to determine whether there was a possible financial motive for murder.
2. Perform analysis of financial data for clues as to possible financial wrongdoing. Once determined, the scope of the reviews would be expanded to identify who may have been involved in that wrongdoing, if not identified in the initial review effort.
3. Attempt to identify possible payments of money in connection with a contract for murder.

In these and other unique assignments, only accountants and auditors who can operate comfortably in such an environment should take on such responsibilities.

It should be noted that not all accountants and auditors are comfortable even in a standard business fraud detection role. Often, that attitude is a cover up for a lack of experience in such a role or, on occasion, a lack of confidence when working on such examinations. The forensic accountant must have confidence in his or her ability to work in such an environment. Such confidence must extend to every phase of such assignment, whether it is an assignment on which he or she is working, or whether he or she is in charge, either coordinating the activities of his or her own staff through the phases of the examination on which the firm is working or coordinating the activities of his or her own staff and all other consultants working in areas for which they have specific expertise, to assure that the total objectives of the review plan are completed properly. The other consultants may be industrial psychologists, computer experts, technology systems experts (e.g., image systems technology, PBX and/or E-mail systems, and so on), security specialists, organizational specialists, noncomputer or computer procedural specialists, information security officers, risk management specialists, and so on.

The key is that the forensic accountant does not have to be an expert in every area, activity, or function involved in a forensic examination. Through their knowledge of accounting, administration, operations, procedures, systems, security, and so on, as well as the maturity and experience to effectively identify the various expert skills required on the review team and coordinate the activities of all team members in any examination, they are the logical person to be in charge of such a team undertaking. Obviously, where no other skills are required, they merely have to direct their immediate subordinates. Their objective, in either situation, is to assure that the review plan objectives are fully accomplished by the examination efforts performed.

To accomplish the objectives of the preceding paragraph, the forensic accountant must have a broad knowledge base in the various aspects of the discipline, as described in Chapter 3. Obviously, they should be expert in accounting and finance from a management, accountant, and auditor perspective. In addition, they also need broad knowledge of a variety of basic business disciplines, including but not limited to the following:

1. Administration.
2. Budgeting and strategic planning.
3. Credit and collection.
4. Customer service.
5. Human resources (personnel) management, including job descriptions and employee benefit plan administration.
6. Management approaches, disciplines, and techniques.
7. Policies, practices, and procedures that achieve the best possible balance between efficiency, effectiveness, and economy, and internal control and check requirements.
8. Operations.
9. Organization.
10. Purchasing, including receiving and materials management.
11. Risk management (insurance).
12. Security.

The benefit of the forensic accountant having a broad understanding of the fundamentals in each of these areas is that it makes them the logical choice to head up and coordinate a team planning the reviews and then assure that all aspects of the review effort are completed as intended.

Management, assuming that its internal auditing function has progressed into operational auditing, receive a false level of "comfort and confidence" when reading the reports on the audits performed. The scope, methodology, and techniques followed in performing such audits are not sufficently deep or broad for management to be so deceived.

This is, however, not the end but only the beginning. The Institute of Internal Auditors, Inc. (IIA), has now encouraged the operational auditor to progress to two levels of internal auditing even more meaningful and valuable to management:

1. *Management auditing:* This is sometimes referred to as the second or upper level of operational auditing. It makes the internal auditing function truly a management function, working in areas of planning and evaluation not dealt with in either financial or operational auditing (e.g., budgeting, strategic planning, merger and acquisition reviews, business continuation evaluations, and so on).

2. *Internal consulting:* In this mode, internal auditors devote only about half of their effort to actual audit work in the mode practiced (e.g., operational or management auditing). The other half is devoted to "special" reviews and analysis of the type previously performed by outside experts. They draw on their knowledge of the organization to perform such reviews since they know more about the business and its strengths and weaknesses than does an outsider.

In 1959, the Institute of Internal Auditors, Inc., adopted the concept of "operational auditing" as its standard. At the time of its adoption, the profession was fundamentally conducting audits in a financial auditing mode, similar to that of the public accountants. The best definition I have seen to date for *operational auditing* is

> Operational auditing is using common sense, or logical audit techniques, with management perspective, and applying them to company objectives, operations, controls, communications and information systems. The auditor is more concerned with the who, what, when, where, why and how of running an efficient and profitable business than just the accounting and financial aspects of the business functions.[1]

To function effectively as an "operational auditor," they should have competency in each of the 12 areas listed earlier. Their reviews should be concerned with efficiency, effectiveness, and economy in systems and procedures as well as the soundness of the internal control and check requirements. Unfortunately, it has been my experience, when performing quality assurance reviews of internal audit functions, that the claim of being "operational auditors" may be a misrepresentation. Some performing the reviews are still fundamentally "financial auditors." The fact that they have added nominal operational auditing scope, methodology, and techniques does not make them operational auditors.

It is essential that forensic accountants always present themselves exactly as they are—nothing more, nothing less. The foundation in basic business knowledge, as indicated, is essential, in addition to the expected accounting and finance skills. Forensic accountants, by having this level of knowledge, must be willing to expand into new and untested waters, as least as far as their experience is concerned. It is not suitable for forensic accountants to always play it safe and stay only within their known areas of expertise. They must be willing to stretch and take on new challenges. Think of how forensic accountants taking on their first examination in a murder case must have felt. This willingness to expand, based on a foundation of knowledge and business competency, is a basic reason why there will be a rapidly increasing demand for the services of forensic accountants in all areas where they can be of service.

Why is this honesty so important? Because, in recent years, it has been my unfortunate experience to encounter practitioners in one profession, internal auditing, who are not always being honest with themselves, their management, or their firms. Let me explain!

The unfortunate thing is that they are not progressing step-by-step into and through operational auditing, into and through management auditing, and, finally, into internal consulting. They are taking shortcuts. Think of these stages of auditing/consulting as steps. From bottom to top they are attest, financial audit, operational audit, management audit, and, finally, internal consulting. Each stage continues to utilize some portion of each lower stage. If internal auditors are not qualified at a given level (e.g., operational auditing), then they cannot properly follow through those approaches and techniques into the higher stages (e.g., management auditing). It is an example of the "Peter Principle." The auditors have passed their level of competency and, therefore, are not adequately skilled and/or experienced to proceed to the next higher stage. Unfortunately, management of most companies cannot evaluate the real strengths and weaknesses of the internal audit function. When they have been misled, they are putting excessive reliance on the report findings and recommendations, which can give them a false level of "comfort and confidence." Why is this important? When functioning in a forensic accounting environment, the audit work, at a minimum, must be at an operational auditing level, because the nature of the work to be performed goes beyond the limits of the purely accounting aspects of business. It must deal with all business risks, necessitating the work be, at a minimum, at the operational auditing level. It is my preference that the forensic accountant/auditor be functioning, at a minimum, at the management accountant and auditing levels. This assures a sound foundation of fundamentals in the subject environment, as well as a management perspective. For the balance of this book, it should be understood that this is the level being assumed for all aspects of the forensic review approaches and efforts described.

My frustration is not limited to internal auditors. Too often, public accountants hold themselves out as having better skills than they actually have regarding operational and management auditing skills. Most are still financial auditors with limited knowledge of operations or skills in effectively evaluating internal controls relative to administration, operations, or organization.

I am pleased that both larger public accounting firms and some internal audit staffs now have specialists in fraud reviews. They may be trained in fraud examination, litigation support, or functioning as an expert witness. Over time, it can be expected that both internal and public accounting practitioners, in the indicated areas, will claim that they are forensic accountants. Are they? Satisfy yourself individually as to their skills, education, experience, and competency in all of the key disciplines before you give them the title forensic accountant. Reserve the title for those with the appropriate credentials. We should not let it be bastardized by unqualified persons assuming such title or the uninformed permitting them to do so.

PHASES OF A FORENSIC ACCOUNTING ASSIGNMENT

A forensic accounting assignment can be broken down into four distinct phases:

1. Problem recognition and review planning. (Note: Most writers combine these two distinct aspects of an assignment. However, I feel that review planning is sufficiently important that it should stand on its own.)
2. Evidence collection.
3. Evidence evaluation.
4. Report findings.

Before going into those four phases, however, we should establish standards for the conduct of a forensic accounting review. We will build these standards from a foundation of those established by the Institute of Internal Auditors, as follows:

Summary of General and Specific Standards for the Professional Practice of Forensic Accounting
100 **Independence: Forensic Acountants Should Be Independent** of the Activities They Review.
    110 **Reporting Responsibility:**
        .01 If internal, the organizational status of the forensic accountant should be sufficiently independent to permit the accomplishment of the review responsibilities, with an alternative line of reporting responsibility to the board of directors if the review is initiated internally or to appropriate law-enforcement and/or regulatory authorities if initiated on the basis of outside direction.
        .02 If independent and engaged by an organization, the reporting responsibility must be to a senior executive, who is assumed to outrank any person perceived as possibly involved in any wrongdoing, with an alternative line of reporting responsibility to the board of directors.
        .03 If independent and engaged by law-enforcement, judicial authorities, or other authorized outsiders, the reporting responsibility must be defined when contracting for the assignment.
    120 **Objectivity:** The forensic accountant must be objective in performing forensic accounting reviews.
200 **Professional Proficiency:**
Forensic accounting examinations should be performed with proficiency and due professional care.
    210 **Staffing:**
    All forensic accounting personnel must have the technical proficiency, education, and experience relative to their role on the review team.

220   Knowledge, Skills, and Disciplines:
The forensic accountant should possess or should obtain (e.g., engaging and utilizing persons with other skills required on the forensic accounting review team) the knowledge, skills, and disciplines needed to carry out his or her review responsibilities.

230   Supervision:
When more than one forensic accountant is engaged on a particular assignment, one should be designated as the "in-charge," who assumes responsibility relative to directing the assignment and assuring all aspects of the review plan are properly completed and documented.

240   Compliance with Standards of Conduct:
Forensic accountants should comply with the highest professional standards of conduct expected of accountants; auditors; the legal profession, including attornies and the judicial; law enforcement, and regulatory authorities.

250   Human Relations:
Forensic accountants must be skilled in interpersonal skills relative to the general business interfaces expected in day-to-day activities, or when interviewing or interrogating (e.g., accusatory interview) people relative to specific matters in connection with the ongoing forensic accounting review.

260   Communications:
Forensic accountants must have excellent skills in communicating review findings (a) orally: to those who engaged their services, or when testifying as to review findings and, as an expert witness, to the conclusions reached based on those findings; and (b) in writing: to those who engaged their services (e.g., "flash" report on a current finding or final report on the complete review findings) or special reporting, summarizing conclusions, as directed by judicial or law-enforcement authorities.

270   Continuing Education:
Forensic accountants should maintain their technical competence through ongoing continuing professional education.

280   Due Professional Care:
Forensic accountants should exercise due professional care in performing forensic accounting reviews.

300   Scope of Work:
The scope of the forensic accounting review should encompass the examination and evaluation of the subject transactions; records, whether manual or computerized; and reports, whether as of a specific date or for a specified period. Such review will cover all management disciplines (e.g., budgeting and strategic planning); policies, practices, and procedures, and the systems of internal control established therein, to evaluate the level of ongoing risks to determine if they have been properly identified and dealt with, relative to effective management of risks; all applicable laws and regulations, as well as any specific activities, functions, transactions, or other specified aspect of the business under review with respect to the goals and objectives of such examination.

Where the work to be performed relates to an individual or group of individuals, the scope of the forensic accounting review should encompass the examination of the subject transactions and records of those persons, relative to the goals and objectives of the examination.

If functioning as the in-charge of a forensic accounting "team" review, then the responsibility as to ultimate "scope of work" must be based on the goals and objectives of the examination.

310   Reliability and Integrity of Information:
The forensic accountant should review the reliability and integrity of accounting, administrative, computer systems, finance, operations, risk management (insurance), and security information and the means to identify, measure, classify, analyze, evaluate, and report on such information.

320   Compliance with Policies, Plans, Procedures, Laws, and Regulations:
Forensic accountants should review the systems established to ensure compliance with those policies, plans, procedures, laws, and regulations that could have a significant impact on operations. They should report on their findings, as to compliance or degree of noncompliance.

330   Safeguarding of Assets:
The forensic accountant should review the means of safeguarding assets and, as appropriate, verify the physical existence of such assets. Protection of those assets through a risk management (insurance) program should be reviewed and evaluated to determine whether the risks retained are deemed to indicate reasonable prudence being exercised relative to the nature and scope of such exposures.

340   Economic and Efficient Use of Resources:
The forensic accountant should appraise the efficiency, effectiveness, and economy with which assets have been and are being employed to determine that reasonable prudence has or has not been exercised by management in that regard.

350   Accomplishment of Established Objectives and Goals for Operations or Programs:
The forensic accountant should review operations or programs to ascertain whether results have been consistent with established objectives and goals (e.g., budgets and strategic planning) and whether the operations or programs are being carried out as planned.

400   Performance of Review Work:
The work involved on a forensic accounting assignment should include (1) a problem recognition (and evaluation), review planning, (2) evidence collection, (3) evidence evaluation, and (4) communication of results.

410   Problem Recognition (and Evaluation):
In this phase, the forensic accountant, assisted by those with other expertise as required, gathers the pertinent facts and circumstances regarding a potential fraud situation. In this phase, as much information about the possible fraud, as possible, is developed without actually undertaking a formal effort to gather evidence. This includes (1) determining how the potential problem was recognized and (2) ascertaining how the matter under review (1) was communicated, as well as where and when the matter of concern was supposed to have taken place. [Note: Forensic accountants do *not* go on exploratory expeditions! There must be some perceived justification for them to become involved on a particular matter.]

420   Review Planning:
Based on the predication under 410, the problem, as it is perceived, must be refined and a review plan developed relative to the data gathering

phase of the undertaking. The plan will identify the goals and objectives of the undertaking. It will include a planned order. It will also indicate the various skills required on the review team and, if possible, name the persons to act in each skill environment. The plan must be flexible, so that rescheduling can readily be accomplished when situations are identified that warrant adding new phases to the review plan or merely reordering the plan, based on review findings.

430   Evidence Collection:
The forensic accountant and other members of the review team will undertake to fulfill the review plan requirements with the objective of developing data relative to the suspected fraud situation. They must focus on evidence relative to the three elements of fraud (e.g., act, concealment, and conversion), reordering the plan to focus on the easiest element based on initial review efforts. In addition, the review team must search for fraud risk environments by utilizing the six basic tools for evaluating internal controls and the six-step approach to control evaluation. [Note: these are described in the next section of the text.] Together, they will help the review team set forth risks in order of their probability and potential materiality monetarily. It is important, in this review phase, to be fully aware of the rights of all individuals who may be contacted by any members of the review team during the ongoing examination.

440   Evidence Evaluation:
The forensic accountant, and other review team members, should be involved in analyzing and interpreting the evidence developed under 430. Identification of any area(s) where additional data are necessary as the foundation on which a conclusion can be drawn requires follow-up on the initial evidence collection efforts under 430.

450   Communication of Results:
The forensic accountant, using the expertise of all other review team members, if and as appropriate, should summarize the evidence evaluations, as under 440, into written report form, stating the facts and conclusions from the reviews. The forensic accountant should be competent to present the report orally.

The Six Basic Tools

The six basic tools for evaluating internal controls, as mentioned in Section 430, are internal accounting control checklists, flowcharting techniques, the walk-through, computer auditing techniques, statistical sampling techniques, and risk exposure worksheets.

Internal Accounting Control Checklists.   To help in evaluating the internal accounting control system, many firms prepare a standardized internal accounting control checklist. Such a form (1) provides a means of ensuring that a comprehensive review of the core set of expected controls for all operating entities is performed, (2) documents review findings, (3) serves as a linkage to the compliance and substantive testing approach to the reviews, and (4) facilitates review of the working papers. It is recommended that the approach be expanded to cover operating controls. The checklists are also useful in evaluating an organization's risk exposure. To assist in evaluating risk, separate the checklists into an overall control environment analysis and a specific control-oriented analysis. The former allows you to evaluate override risk, employees' competency, effectiveness of control policies, and the extent to which nonroutine processing of transactions is documented. Those reviews can be extended where the objective is to evaluate a specific control.

Flowcharting Techniques. Do *not* use the short-form flowcharting techniques developed by Big 6 firms (e.g., transaction flow auditing [TFA], SEADOC, etc.). They do not focus sufficiently on internal check criteria, competency of personnel, and risks when new documents come into transaction stream. The old form step-by-step flowcharting should be done relative to risk or fraud reviews, or both.

The Walk-Through. This approach enables you to see whether transactions are processed as expected as the reviewer accompanies transactions through the system, or walks through the audit trail generated by a set of transactions.

Computer Auditing Techniques. The auditor should use audit software that is directed primarily at testing data. Those tests should be supplemented by systems-testing techniques (e.g., using test decks, tagging and tracing, parallel simulation, and so on). The two approaches can be expected to overlap somewhat in evaluating performance or risks, or both.

Statistical Sampling Techniques. This approach results in the sampling of transactions being made using mathematical theorems of probability to arrive at quanitative measures of the likelihood that the sample results will reflect the larger group's characteristics and the accuracy with which the sample results are measured.

Risk Exposure Worksheets. In either designing controls or evaluating the cost-benefit picture for the adoption of new controls or the elimination of existing controls, as well as assessing the overall risk exposure from existing weaknesses in control, risk exposure worksheets can prove to be a valuable tool.

Quantifying Risk

There are two dimensions of the risk exposure form related to control weaknesses:

1. The expected error or loss from one occurrence.
2. The frequency with which this one occurrence is likely to be observed.

Risk Exposure Worksheet.   To facilitate an analysis of the range of the risk exposure for a particular accounting control, a worksheet is recommended on which all of the possible risks can be summarized. For each risk, the worksheet should show on the horizontal line the frequency of occurrence and, on the vertical line, the magnitude of expected error or loss.

Other Risk-Related Considerations.   The reviewer should document the explicit considerations in deriving the cost and frequency parameters. Also to be considered are those factors that were purposefully excluded from the analysis. In considering problems to benefits, you must be careful to identify what could go wrong and then determine controls that would prevent or detect such situations earlier.

The six-step approach to control evaluation is illustrated by the following:

Step	Procedure
1. Obtain and record an understanding of the internal control system relative to accounting, administration, operations, and data security and integrity.	Conduct site interviews; identify transaction types and supporting data relative to each; and prepare flowcharts.
2. Develop a sound understanding of the system.	Review documentation flow based on walk-through of one transaction of each type and modify flowchart, if necessary.
3. Evaluate the system to determine where it contains any fundamental/inherent control weaknesses.	Complete internal control questionnaire using internal control manual or base it on procedural walk-through.
4. Assess all identified weaknesses to determine whether any of them represent material risk as to amount or frequency of possible occurrence.	Complete a detailed record of control weaknesses identified. Place a "risk" rating on each: 1 = low, 5 = high.
5. Assess controls in place to determine if they are functioning as intended and if they are, in fact, holding specific risks to the desired range-of-risks.	Perform functional tests to evaluate controls using several transactions of each type, to gain a reasonable assurance that procedures are being applied as prescribed. Complete a record of control-operation exceptions.
6. Report to senior management the internal control weaknesses identified and actions needed to reduce related risk.	Draft report on overall and specific activity/function systems reviews.

The Summary of General and Specific Standards for the Professional Practice of Forensic Accounting should be viewed as a first attempt to set such criteria. They are stated in an effort to indicate the high level of professionalism that should be expected of anyone presenting themselves as a forensic accountant. At the present time, there is no professional association for them. Should there be? With the rapid growth in importance of the designation *forensic accountant,* this would seem to be the perfect time for such professional recognition to be given to those professionals. Rather than a new or separate organization, it would seem that the Association of Certified Fraud Examiners (ACFE or "the association") would be the ideal organization to provide those professionals with appropriate recognition. For example, they could add a class of "Certified Forensic Accountant" to their present Certified Fraud Examiner (CFE) recognition. If broader than accounting, to include all forensic skills, then the title would be "Certified Forensic Expert." Either would have special experience requirements over and above the present requirements to qualify as a CFE and, possibly, require passing some form of oral or written examination. If that or something similar is not done, the profession of forensic accountant may suffer, over time, because it is almost inevitable that persons who are not fully qualified will inappropriately present themselves as experts in the field.

Working within the framework of the forensic accounting standards, stated earlier, let us now consider the phases of the forensic accounting assignment.

Phase 1: Problem Recognition and Review Planning

Most writers on the subject treat these two subjects together. However, they are, in my opinion, too important to be combined. Therefore, they are treated as two distinct and separate subjects in the following text.

Problem Recognition

The forensic accountant must answer several questions. First, how was the actual or potential problem identified and communicated? It may have been identified in a number of ways. For example, it may have been discovered by an internal or external audit or, where applicable, by a regulatory examination; or a clerk, supervisor, or manager may question a procedure or internal practice that, on follow-up by persons involved in the line or staff activity or function, is identified as a possible fraudulent situation. In addition, the problem may be identified by a "tip." This is information provided by a person *not* involved in or *not* benefitting from the apparent fraudulent situation. This information can be transmitted through a telephone "hot line"; contact with someone from audit, law, or security, or other staff function; or an intermediary (e.g., an immediate superior, that individual's immediate superior, or a friend in a supervisory or management position). This information also may be provided by a "lead," someone who is involved in a fraudulent activity or who is not actually involved in such activity but who is benefitting from it (e.g., a girlfriend or boyfriend of the person actually participating in the fraud).

Where was the fraud supposed to have taken place? Information can come from any source or informant identified above. That information would be supplemented by "historical" data on fraud situations that had occurred in the area where the current fraud was supposed to have occurred to get an immediate perspective of "historical" weaknesses in that environment. This information can come from audit, law, risk management, security, or senior management.

During what time period was the fraud supposed to have taken place? Again, this information can come from any of the sources of information identified above.

Who are the potential fraud perpetrators? The forensic accountant should learn as much as possible about them. This would include

1. Determining their position(s) on the organization chart.
2. Ascertaining the authority/responsibility assigned to them, based on a review of their job descriptions. Determine their specific duties; to whom they report; who, if anyone, reports to them; with whom they interface in the organization. Identify specific job skills required (e.g., computer programmer, cash management professional, and so on).
3. Reviewing their personnel files to ascertain their education, experience, and the perception of each individual (e.g., good employee, troublesome employee, and so on).
4. If deemed appropriate, having background and/or lifestyle checks performed relative to any individual(s) possibly considered to be involved in the suspected fraud.

In addition, the forensic accountant should review any and all documents that may have identified the possible fraud (e.g., mailed in to the audit department, left on the desk of a manager, and so on) and have background checks performed relative to possible environmental or social audit violations.

After all the preceding work has been performed, all information developed on the possible problems is refined, summarized, and evaluated. Based on this evaluation, a decision will be made whether to proceed or to abort the fraud examination at this point. This is considered "predication." Related definitions are

Predicate: "Something that is affirmed or denied of the subject in a proposition in logic."[2]
Predication: "The logical affirmation or something about another."[3]
Predication has been defined, specifically regarding fraud, as

Predication is the totality of circumstances that would lead a reasonable, professionally trained, and prudent individual to believe a fraud has occurred, is occurring, and/or will occur. Predication is the basis upon which an examination is commenced. Fraud examinations should not be conducted without proper predication.[4]

For example, it is possible that the problem may prove to be nothing more than mistakes or unintentional errors but not a fraud. If it is decided that a fraud examination is not warranted, it may still be considered appropriate to have a special review performed in the area of concern (e.g., organizational deficiency, procedural weaknesses, or internal controls). If the facts indicate that a probable or actual fraud exists, then it is necessary to initiate the review planning for the examination. There must be valid reasons to proceed with a fraud examination because the forensic accountant does *not* engage in fishing expeditions!

If a fraud examination is determined to be warranted, then the following fraud theory approach is applicable: "Each fraud examination begins with the proposition that all cases will end in litigation."[5] The more complex the fraud, the more important this theory is to the fraud auditor.

> The fraud theory begins with the assumption, based on the known facts, or what might have occurred. Then that assumption is tested to determine whether it is provable. The fraud theory approach involves:
>
> • Analyzing available data
> • Creating a hypothesis
> • Testing the hypothesis
> • Refining and amending the hypothesis.[6]

Review Planning

This is not as simple as the planning for a specific audit because this phase is only required when there is valid reason to believe that a fraud exists. Therefore, the review plan must cover all the possible bases, because the "problem recognition" reviews are designed to identify and confirm a problem but not to provide full details as to all aspects of the wrongdoing. The true fraud examination should be approached following the general framework of a management audit, as follows:

Unique Characteristics.

1. *Purpose.* The goals and objectives of the fraud audit must be clearly identified.

2. *Information Base.* The fraud examination is as dependent on factual evidence as is the financial or operational audit. But it must be more focused on weaknesses identified, deficiencies determined, evidence as to wrongdoing, and the range of actions that should be taken based on the information base developed.

3. *Range of Injury.* In a fraud examination, there is a broader range of qualitative evaluation than in either a financial or operational audit. The scope is flexible so that reviews can be expanded or reduced based on review findings from the initial examination plan.

The review work must consider management strengths and weaknesses; organizational integrity and effectiveness; soundness of goals, objectives, and strategies; and the relative strengths and weaknesses in accounting, administration, and operations, as well as the systems of internal control relative to each activity, function, or discipline reviewed.

4. *Frame of Reference.* The fraud examination looks at the past management decisions and actions and evaluates them relative to the impact on each of the activities, functions, or disciplines covered under (3).

Structural Variables.   Although all fraud examinations have a common purpose and employ a similar analytical approach, their structure can vary markedly, depending on how the following key elements are defined.

1. *Role of the Parties.* Each team member on a fraud review team has specific assigned duties and responsibilities. This may involve working alone or actively participating with other team members on any phase of the review.

2. *Scope.* Depending on the goals and objectives of the fraud examination, the audit can be comprehensive (scrutinizing everything) or limited to a particular activity or function (e.g., purchasing, accounts payable, inventory, and so on). All team members should understand the background and events leading up to the fraud examination, as well as one another's particular interests and concerns.

3. *Objectives.* Fraud examination objectives are focused on identifying where the fraud occurred; who was involved; what transactions, records, reports, goods, materials, or other assets are involved; what laws or regulations are being breached (noncompliance); when it started; how it got past the systems of internal control and check; and why the situation wasn't identified earlier.

4. *Depth of Analysis.* The general rule of balancing level of scrutiny between needs and costs is discarded in any fraud examination. In such examinations, "costs" represent past/present/future losses if fraud is not found and stopped and steps are not taken to prevent repetition. Therefore, the depth of analysis should be as extensive as necessary to achieve the goals and objectives of the fraud examination, as described earlier.

Common Pitfalls.   Some common pitfalls relate to communication of costs, lack of agreement about team structure, failure to establish confidentiality provisions, insufficient corroboration of data, and imbalances in the portrayal of analytical results.

1. *Communication of Costs:* There is always a real risk that the fraud examination sponsor, management requesting the examination, may not comprehend how much more effort and cost is involved in a fraud examination as opposed to a standard financial or operational audit.

Some years ago in Chicago, one of the two partners in a successful local firm stole $9 million and left the country. The theft forced the firm into Chapter 11 bankruptcy and eventually into liquidation. When the fraud was first discovered, a reporter asked a partner of a Big 6 CPA firm, "Why don't you auditors find more of these frauds sooner?" The partner responded with an excellent answer:

> Let us assume that my firm contracted to perform an audit of your firm which we anticipated would result in clean certified financial statements being issued for a contract price of "X" dollars. If you asked us to contract to perform a fraud audit at your firm, we would indicate to you a starting price of "20X" dollars, and an all-in price of several times that amount, depending on the findings of that examination.

If there are no surprises as to cost, there is never any pressure for shortcuts or to finish the fraud examination before all the facts on the fraud have been developed.

2. *Lack of Agreement about Team Structure.* Regarding the fraud examination team, it is important that, before the review begin, agreement should be reached as to who is in charge, the role of each team member, and the liaison contact either within the firm or outside the firm, if the examination has been initiated under their direction (e.g., regulatory authorities).

3. *Failure to Establish Confidentiality Provisions.* A fraud examination will inevitably involve extensive interviewing. As a result, it is important that confidentiality be confirmed (also preferably in writing) to encourage personnel with whom the fraud examination team members are dealing to share knowledge and viewpoints that may potentially prove helpful as the review effort continues. Without such a provision, personnel may be reluctant to communicate openly and fact-finding efforts may prove much more difficult than they have to be.

4. *Insufficient Corroboration of Data.* The conclusions of virtually every fraud examination are based on information from a variety of internal and external sources. Such data must be corroborated in a manner deemed appropriate before they are included in any final analysis. Factual errors can seriously undermine the credibility of the analysis, and arguments about accuracy can distract attention from substantive findings.

5. *Imbalances in the Portrayal of Analytical Results.* There is always a danger that too much information will enable those under investigation for a fraudulent activity, or their supporters, to label the examination report as either a "whitewash" or a "witchhunt" in an effort to divert attention from important review findings that are being reported. It is very important that the report be based on the old Jack Webb school of information—just present "the facts": maximize the facts presented and reduce the amount of opinion necessary in a report.

Phase 2: Evidence Collection

The purpose of this phase of the fraud examination is twofold: First, the fraud examiner should ascertain whether the evidence developed during the problem recognition phase is reliable or misleading. If considered misleading, then an evaluation should be made as to whether the examination plan should be completed as established or a reassessment be made relative to continuing the reviews.

Assuming the data are considered reliable, then action should be initiated to cover all aspects of the examination plan and develop the evidence considered appropriate and relevant to that undertaking. It is critical that the evidence as developed is sufficent to prove the conclusions reached; competent and relevant to resolve the fraud situation.

Remember when collecting evidence that an objective is to identify the three elements of fraud: act concealment, and conversion. As the work progresses, focus the effort on the easiest of the three elements, which is the "keystone" on which the subsequent review efforts will be focused. Use of vulnerability charts and internal control critical combination charts can be helpful in determining weaknesses in procedures and practices and areas where reviews should be focused to develop data on identified weaknesses.

These charts isolate fraud opportunities. Document examination is a technique that, if used properly, may uncover efforts by the fraud perpetrator to conceal some wrongdoing. However, it must be remembered that documents can be other than what they appear to be. They can be altered, created, duplicated, forged, or destroyed, lost, or misplaced. Historically, we know that many internal frauds are concealed by manipulating source documents in a variety of ways. It should always be remembered that documents are more meaningful evidence than notes relative to discussions or interviews undertaken in regard to some specific aspect of the review. Remember that original documents are preferred by the court over copies, although some courts accept a certified copy of the original with roughly the same value.

It must be recognized that obtaining evidence and evaluating it (Phase 3) constitute the essence of both auditing and fraud examinations. It is essential to recognize that objectivity is the process of obtaining and evaluating evidence that must be adequately distinguished from the objectivity of the evidence itself. "Objectivity of evidence is one of several factors related to the usefulness of the evidence in achieving the purposes for which it was gathered . . . Objectivity of the process refers to the [fraud examiner's] ability to maintain an impartial attitude in selecting and evaluating evidence." That is, in fact, part of the fraud examiner's independence.

While the fraud examination may include such actions as desk checks, lockers, lunch boxes, and so on, it is important that the fraud examiner never overstep the line that is a violation of a person's rights, specifically, the Fourth Amendment to the U.S. Constitution, which states, "The right of people to be secure in their persons, houses, papers, and effects, against unreasonable searches . . . shall not be violated." If an improper search is conducted, it is probable that the evidence will be declared inadmissible, as it was illegally obtained.

The evidence-gathering exercise should include investigating an individual's background. This would include affirming professional qualifications, education, credit rating, secured debts, and other factors relative to lifestyle. Public domain information should be utilized whenever appropriate, whether on an individual or a business.

External and internal auditors tend to classify evidence into one of the following classifications:

1. Analytical procedures—using comparisons.
2. Confirmation—positive or negative response from an independent third party.
3. Document—supporting the subject transactions or records.
4. Inquiries—supplying written or oral information.
5. Mechanical accuracy—rechecking computations or transfers of information between records or functions.
6. Observation—actually seeing certain things are done (e.g., walking through a system, observing the movement of inventory of materials or supplies from receiving in the materials management warehouse to user function).
7. Physical examination—actual inspection or count.

Fraud examiners tend to use the following additional classifications: people, documents, physical evidence, and personal observations.

Phase 3: Evidence Evaluation

Others contend the most critical phase of a fraud examination is the review planning or evidence collection. In my opinion, though, evidence evaluation is the most critical phase. My reason for feeling this way is that it is the last phase where the review effort can be extended or expanded to develop additional information before having to make a conclusion and including it in the report on the undertaking.

When making an evaluation of any factor or element of the review, the fraud examiner can make a value judgment that there is not enough evidence or information available on which to make a conclusion or recommendation. How can the fraud examiner get out of this dilemma? It is simple! Because the work is not considered complete until the report is issued, it merely requires the fraud examiner to identify what additional reviews or interviews should be performed in any given activity, function, or other environment relative to the examination or request a specific piece of information (e.g., a letter, interoffice memorandum, and so on) that will support a conclusion drawn in the review workpapers. That document(s) may be all that is necessary to enable the reviewer to either agree or disagree with the conclusion drawn in the review workpapers. Since the time dimension on such reviews is normally open-ended, this extra effort to assure all the facts are fully supported is essential.

Phase 4: Report Findings

In the general auditing environment, it has been interesting to note that there are many internal auditors who are extremely competent in planning, managing, collecting evidence, and evaluating evidence. However, relative to writing audit reports, they are

1. Afraid to write a report, being uncomfortable with what should or should not be included. For those items that should be included, they are unsure as to how much detail to provide, so, to protect themselves, they tend to provide too much information for any review finding or conclusion thereon.
2. So unsure of their competency in English, the written word, that they feel they will embarrass themselves if they write the report on any assignment.

Forensic accountants must have confidence in their ability to take any data developed, put them into proper perspective, and report the information so that the reader will accept the facts presented and feel comfortable in their understanding of them. They should also feel competent in the English language so they can clearly, concisely, and effectively communicate the reported facts to the reader and make him or her aware that there are additional details behind each fact reported, should the reader feel the need for more information on any matter included in the report.

With respect to the opinions in the end product report, "sufficient competent evidential matter is to be obtained through inspection, observation, inquiries, and confirmation to afford a reasonable basis for an opinion regarding [the matter(s)] under examination."[8] The philosophy when preparing the report is simply to present the facts in an order that will support the conclusions reached or the inferences stated.

NOTES

1. Dale L. Flesher and Steward Siewert, *Independent Auditor's Guide to Operational Auditing* (New York: John Wiley & Sons, 1982), p. 5. Copyright © 1982. Reprinted by permission of John Wiley & Sons, Inc.

2. *Webster's Ninth New Collegiate Dictionary* (Springfield, MA: Merriam-Webster, 1986), p. 926.

3. Ibid.

4. National Association of Certified Fraud Examiners, Advanced Fraud Symposium—Investigation, April 16, 1992, p. 1.

5. Ibid.

6. Ibid.

7. Jerry D. Sullivan, Richard A. Gnospelius, Philip L. Defliese, and Henry R. Jaenicke, eds., *Montgomery's Auditing*, 10th ed. (New York: Ronald Press, 1986), p. 7. Copyright © 1986 by Ronald Press. Reprinted by permission of John Wiley & Sons, Inc.

8. Ibid., p. 68.

PART 2

PRACTICAL ASPECTS OF FORENSIC ACCOUNTING

CHAPTER 5

"ON-BOOK" ACCOUNTING AND FINANCIAL STATEMENT FRAUD

It is not only what we do, but also what we do not do, for which we are accountable.

Molière

INTRODUCTION

To understand how "on-book" fraud can occur in any aspect of government or business, the forensic accountant must start with a strong foundation, in both theory and practice, in each of the following areas:

1. Accounting Basics.
2. Accounting Systems.
3. Financial Statements.
4. Financial Analysis.

This chapter will provide examples of actual fraud situations to indicate how easily fraud can occur relative to (a) the improper application of accounting basics, (b) poor design and/or implementation of accounting systems, (c) misrepresentations in financial statements, and/or (d) improper or ineffective use of financial analysis. Each fraud case used provides a warning as to how easy it would be for the forensic accountant to miss a specific fraud situation. Now let us briefly consider the four areas mentioned at the beginning of this chapter:

Accounting Basics

This involves the recording and reporting of transactions and would include

1. Occurrence/emergence (e.g., timing, quantification—either in physical units or in money terms).
2. Processing (e.g., procedures/systems design and the internal controls/checks therein).
3. Recordation (e.g., maintenance of general and subsidiary records).

4. Internal reporting (e.g., position statements at a point in time [trial balances], activity reports [for a period of time], and exception reports for irregular situations/conditions).
5. Continuous review and testing of transactions (e.g., internal auditing) or periodic review and testing (e.g., by examiners and public accountants).
6. Summarization of account groups into conventional patterns (e.g., balance sheet—assts, liabilities, and owners' equity; and income statement—income and expense).
7. Periodic reporting to outsiders (e.g., investors, governmental agencies, and the public).
8. Transaction projection (e.g., capital and operational budgeting and strategic planning).
9. Internal or external review of and recommendations on organizational functioning (Note: This is an outgrowth of the increased involvement of accountants with organizational structure and management functioning).

An AICPA committee on terminology proposed that accounting be defined as "the art of recording, classifying, and summarizing in a significant manner and in terms of money, transactions and events which are, in part at least, of a financial character, and interpreting the results thereof." These are the accounting basics!

Accounting Systems

Systems Defined

In its most basic form, a system is a set of elements or components that interact to produce a cohesive unit. In both its physical and abstract forms, a system consists of elements or components, boundaries, environment, and input/outputs.[1]

Manual Accounting System

A manual accounting system requires the handwritten entry of all financial transactions for a business. Source documents are forwarded to the bookkeeper who logs the transactions into the correct ledgers.[2]

Information System Defined

A set of elements working together to produce information. This set of elements may take the form of an informal or a formal system. An informal information system is characteristically a loosely structured arrangement . . . not officially recognized by an organization and their behavior is not predictable . . . A formal information system is a set of elements working together under a well-defined set of operating rules or guidelines to produce information.[3]

Accounting Information Systems

The American Accounting Association, in its statement on *Basic Accounting Theory* (p. 64), defines accounting as

> Essentially, accounting is an information system. More precisely, it is an application of a general theory of information to the problem of efficient economic operation. It also makes up a large part of the general information systems which provide decision-making information expressed in quantitative terms.[4]

Financial Statements

Financial statements are discussed in Chapter 12.

Financial Analysis

Financial analysis is discussed in Chapter 12.

FRAUD RISK SITUATION

The following are actual "on-book" fraud cases. They are intended to identify and review a number of the risks that exist in the transactions, records, and financial reports of any entity. In none of these cases was the computer a primary element or factor in the fraud described. Later in the text, this book will cover "off-book" noncomputer fraud matters and "computer" fraud matters, providing actual fraud cases to support the text and dealing with principles and practices in each of those environments.

Case 1: Excessive Improvement in Current Ratio

Company A, a manufacturer of textiles, was the primary provider (i.e., over 80 percent) of fabric (raw materials) to Company B, a manufacturer of finished men's and boy's clothing (e.g., two- and three-piece suits, trousers, sports jackets, as well as lined and unlined raincoats). Company A financed the raw material inventory of fabric sold to Company B by holding a lien on

1. The entire inventory held by Company B (e.g., raw materials, work-in-process, and finished goods).
2. The machinery and equipment owned by Company B.
3. The finished goods inventory held by Company C, which had been provided to it by Company B. Company C was a wholly owned subsidiary of Company B that operated a chain of retail clothing outlets in several states.
4. The furniture and fixtures owned by Company C.

For this financing, Company A was paid 22 percent of the total retail sales of Company C, with settlement monthly. It was also paid 25 percent of the sales of Company B made to other companies, with settlement monthly. (The sales by Company B to firms other than Company C represented approximately 20 percent of their total sales.)

Once a year, as of the close of business on May 31, using the public accounting certified financial statements, the value of materials on-hand was compared to the debt then open to Company A on raw materials provided by them. If the value of the materials was equal to or in excess of the debt, no inventory adjustment paydown was required. If, however, the debt exceeded the inventory valuation as calculated, a paydown of the debt to that amount was required. Such calculation and paydown, if required, was to be finalized within 30 days following issue of the annual certified financial statements. The calculation was made by the certified public accountants: First, the value of raw materials, work-in-process, and finished goods held by Company B was determined, then the value of finished goods held by Company C that were produced by Company B were determined at 22 percent of their current retail value, as then marked.

The other financing requirements of the agreement with Company A were that Company B and Company C, as consolidated, would

1. Maintain positive working capital.
2. Maintain positive net worth equal to not less than $1.2 million.
3. Hold finished goods at no more than 25 percent of annual sales of Company C for suits, sports jackets, trousers, and rainwear (i.e., four turnovers a year).
4. Not sell any furniture, fixtures, or equipment, as Company A held a contractural lien on them.
5. Provide Company A with annual certified financial statements and semi-annual "break-even" inventory financial statements.

When the most recent year-end certified financial statements came in, a financial analyst at Company A reviewed them and noted a "very favorable" change in working capital.

	May 31st		
	1993	1992	1991
Current assets	$735,000	$693,000	$616,000
Current liabilities	$350,000	$630,000	$560,000
Current ratio	2.1:1	1.1:1	1.1:1
Working capital	$385,000	$ 63,000	$ 56,000

Shouldn't an increase in the current ratio be considered a positive change? Isn't an increase of $322,000 in working capital, a 511 percent change, a good thing? What could be bad about the indicated change in the current year? Some possible scenarios are:

1. Are they leasing fixed assets (e.g., furniture, fixtures, equipment [forklifts, sewing machines], automobiles, and so on) instead of buying them to conserve working capital?
2. Are the accounts receivable overstated?
3. Are the accounts payable understated?
4. Have accounts payable been refinanced, in full or in part, with senior (collateralized) long-term notes? This would have provided cash, increasing current assets. It also would have reduced accounts payable and total current liabilities, as a result of reclassifying the liability to long-term, if it is not due for more than one year. The question is, what assets were pledged to collateralize these notes?
5. Have accounts payable been refinanced, in full or in part, with junior (uncollateralized) long-term notes? This is the same as #4, but there would be no assets pledged to collatalerize the debt. Usually, this type of note would bear a higher interest rate than for debt that is collateralized.
6. Have accounts payable been refinanced, in full or in part, with capital injection by owners (e.g., bonds or preferred stock)? This would have provided cash to enable Company B to reduce accounts payable. Such debt could have been structured to place the investors in such new issue in a preferred position in event of liquidation. This can be manipulative if the original owners sold back some of their common stock to the company and converted the proceeds and additional cash into any debt or equity instruments that would give them a preferred position in liquidation.

Since the analyst seemed satisfied merely to report what he considered a favorable finding on his review of the financial statements of Company B consolidated with Company C, the corporate comptroller of Company A assigned a forensic accountant to follow up on the matter. His assignment was to determine what caused the substantial reduction in the current liabilities in the certified financial statements of Companies B and C.

Review Findings Developed by Forensic Accountant

Follow-up with the public accounting firm that had prepared the annual certified financial statements identified that Company B had issued $400,000 of senior (collateralized) notes. These were three-year notes with interest only due quarterly and the entire principal amount due at the end of the three-year term. To obtain this financing, Company B had hypothecated as collateral all of the furniture and fixtures of Company C, which were located in its retail outlets. As of the audit date, those assets had a net book value of $225,000. The senior notes had a variable interest rate of prime + 5 percent, adjustable quarterly.

All of the money paid-in on the senior notes was new money and Company B had used the note proceeds to pay down accounts payable. That explains the drop in current liabilities and the increase in the current ratio and working capital, when comparing the most recent year-end certified financial statements with those of the preceding two eyars.

The forensic accountant, however, had several concerns. First, the interest rate being paid on the senior note debt seemed too high in light of the fact that it was better than 50 percent collateralized. Follow-up determined that all of the senior notes had been sold to family members and friends of the original investors in Company B. It was determined that the sale had to be to those individuals at the higher rate because no other financing source they approached indicated any interest in investing in the company. Management wanted the new funds so they could improve their working capital position and ease the pressure to maintain that as a positive figure for their ongoing operations.

Why hadn't the public accountants, in the footnotes to their certified financial statements, noted the hypothecation of the fixed assets of Company C as collateral on the senior note debt? Weren't they aware that those assets were pledged to Company A in a covenant in the financing contract between that firm and Company C? The public accountants claimed that they had footnoted the issuance of the senior note debt, which was all they were required to do. They claimed that the hypothecation of the fixed assets for that senior note debt would only be of concern to the going concern prospects of Company B should they fail to pay the interest and principal payments on that debt when due. They indicated they were aware that those same fixed assets were pledged as collateral in the financing agreement with Company A. They had not footnoted that potential lien on the subject fixed assets since it did not affect the going concern prospects of Company B unless and until they failed to comply with any of the covenants protecting the creditor under that financing agreement. They noted no liens had been filed on the subject fixed assets relative to either potential claim.

The forensic accountant disagreed with the position of the public accountants as to the potential claims on the fixed assets of Company C. His position was that the claim on those assets, as stated in a covenant in the financing agreement with Company A, should have been footnoted in the financial statements since that agreement went into effect. His employer firm had been negligent, in his opinion, for not requesting such presentation in the footnotes to the financial statements of Company B. Had that been done previously, the public accountants, in his opinion, would not have permitted those same fixed assets to be hypothecated as collateral for the new senior note debt issuance. Without the collateral provided, would it have been possible for Company B to have sold the senior notes at the interest rate stated thereon? Because of the high risk of the investment, it is thought that even insiders and their friends would have been reluctant to put more money into the business.

It was concluded that, without the investment resulting from the sale of the senior notes, Company B would not have been able to maintain a positive working capital figure at their fiscal year-end. That is based on their having working capital of only $385,000 as of the indicated date, after having added $400,000 into working capital from the sale of the subject senior notes. Therefore, without that transaction having occurred, Company B would have had negative working capital of $15,000 as of their fiscal year-end. That put Company

B in default of the covenants of their financing agreement with Company A as of that date.

Actions Taken on Basis of Forensic Accountant's Findings

Based on the preceding findings, Company A took the following actions. First, Company A called and canceled their inventory credit facility. On the basis of that action, they took possession of all raw material, work-in-process, and finished goods at the manufacturing facility of Company B. They also took possession of all finished goods of the specific types covered in the financing agreement at Company C. This consisted of most of the suits, trousers, jackets, and rainwear at those retail outlets.

Company A went to court quickly and had their first lien on the furniture and fixtures at Company C validated. When that was accomplished, they took possession of all furniture and fixtures of Company C. They also took possession of all furniture, fixtures, and equipment at the manufacturing facilities of Company B.

Company A then sold at an auction within days after taking possession all of the raw materials, work-in-process, and finished goods inventory from both Companies B and C. Unsold lots of finished goods and work-in-process were given to charities who wanted them, for appropriate tax write-off. Company A also sold all of the furniture, fixtures, and equipment, from both Companies B and C by lots to two dealers who dealt in such items. All lots were disposed of in that manner.

Company A achieved 98 percent recovery of the amount of their credit exposure due to these actions, net of legal and other costs relative thereto (e.g., moving and storage). Finally, they negotiated a settlement with the certified public accountants for the 2 percent balance in lieu of suing then for negligence.

The result of the preceding actions was that Company A achieved full recovery against its inventory credit facility exposure. In addition, Company B and its subsidiary Company C were put out of business. The general creditors of those companies received only 10 percent of the amount of their validated claims.

By the due diligence of the comptroller of Company A, who was concerned with the favorable increase in working capital identified by a financial analyst, which resulted in his assigning a qualified forensic accountant to look into the matter, they were able to protect the interests of their company. Where the financial analyst saw good, the comptroller recognized that it was too good a favorable change in working capital and the current ratio. He remembered the definition of fraud from Michigan Law, Chapter 86, Section 1529, which states:

> Fraud is a generic term, and embraces all the multifarious means which human ingenuity can devise, which are resorted to by one individual, to get an advantage over another by false representations. No definite and invariable rule can be laid down as a general proposition in defining fraud as it includes all surprise, trick, cunning, and unfair way by which another is cheated. The only boundaries defining it are those which limit human knavery.

Conclusion

In my opinion, Company B's management, with the help of poorly footnoted certified financial statements, attempted by "cunning" and in an "unfair way" to misrepresent the actual situation to Company A. They were willing to "cheat" Company A through their misrepresentation. The excessively favorable change in working capital and current ratio was considered by the comptroller as a "red flag." Only because of his curiosity and the investigative skills of the forensic accountant did Company A avoid sustaining a loss in its dealings with Company B.

Case 2: How Does "Standard Cost" Make a Fraud Work?

Company X, a subsidiary of Company ABC, a Fortune 100 firm, manufactured a variety of stainless steel–based products, including bulk milk storage tanks and cooler systems for dairies; pots and pans for cooking, some with copper botoms; trash receptacles; and telephone booths. All the products were sold throughout North America. The bulk milk storage tanks and cooler systems were sold around the world through distributors. They represented 70 percent of the total sales volume of Company X.

The parent company adopted a new bonus system for the senior executives of its subsidiary companies. Half of their bonus would be based on gross margin, that is, sales less cost of goods sold. The other half of their bonus would be based on net profit after taxes. The thinking behind the plan was that, if any subsidiary could increase their gross margin, they would probably run a "tight ship" that would help carry more of that amount down to net profit after taxes.

The management of Company X took every action they could imagine to reduce costs (e.g., just-in-time inventory purchases, reduction of staff, more efficient production techniques and approaches, redesign of some products to reduce materials cost per finished unit, and so on). It still did not help their sales either in dollars or in number of units, which showed only nominal increases on a period-by-period comparison.

The president, comptroller, and chief engineer came up with a simple scheme. The only product line to be affected by the fraud scheme would be the bulk milk storage tanks and cooler systems for dairies. First, the engineer would revise the standard cost calculations on all cooler tanks and related products by increasing the finished product cost to double what it had been. The comptroller would approve these revised standard cost amounts and input them into the computer system. The comptroller would then close the variance accounts in the cost accounting system that had been set up in the general ledger of Company X. After all of this had been accomplished, each finished unit of the subject products would come in at an actual cost materially below the standard cost. Therefore, when transferring any unit from work-in-progress to finished goods, there would be a favorable variance. Because the variance accounts had been closed, the favorable variance was credited to cost of goods sold. An example would be

(1) Standard cost of bulk milk tank		$8,000
(2) Work-in-process		
Labor:	$1,400	
Materials:	1,400	
Overhead:	1,400	4,200
(3) Favorable variance [(1) − (2)]		$3,800

The accounting entry when moving the unit from work-in-process to finished goods would be

DR.	Finished Goods	8,000
CR.	Work-in-Process	4,200
CR.	Cost of Goods Sold	3,800

Obviously, this would increase the gross profit margin that could carry down and have a similar impact on net profit after taxes. Both factors would increase the bonus for the senior executives of Company X.

However, to have the scheme work to their advantage, it was necessary for them to produce more finished units than they sold. The sale of any product unit involved in the fraud scheme would eliminate the profit advantage generated at the time the product was completed and moved from work-in-process to finished goods. An example of what happens when a sale occurs follows. It indicates a sale price of $9,000 for the finished unit. Otherwise, the entry uses the data from the earlier entry when moving the unit from work-in-process to finished goods.

Part 1

DR.	Cost of Goods Sold	8,000
CR.	Inventory (Finished Goods)	8,000

Part 2

DR.	Accounts Receivable	9,000
CR.	Sales	9,000

Combining the preceding entries, we would arrive at

DR.	Cost of Goods Sold	8,000	3,800
DR.	Inventory (Finished Goods)	8,000	8,000
DR.	Accounts Receivable	9,000	
CR.	Sales		9,000
CR.	Inventory (Work-in-Process)		4,200

The CR. Inventory (Work-in-Process) of $4,200 represented exactly that amount in charges for labor, materials, and overhead [Note: for our example, 50 percent of the combined total of labor and materials]. The gross profit margin per the books of account using the earlier figures was

CR. Sales	$9,000
Less: DR. Cost of Goods Sold (actual cost)	(4,200)
Gross profit margin	$4,800*

Actual gross profit using the earlier figures was

CR. Sales	$9,000
Less: DR. Cost of Goods Sold (based on standard cost)	(8,000)
Gross profit margin	$1,000*

* Difference of $3,800 is the result of the cost standard for the product unit being revised.

It was never the intention of Company X management to try and increase unit sales of the subject products. They had tried that since the new bonus plan went into effect with little success. Their plan was to produce far more finished product than they sold. Since they did not have the storage facilities to keep that finished product on hand, they came up with a scheme to load up all of their worldwide distributors with consigned inventory of the finished units. They would properly document the transactions so, if reviewed, everything would appear proper. They would try hard to add new distributors so they could operate the scheme over a larger base.

They projected that, at some point in time, the finished goods inventory figure on the balance sheet would begin to get so big that someone at the parent company would question it. Therefore, phase two of the plan would have them continue to ship finished product to the distributors. However, instead of reclassifying those amounts from finished goods inventory to consigned inventory, the reclassification would be to accounts receivable. They would set up documents in each distributor's file to make it appear the product units were sold. The comptroller would also re-age those receivables every two months so that none of them was ever more than two months past-due. The policy of Company ABC, which was followed by all of its subsidiaries, was to set up a specific reserve for possible loan losses for any accounts receivable more than two months past-due. The percentage of the reserve increased as the delinquency on any receivable increased.

At the head office of Company ABC, the comptroller began to worry about two of the figures his financial analysis was developing on Company X: the causal ratio and the effect ratio.

Causal Ratio

$$\text{Causal Ratio} = \frac{\text{Net Sales}}{\text{Inventory}}$$

The figures developed, in thousands of dollars, were

	June 30th*		
	1993	1992	1991
Net sales	$3,800	$3,700	$3,600
Inventory:			
Finished goods†	$2,000	$1,200	$ 400
Work-in-process	600	400	200
Raw materials	300	200	100
Total	$2,900	$1,800	$ 700
Accounts receivable	$ 500‡		

* June 30 is the fiscal year-end for Company X. All figures shown were as of their fiscal year-end.

† Consigned inventory was not separated from finished goods for financial reporting purposes. The parent company management was not aware that consigned inventory was being merged with finished goods inventory and was not shown separately.

‡ This represents the overflow of consigned inventory that the management of Company X wanted to hide from its parent company. This figure was not known to parent company management at this time.

Using the known information only, the comptroller calculated the following causal ratios:

June 30, 1993

$$\frac{\$3,800}{\$2,900} = 1.31:1$$

June 30, 1992

$$\frac{\$3,700}{\$1,800} = 2.06:1$$

June 30, 1991

$$\frac{\$3,600}{\$ 700} = 5.14:1$$

The increase in inventory in relation to sales is obvious and is certainly a "red flag" that something is questionable and needs to be checked out further.

Effect Ratio

$$\text{Effect Ratio} = \frac{\text{Inventory}}{\text{Working Capital}}$$

The figures developed, in thousands of dollars, were:

	*June 30th**		
	1993	*1992*	*1991*
Inventory (total)	$2,900	$1,800	$ 700
Working capital	$2,300	$1,400	$ 400

* June 30 is the fiscal year-end for Company X. All figures shown were as of their fiscal year-end.

Using the known information only, the comptroller calculated the following effect ratios:

June 30, 1993

$$\frac{\$2,900}{\$2,300} = 1.26:1$$

June 30, 1992

$$\frac{\$1,800}{\$1,400} = 1.29:1$$

June 30, 1991

$$\frac{\$ \ 700}{\$ \ 400} = 1.75:1$$

From these figures, it can be seen that inventory is growing faster, in dollar amount, than is working capital. Restated, the increase in inventory exceeds the increase in working capital, another "red flag" warranting follow-up and explanation.

The comptroller of Company ABC called in a forensic accountant as he did not have such skills on his staff. Based on a review of the Company X financial statements, starting with a review of the ratio figures shown above, he agreed to undertake the assignment. He promptly traveled to the headquarters city of Comapny X in another part of the country. Before making that trip, he reviewed the financial statements of Company X for five years. While receiving answers for certain questions raised from his review, he was informed about the new bonus plan that Company X had put into effect at the beginning of the fiscal year ending June 30, 1992.

Review Findings Developed by Forensic Accountant
His first action was a walk-through of the production and warehouse portion of the Company X single plant facility. He noted that it was a relatively small operation, as indicated by the most recent fiscal year sales of $3.8 million. He particularly noted that the production operations were relatively old-fashioned, being very labor intensive, with little in the way of robotics or high-technology

equipment in use, and there was very little finished goods inventory in the warehouse area.

He next reviewed the shipping documents for all shipments made during the preceding 30 days, focusing on milk bulk storage tanks and cooler systems, which represented the majority of the production of the plant.

He then reviewed the processing of the shipping documents for finished product shipped to see how the billing was done. Through this effort, he identified that many of the shipments were consigned inventory to the indicated distributor, not sales.

Finally, he reviewed the cost accounting system back for a three-year period. From this review, he identified the following. First, the variance accounts, favorable and unfavorable, had been closed two years earlier. This action was approved by the company president, chief engineer, and comptroller. With the closing of the variance accounts, actual variances between work-in-process and cost standards were taken directly into cost of goods sold. In addition, the cost standards for standard production items had been changed locally, again approved by the company president, chief engineer, and comptroller, nearly doubling the finished goods standard costs on a number of items. The head office of the parent company was never advised of any of these actions.

The forensic accountant then selected a number of production items on which the cost standards had been changed and followed them through work-in-process, the accounting reassignment to finished goods, and then to the sale. The work-in-process procedures had not changed. When the production on a given item was completed and the unit reassigned to finished goods, the adjustment for book inventory purposes approximately doubled the actual production costs. The difference between work-in-process costs and amount placed on the item as finished goods was credited to cost of goods sold. This increased the gross profit margin on sales at that point in the bookkeeping process. From this, the forensic accountant determined that, if production exceeded sales, both gross margin and net profit after taxes would be favorably influenced, thus benefiting the three officers in their individual bonuses. They were the only three officers at Company X who qualified for that specific bonus plan.

Transactions were selected from each month of the 36-month review period and followed through from production to shipment of the finished product from the plant. This effort highlighted the high consignment inventory level at virtually every distributor of the company's products throughout the world. The only distributors who did not have high consigned inventory positions with the company were those who threatened to drop its product line if they were required to carry any additional finished goods inventory.

For the most recent months of the 36-month review period, the forensic accountant identified that finished product consigned to some distributors had merely passed through consigned inventory and ended up in accounts receivable. He identified that the company at the last fiscal year-end was carrying approximately $500,000 of such fictitious receivables. This amount was approximately $650,000 by the time of his reviews in late September 1993.

His reviews also indicated that the company had only $1.1 million of inventory on hand, as contrasted with a book figure of $3.2 million. Of this difference, $1.8 million was in finished goods, $200,000 in work-in-process, and $100,000 in raw materials.

Based on his findings, he flew to a nearby major city to meet with the comptroller of Company ABC, the parent company of Company X. They reviewed his findings. The forensic accountant was authorized to return to the Company X plant and interrogate each of the three officers who had obviously been involved in the fraud scheme to generate increased bonuses at fiscal year-end 1992 and 1993. The comptroller would report back to executive management at the Company ABC head office.

As requested by the forensic accountant, the public accountants used by Company ABC would provide additional personnel to speed up completion of the full fraud audit. Also, he would send an attorney from the secretary's office of the Company ABC head office to handle any legal problems resulting from finalization of the full fraud audit. The attorney would have letters to the president, comptroller, and chief engineer of Company X indicating to that they were being suspended at this time with full pay and benefits and they should pack up and remove their personal effects from the offices of Company X while the fraud audit was in progress. The public accountants and the head office attorney showed up the following Tuesday. The indicated actions were taken against the three executives.

Actions Taken on Basis of Forensic Accountant's Findings
On completion of the full fraud audit, the president, comptroller, and chief engineer of Company X were discharged and arrested for their fraudulent activities. The three co-defendants countercharged management of Company ABC with gross negligence, ineffective policies and procedures, and lack of responsible staff support in the areas of cost accounting, general accounting procedures and practices, and internal auditing. Their attorney was obviously taking the position that a good offense is the best defense.

Management of Company ABC, on the recommendation of the forensic accountant (who had formerly been a senior corporate financial executive), decided to take Company X into bankruptcy and liquidate its assets. They were able to sell the production, warehouse, and office facilities at a nominal profit. They were able to sell tools, dies, logos, trademarks, and patents at a nice profit. They reclassified consigned inventory hidden in accounts receivable to inventory. They then sold off all finished goods inventory both on hand and on consignment to the same firm that purchased the tools, dies, and so on, at a discount of 10 to 20 percent below book cost. The quality of the overall receivables portfolio was only fair.

As a result, they had to be sold at a discount of 20 percent to the book amount since most of them involved sales of bulk milk cooler systems to dairy farmers who paid for them on a unique basis: the "Milk-Minder" Finance Plan. This was based on the favorable differential that dairy farmers received for shipping to the co-op with whom they worked on a bulk transfer from cooler system to trucks, as opposed to shipping in 30-gallon cans. The size of herds can change, some of the herd would be sour and not producing, and acts of God (e.g., floods, fires, blizzards, and so on) could have an impact on the volume shipped in any period. That, of course, would be reflected in the amount paid by any dairy farmer against their cooler system finance debt. The net impact in liquidating the assets of Company X was a net book loss of $3.4 million.

Once these actions had been completed, the legal action against the fraud perpetrators was pushed rapidly. Company ABC had not wanted to do so until the net loss from liquidating assets of Company X was known. The judge handling the bench trial (i.e., no jury) in the midwestern state where Company X had its plant and offices was, from the beginning of the trial, quite upset at the management of Company ABC. After reviewing all of the evidence presented, the judge concluded that the fraud should not have occurred and, if it did occur, discovery should have been earlier, had Company ABC exercised "due diligence" in monitoring and controlling the activities of Company X. His attitude was that the management of Company ABC had not, for a number of years, properly or effectively performed its duties in monitoring and controlling the activities of Company X. The judge in the case assessed a small fine against each of the three fraud perpetrators and directed that they were entitled to any retirement benefits earned and any profit-sharing funds held in their names at either Company X or Company ABC.

Conclusion

If there can be a lesson learned from this case, it is that executive management has a day-to-day responsibility to monitor, evaluate, and control each function, activity, or entity under their direction. Failure to do so can result in the court assigning executive management partial or full responsibility for wrongdoing by others and criticizing them for not having controls in place to reduce the possibility of fraud and/or ongoing staff reviews to increase after-the-fact identification of such wrongdoing. Their failure, in this instance, enabled the fraud perpetrators to walk off with a net profit (that is, total stolen less amount of fine assessed by the court) from their fraudulent activities, even though their actions resulted in Company X having to be liquidated and costing a number of people jobs in the city where the plant had been located.

Case 3: The Criss-Cross Scheme

In Chapter 13, there are five features indicated as possible additions to those features named in APB No. 4, two of which deal with the conditions in this case: conservatism and consistency.

A major defense contractor, Company Y, found itself about to have overruns on a number of fixed fee contracts (FFCs). The comptroller's department of that firm came up with a scheme where they could divert some of the costs from FFCs and roll them into cost plus contracts (CPCs). If this was done properly, they were convinced that neither the public accountants nor Department of Defense (DoD) auditors would be able to identify what they were doing. For each FFC where an overrun was about to occur, they would pair it up with a CPC. For all government contracts, both FFCs and CPCs, they would roll all labor, materials, and overhead charges into a suspense account at the end of each shift. The charges would then be manipulated between contracts so that, whenever they wished, a part of the costs applicable to one or more FFCs would be reallocated to one or more CPCs. In some cases, they would make complete switches between one FFC and one CPC for a shift, making such change appear to be a clerical error.

There was absolutely no valid reason for the suspense account except to assist in the reallocation of expenses, as described. That was, of course, intended to keep FFCs from any material overruns by reallocating such amounts to CPCs. The management of Company Y defended setting up, for each contract, the suspense account used to clear shift charges into the master contract file on the basis that "on occasion they had some indirect overhead charges which would be merged in the 'suspense' account with other charges on any contract and the total amount then cleared to the various contracts." Obviously, the described manipulation of charges on any contract to another contract breached the intent of conservatism and consistency for which sound accounting principles should strive at all times.

The DoD auditors had picked up "tips" from several sources that Company Y was doing some "creative accounting" with costs involving FFCs and CPCs. After the third such "tip" was received, it was decided to conduct a "special" audit at Company Y, specifically to review development of shift costs on contracts and follow such amounts through to the appropriate contracts. A top DoD forensic accountant was assigned to head up this audit team.

The review team consisted of eight persons: one forensic accountant in charge of the review team, five non-EDP auditors (two managers and three seniors), and two EDP auditors (one manager and one senior). The team initially picked 20 contracts for the first phase of their audit effort: 10 were FFCs and 10 were CPCs. In this first phase, they identified the manipulative practices of reallocation of some charges of an FFC to one or more CPCs. Based on those initial findings, the audit team expanded their review to cover cost accounting procedures and practices on all then-open contracts between the government and Company Y on which some costs had already been incurred and charged to the contract and 20 government contracts on which all work had been completed within the 12 months preceding their selected audit date. They again selected 10 FFCs and 10 CPCs.

The type of manipulation that they had identified in the original test is illustrated in the following diagram. In the example, one FFC and one CPC for one shift are used.

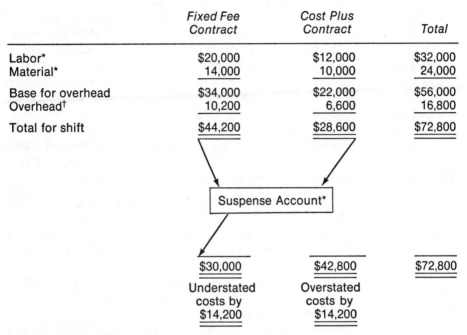

	Fixed Fee Contract	Cost Plus Contract	Total
Labor*	$20,000	$12,000	$32,000
Material*	14,000	10,000	24,000
Base for overhead	$34,000	$22,000	$56,000
Overhead†	10,200	6,600	16,800
Total for shift	$44,200	$28,600	$72,800

Suspense Account*

	$30,000	$42,800	$72,800
	Understated costs by $14,200	Overstated costs by $14,200	

* Starts and ends each shift at zero.
† Overhead rate is 30 percent of combined labor and materials.

Review Findings Developed by Forensic Accountant

It was determined that the Company Y comptroller or his designate would, at the end of each week, select which FFCs were to have part of their charges the following week reallocated to one or more CPCs, the shift(s) on which such reallocation would take place, and the amount of the reallocation to be made to each CPC selected.

The Company Y comptroller or his designate would have the entries for the reallocations prepared by a subordinate during the first shift for the entire 24-hour period, including the second and third shifts. The entries would then be approved by the authorizing official. The appropriate entry(ies) would be processed into the suspense account set up in the firm's cost accounting system as close as possible to the closing of each shift's production records for all contracts. Those production records covered labor and materials and a percentage of those combined amounts as overhead. This would enable the reallocation of FFCs to CPCs while the shift production data were temporarily held in the suspense account set up as an interim step between the production records and the general ledger contract subsidiary records.

The review identified that a total of 23 open contracts and 14 completed contracts between the government and Company Y had been improperly debited (costs increased) or credited (costs decreased) through this manipulation format. For the 12-month period through the examination date, the audit team identified total reallocated charges from FFCs to CPCs of $39.7 million.

On the basis of the materiality of these review findings, the audit was extended back for another 12 months on both open and completed contracts. Nothing was found in the oldest 8 months of the period. However, in the 4 most recent months of this expanded audit period, they found more creative accounting. There findings involved a total of six contracts: two FFCs and four CPCs. The total manipulated amount was $363,000. This finding was perceived by the audit team as the "test period" for the creative accounting fraud scheme. Since it had worked out all right in this period, it was expanded substantially.

The audit team wondered why neither the internal auditors nor the public accountants had identified this scheme. In reviewing their procedures against the diagram given earlier, they identified that both groups of auditors:

1. Tested the charges of labor and materials to selected contracts, both FFCs and CPCs.
2. Tested the calculation of overhead on the same contracts tested in #1 to assure that the company-established overhead rate was properly applied.
3. Verified that the shift total on the selected contracts, combining labor, materials, and overhead, was properly closed out at the end of the shift into the appropriate suspense account.
4. Aggregated the total amount of the close-out for all contracts that had incurred costs in the subject shift into the appropriate suspense account.
5. Aggregated the total amount cleared from the suspense account to the appropriate contract subaccount in the general ledger of the company, prior to the end of the following shift.

On first review, the indicated procedures seemed both proper and adequate. However, it contains a clearcut deficiency. What do you think it is?

The deficiency in audit approach is in #4 and #5. It is necessary to follow the amount closed into a suspense account for any specific contract at the end of any shift. This must be done directly from the records accumulating labor, materials, and overhead charges on that contract. Then that amount must be followed out of the suspense account for that specific contract to the general ledger subaccount for it.

In other words, the amount going into the suspense account must be the same amount clearing from that account into the general ledger subaccount for that contract. That was not done. Failing to do so enabled the fraud perpetrators to shift costs from an FFC to a CPC whenever they wished. Closing procedures must be on a contract-by-contract basis, not on an overall or group-of-contracts basis. Had that closing approach been followed, the fraud as described would have been identified.

The comptroller and three of his deputies were interrogated regarding the audit findings and the manipulation of costs between FFCs and CPCs. When confronted with the findings, they all confessed to their participation in the scheme. Further, all identified that the president of the firm had directed them "to find a way to transfer part of the costs on FFCs, nearing the maximum contract price, to CPCs so it wouldn't be found."

The president was then confronted with the audit findings and the statements that the comptroller's department officials were merely following his instructions in perpetrating the fraud. He readily confessed to his having encouraged "creative accounting" to avoid having FFCs with unreimbursible overruns.

Actions Taken on Basis of Forensic Accountant's Findings

The officials who confessed to having participated in the fraud, either actively or passively, were discharged, arrested, and given jail sentences ranging from one year and one day to five years. Company Y was assessed fines in excess of $100 million and was removed from the "approved vendor" list and could not bid on any new government business for a six-month period.

It is interesting to note that less than two years following the discovery of this fraud, the Department of Defense auditors encountered another "creative accounting" situation involving another defense contractor. That fraud involved deliberate overbilling of costs on CPCs held by that contractor. Again, the original tip came from a person who thought something was wrong but was not in a position to definitively state the details of what was going on or who was involved. The total fines exceeded those assessed against Company Y. The period for which that contractor was not permitted to bid on new government contracts was even longer than the period assessed against Company Y.

In both cases, tips were the first red flags of possible fraud.

Case 4: Murder He Wrote

Let me note the fact that the Canadian government had used forensic accountants in connection with a number of murder investigations. To put this into perspective, consider the *criminal equation* formula:

$$\text{Target} + \text{Motive} + \text{Access} + \text{Opportunity} = \begin{array}{c}\text{Potentially successful}\\ \text{fraud situation}\\ \text{(or criminal attack)}\end{array}$$

Let us consider the four elements in this equation:

1. *Target:*
   a. The object of the possible crime or the *target* must be established; or
   b. The objective of the crime, or the *target,* must be established.
2. *Motive:*
   a. Identifying who might have a *motive* for the crime; or
   b. Identifying who might have had a *motive* for the crime.
3. Access: This phase of the formula focuses the investigation on those whose personal habits or history suggest they have antisocial behavior problems (e.g., criminal record, alcohol or drug abuser, history of petty theft, poor work record, and so on). It is necessary, relative to *access,*

to determine who can be placed at the scene of the crime. Restated, who could have had *access* to the *target* at the time the crime occurred.
4. *Opportunity:* The weakness that gave rise to the *opportunity* for the crime must be identified, as well as those who had the knowledge to be able to take advantage of it.

The forensic accountant would usually be engaged to identify a motive or a target, or both, for any assumed wrongdoing. In the case of a murder investigation, the reason for the crime may have been to prevent someone from discovering a fraud scheme, recognizing that if discovered it could be reported to law-enforcement or other authorities, or prevent someone who has already discovered the fraud scheme from reporting it to the authorities. Another factor may be that someone knowing of the fraud but not involved in it may be attempting to blackmail a person(s) participating in the fraud scheme. Some of the fraud schemes that may be involved are "cooking the books" (that is, creative accounting), skimming, money laundering, and off-the-book fraud.

While the initial reasons for engaging a forensic accountant may be relative to motive or target, or both, once the fraud scheme has been identified, the focus shifts to access and opportunity. When a crime as serious as murder occurs in relation to any financial matter, it will normally require extraordinary imagination and curiosity on the part of the forensic accountant to identify all aspects of the situation, not merely the amount involved or the duration of the wrongdoing. He or she must identify the point of origination of the fraudulent act, whether it is on-books or off-books, or both, and then each step along the way until the end objective of the fraud perpetrator(s) has been accomplished. As is typical for nearly all reviews involving a forensic accountant, it is necessary to go the extra step—perform the extra review stage, check out the additional detail, and interface with every person potentially involved through effective interviewing or interrogation, or both.

Case 5: Escrow Is a High-Risk Business Area

Introduction
It had come to light at a major bank that they had, in their escrow function, actually processed a large number of irregular transactions.

At this point, let us define some of the terms we will use in this case.

1. *Escrow:*

A legal document (such as a deed), money, stock, or other property delivered by the grantor, promisor or obligor into the hands of a third person, to be held by the latter until the happening of a contingency or performance of a condition, and then by him delivered to the grantee, promisee or obligee. A system of document transfer in which a deed, bond, stock, funds, or other property is delivered to a third person to hold until all conditions in a contract are fulfilled; *e.g.* delivery of deed to escrow agent under installment land sale contract until full payment for land is made.[5]

2. *Escrow account:*

A bank account generally held in the name of the depositor and an escrow agent which is returnable to depositor or paid to third person on the fulfillment of escrow condition; *e.g.* funds for payment of real estate taxes are commonly paid into escrow account of bank-mortgagor by mortgagee.[6]

3. *Escrow contract:*

Agreement between buyer, seller, and escrow holder setting forth rights and responsibilities of each.[7]

4. *Land flip:*

A land flip is the practice of buying and selling a parcel [of land or land and building] very quickly, often in a single day or month, at a successively higher price to related parties, until a lender (who believes the buyer is arm's length) takes everyone out with an unrealistically inflated loan amount.[8]

5. *Straw man* or *party:*

A "front"; a third party who is put up in name only to take part in a transaction. Nominal party to a transaction; one who acts as an agent for another for the purpose of taking title to real property and executing whatever documents and instruments the principal may direct respecting the property. Person who purchases property for another to conceal identity of real purchaser, or to accomplish some purpose otherwise not allowed.[9]

Review Efforts Internally

The bank chairman had previously ordered the internal audit function to *not* review the escrow function. Why? Because they did not have the required expertise on their staff. Their prior internal audit reviews into the escrow function had been very unsatisfactory, as to both the findings of their reviews and the contents of the related audit reports.

Management had received some "tips" regarding possible improper activities in the escrow function in its five offices throughout the state. These tips focused on possible problems in one particular escrow office. That office, the largest of the escrow function, was located in the largest city in the state where the bank was headquartered, but not the headquarters city of the bank. Because management had no confidence in the internal audit function relative to review work involving the escrow function, they had to go outside for review personnel to follow up on the tips received of possible fraud. Management engaged the audit and consulting arms of the public accounting firm regularly used by the bank to perform a full fraud audit of the bank's escrow function, starting with the office on which tips as to possible fraud had been received. Before commencing the fraud audit, the public accounting personnel performed a full familiarization of the bank's escrow functions to understand the strengths and weaknesses in the related accounting, administrative, operational, and control environment. This familiarization effort proved to be very worthwhile. It identified that the work environment

1. Put excessive authority and responsibility in the hands of the intermediate (VP and 2nd VP) and junior (escrow officer) level management personnel. They could make yes, no, or pending decisions on any transaction they processed without any second opinion or review of the decisions made performed by anyone else.
2. Gave those intermediate and junior management personnel the ability to authorize payment without their instructions being reviewed. Therefore, if they made an error in the disbursement, there was no internal check on their actions prior to drawing and disbursing the funds.
3. Allowed those intermediate and junior management personnel to prepare or direct the preparation of any forms or documents for any escrow transactions. There was no internal check on their actions to verify that all proper forms were prepared and no unneeded forms were prepared that, under law, might confuse the finalization of any escrow transaction.
4. Did not maintain either the manual or computer ledger/logs properly, and the internal check objective of matching one record to another at different stages of the processing of a given transaction was not properly performed and was either not performed at all or not performed on a timely basis.

In addition, the manual and computer systems did not contain adequate internal control, in general, and internal check, specifically, to assure proper recording and control over each escrow transaction processed.

The public accountants were very concerned by their findings. When added to the tips received by management, it clearly indicated the possibility of a fraud situation existing somewhere within the escrow operations of the bank. On that basis, they obtained the services of the senior forensic accountant on their staff. He was the head of their primary litigation support services group, headquartered at another office of the firm. He took charge of the review team upon his arrival on site. Based on the tips and the findings of the familiarization reviews, he directed that a full fraud audit commence at the selected escrow office. Based on the same reasons, he selected the work of three junior management personnel as the initial stage of their fraud audit undertaking.

The audit work performed on the work of two of the three selected-focus officers reaffirmed the deficiencies of the systems (computer and manual), procedures, and practices within the escrow function.

The audit work performed on the work of the third selected-focus officer identified an ongoing fraud situation of major proportions. The review work discovered the following written memoranda in the bank files:

1. The chairman had written to the subject-focus officer's immediate superior and his immediate superior and informed them that they no longer needed to supervise or monitor the work of that focus officer.
2. The chairman had written to the general auditor and informed him that internal auditing, because it did not have the necessary experience or expertise, should no longer audit the escrow function.
3. The audit review officer had reviewed the audit reports on the escrow function as issued in the past and indicated that "while we can be proud

of many of our audit reports, we certainly cannot be proud of those issued on the escrow function."

4. The chairman had written a letter similar to #2 to the head of the bank's loan review, directing that that function no longer needed to review records or activities of the escrow function.

Fraud Findings

This was a "complex" fraud in that it involved both an insider and outsiders. The participants were

1. Insider: A junior escrow officer in the bank's largest escrow office.
2. Outsiders:

   a. A different senior executive at each of two real estate development firms. Both firms operated statewide, but the bulk of their properties and work was in the city where the subject bank escrow office was located or its immediate suburban areas.

   b. A senior executive at a mortgage finance firm that also operated statewide but did most of its work in the city where the subject bank escrow office was located or its immediate suburban areas.

   c. One real estate appraiser who operated throughout the state but did most of his work in the city where the subject bank escrow office was located or its immediate suburban areas.

All of the indicated fraud co-conspirators had colluded to put the fraud in place and keep it operational on an ongoing basis.

The escrow officer of the bank would process and approve properties submitted by three of her co-conspirators, often using appraisals prepared and submitted by the fourth co-conspirator. These could be either

1. Nonexistent properties: Each property supported by fraudulently prepared financial statements, including cash-flow projections; documents appearing to support the existence of property (e.g., deeds, and so on, prepared on standard legal forms), fraudulently notorized, if deemed warranted. These were developed by persons at the real estate development firm or the mortgage finance firm. If deemed warranted, they would be supported by a real estate appraisal, fraudulently prepared by the real estate appraiser.
2. Documents on real property: Each properly supported by fraudulently prepared financial statements, including cash-flow projections prepared by persons at the real estate development firm or the mortgage finance firm. It was always accompanied by a real estate appraisal, fraudulently prepared by the real estate appraiser. On occasion, the co-conspirator would complete a land flip on a specific property to create a fictitiously high valuation. On other occasions, the co-conspirators would use straw men to act on their behalf, so as to raise the apparent value of the subject properties.

The fraud audit team, headed by an experienced forensic accountant, was able to identify fraudulent transactions of the various types described, in the aggregate amount of $188 million, that had been processed through the one internal participating escrow officer.

How would you proceed from this point in the case?

The following steps were taken by the forensic accountant in charge of the fraud audit team. First, the chairman was asked to explain the reason for his three internal memoranda that left the escrow officer, the sole insider involved in the large discovered fraud, totally free of any direct internal supervision (e.g., preventing her immediate superior and his imediate superior, a VP and an SVP respectively, from directing or monitoring her day-to-day activities).

His first response was that, by freeing her up from direct supervision, it was hoped that she would increase her income generation. She had pleaded for "more freedom of action," which she contended would make her even more productive. (Note: Her income generation was already three to five times that of any other escrow officer in the organization. That would be a red flag to me to determine if she was generating such income properly.)

In addition, in his opinion, neither internal audit nor loan review were qualified to review and evaluate the escrow activities or any of the officers working in that activity. As a result, he viewed them as being potentially disruptive with no offsetting values.

Next, the internal audit review officer who reviewed and evaluated internal audit review work, findings, and the reports thereon was asked why he had been so critical of the internal audit reports on the escrow function.

In response, he indicated that the audit reports on escrow that had been reviewed by him clearly indicated that the senior management of the internal audit department did not understand the principles of escrow and the reports were written in a style indicating that deficiency. In addition, there was no continuity in the reports, because the auditors did not understand how the various work phases interconnected. Finally, his review of the audit programs and workpapers reaffirmed that the auditors did not have the knowledge required to properly perform audits in the escrow environment. He had not criticized the programs and workpapers because he thought his comments on the audit reports on escrow made the lack of competency in the internal audit function relative to escrow function quite clear. He felt that the chairman's follow-up memorandum directing that audit no longer review the escrow function was, in fact, a follow-up on his memorandum.

It was the evaluation of the forensic accountant that management had acted improperly by removing all supervision (that is, two superiors neutralized relative to directing or controlling the activities of the subject escrow officer) and internal check (e.g., loan review and internal audit). That was clearly mismanagement. This could also be considered gross negligence on the part of the chairman.

The fraud audit scope was expanded, and the general operations of each escrow officer in the system were reviewed. While each of them had inadequate procedures, practices, and records, and deficient internal controls and checks relative thereto, no fraud was encountered. further review work at the escrow office where the fraud had been identified revealed the same inadequacies and deficiencies elsewhere in the escrow system. It did not reveal any other fraud.

A series of interviews with other personnel at the escrow office where the fraud had been identified affirmed that everyone knew the procedures, practices, and records were inadequate. They also knew that the internal control and check requirements were deficient. The personnel interviewed ranked the office environment from chaotic, at worst, to poor, at best. Criticisms had been raised to management with no improvements seen to procedures, practices, records, or controls. This confirmed the earlier conclusion of mismanagement and gross negligence on the part of executive management. It now established the same evaluations for management of the office. Repeating the interviews at the other escrow offices obtained the same opinions. This established the same evaluations for the entire bankwide escrow function.

Shortly thereafter, the chairman resigned, as did a number of middle and senior management officers (that is, 2nd VP and higher, up to the EVP level). New management was placed in charge of the escrow function bankwide. A new facility manager was assigned at each escrow office. The public accounting firm's consulting arm was engaged to develop a formal policies and procedures manual for the bankwide escrow function. This six-volume set of criteria was put into place as it was developed over a nine-month period, with the first volume in place six months after the work began.

It is interesting to note that, while the preceding was occurring, none of the fraud perpetrators provided any information. The insider, a female escrow officer, and all four of the outsiders identified earlier had apparently taken an "oath of silence." They did not cooperate in any way. They did not acknowledge that they had, in any way, participated in a fraud scheme. They hid behind the Fifth Ammendment to the Constitution.

Fortunately, the paper document trail and data developed for each property (e.g., overvaluations on actual properties or financing of nonexistant properties) were adequate to build a criminal case around the five co-conspirators. It should be noted that some transactions involving two or more of the five fraud co-conspirators were found to be legitimate with the subject properties properly valued. Each co-conspirator had his or her own attorney. All five of the attorneys contended that the fact some properties did exist and were properly valued was proof that their client had not been involved in any fraud scheme against the bank. This was not accepted by the court. As a result, all were convicted of fraud in this matter and received prison sentences.

The following table summarizes the information known with respect to the losses resulting from this fraud (figures are given in millions of U.S. dollars).

Total fraud amount	$188
Less: Recovery obtained through actions against legitimate properties and the business interests of the two real estate developers, the one executive of a mortgage finance firm, and the one real estate appraiser	(58)
Net fraud loss	$130
Time value of money (from time of fraud occurrence until submission of this claim)	$ 20
Total claim against insurers*	$150

* The bank carried a $300 million employee bond coverage with a $5 million deductible. The amount here ($150 million) less that deductible left a net claim against the insurers of $145 million.

The employee bond coverage consisted of a group of insurers providing coverage from $5 to $300 million; in groups as follows $5 to $100 million, $101 to $200 million, and $201 to $300 million. One firm was in all three groups, while two others were in two groups. All other insurance companies involved were in only one group.

Negotiations dragged on because the insurers were only offering settlement based on a percentage of the claim. Their position was based on the four documents that they contended indicated mismanagement and gross negligence. Just prior to depositions of all concerned parties, preliminary to taking the matter to court, the bank agreed to a settlement. While the settlement was above the original offer by the insurers, it was substantially below the amount of the claims against them by the bank. Based on what is known about this case, the final settlement of the $145 million claim was less than $100 million.

Lessons Learned

1. No one should be permitted to operate in any business, not just banking, without an adequate level of control over his or her activities. Remember the rule of sound internal control that states, "No person or group of persons should have total control over any transaction or group of transactions." Such situations, should they exist, establish a premise for claiming mismanagement by middle or executive management of the organization.

2. Policies, procedures, and practices must be established with adequate internal controls/checks built in to assure effective day-to-day accounting, administration, and operations. Failure to have such disciplines in place clearly indicates gross negligence on the part of middle and executive management.

3. Management has a responsibility to assure independent monitoring of every activity or function of an organization. Usually this is done by staff functions within the organization, for example

    a. Internal auditors, including EDP auditors, reviewing any activity, function, facility, or entity of a business organization.

    b. Loan review, reviewing credit decisions and risks in a financial organization (e.g., depository institution, finance company, insurance company, and so on).

    c. Information security officer and staff in the EDP environment in any organization using computers, whether in-house or out-sourced.

The public accountants can be engaged to supplement the internal staff functions or, in some instances, to perform the full independent review. Failure to ensure such independent review, on an ongoing basis, is clearly mismanagement.

In this case, the fraud audit team reviewed over 1 million bank documents, in addition to reviewing procedures, practices, and controls and interviewing some 200 people. The attorneys for the insurers took copies of nearly 800,000 documents for potential evidence purposes. From this mass of documents they identified the four key documents, described at the beginning of this case. These were enough to have the bank negotiate a settlement substantially below the original amount claimed.

Transaction Flow of the Fraud

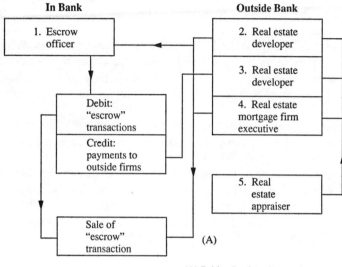

(A) Paid to bank and passed on to
purchasers of property.

Sequence:

1. #2, #3, and #4 submit false documents to #1, who reviews transactions. Occasionally, rejected items are returned to submitters for "window dressing," making it appear that #1 is doing the job properly.
2. Approved transactions by #1 are booked, with funds paid to #2, #3, and #4, with #5 paid for services provided, as appropriate.
3. Kickback provided to #1 from #2, #3, #4, and #5.
4. New deals provide funds so periodic payments on previously booked transactions can be made on time.

Case 6: Watch It Disappear—Watch It Reappear

The chairman of a bank had created a fictitious company, unincorporated, that we will call Company Z. He rented a mailbox at a local package service facility for its mailing address and then opened a demand deposit account (DDA) at his own bank in the name of Company Z. He also set up a complete credit file on the firm, including created "unaudited financial statements." From these he prepared normal financial analysis spreadsheet for Company X. On the basis of the preceding, he made a $490,000 loan to Company Z. He set up the loan for a five-year term, with interest payments to be made quarterly and principal payments to be made at 5 percent quarterly starting in the first quarter of the fourth year of the loan term. There was a 65 percent principal repayment bullet due as the last payment on the loan. Because of his rank, he could both initiate and approve the loan, and because the credit facility was under $500,000, it did not have to be cleared through the bank's credit committee.

Six months later, he repeated the scheme using Company Y, with exactly the same loan amount and terms as for the loan made to Company X. The funds for the loans to Company Y and Company Z were deposited into the DDAs set up for those two companies. The chairman could draw them down at his discretion.

As October 31 approached, the chairman became nervous. Why? Because the public accountants had historically used the close of business on the last business day of October as the date on which they selected credit files for review and accounts, both loan and deposit, for confirmation mailing and test reviews.

He had to come up with a scheme that would permit him to leave the two loans as described open but hide them from the public accountants as of the specified date. How could he do that?

The scheme was simple! On the last business day of October, just before the close of business, the bank chairman prepared tickets. (Note: Banks use separate debit and credit tickets to pass accounting entries, rather than journal entries used by most other businesses.) The amounts shown are for illustrative purposes. The entries made were

DEBIT:	Demand Deposit Accounts:		
	Company Z	$180,000	
	Company Y	240,000	
CREDIT:	Loan Receivable:		
	Company Z*		$498,000
	Company Y*		498,000
Subtotals		$420,000	$996,000
CREDIT:	Suspense Account	576,000†	
Total		$996,000	$996,000

* Includes $8,000 of accrued interest on loan.

† This balance would be combined with the debit and credit balances in other suspense accounts then in use on the general ledger of the bank, with those balances shown under either Other Assets or Other Liabilities.

The chairman, not an accountant by training, knew that the public accountants had, in the past, always selected the items to be tested in the following areas as of the close of business on October 31:

1. Loans for review, from the trial balance of open and in-use credit facilities, to evaluate their soundness or risk, or both.
2. DDAs, NOW, savings accounts, and certificates of deposit (CDs) for confirmation purposes and such other reviews of those accounts as they deemed appropriate (e.g., proper classification of "dormant" acounts, account opening documentation, and so on).

On the other hand, he knew that historically the public accountants did little, if any, reviews relative to the amounts in any suspense accounts and, if they did, their tests would be limited to items that had been open for some time. Since the loans had been closed into the suspense account on the last business day of October, he assumed quite correctly that it was probable his closing entries would not be reviewed by the public accountants. He was correct!

Midday on the first business day of November, the chairman reversed the entries, as detailed earlier. The tickets indicated that the "original entry had been made in error."

With respect to the elements of APB No. 4., as discussed in Chapter 13, the chairman violated the requirement for integrity in each of the "time periods." The chairman also breached the reliability, consistency, and disclosure elements that are supplemental to APB No. 4.

A year went by and the chairman repeated the same closing procedure as of the close of business on the last business day of October. One of the operations people questioned the entries this time and advised internal audit of the tickets. They followed up on the two loans, back to their origination, and identified that the same tickets had been processed one year earlier and reversed the following day, the first business day of November. A "light" then came on and the audit officer remembered that the public accountants usually used the close of business on the last day of October as the day for many of their interim reviews and tests, including credits outstanding and confirmation mailings on DDAs.

The auditors then affirmed that the chairman had directed the opening of the two DDAs and both initiated and approved the two credit facilities. Follow-up on the loan addresses found them both to be the same address but with different boxes. The general auditor sent a security man back with an auditor and a picture of the chairman. The owner of the mailing firm that rented the mailboxes identified the picture as the man who rented the two mailboxes. He indicated that the person came to pick up mail from the two boxes once a month. There was very little mail for either box, usually the bank statement and some promotional advertising pieces.

With that information, the general auditor contacted the three members of the audit committee of the board of directors and informed them that the chairman appeared to be involved in a fraud scheme. Once they had reviewed the information developed, they agreed. After the chairman was confronted by a member of the audit committee and the general auditor, he broke down and confessed to the fraud scheme. He also confessed that he had passed tickets at the close of business on the last day of October for two years to minimize the probability of the public accountants reviewing either the two loans or the DDAs set up for those companies. The fraud situation was reported to the appropriate law-enforcement and regulatory authorities.

SUMMARY

In some of the cases described, I specifically indicate that a forensic accountant was involved. In one case, there is no mention of a forensic accountant being involved. Why? Because even an accountant or auditor who does not have all of the training, experience, and skills of a forensic accountant can apply the principles and standards they use. In a standard accounting or auditing environment, the biggest drawback traditionally is that they are under severe time pressures to complete a specific phase of an audit (e.g., treasurer's office, accounts/loans receivable, and so on). In a given situation, the forensic accountant will normally not face the clock pressures to complete, as does the regular practitioner. In either case, the practitioner must exercise due diligence, have appropriate curiosity, and have the confidence in his or her judgment to reallocate time so that he or she can follow up on matters identified during reviews that are of concern and warrant such action. The forensic accountant does not need to be as structured as do normal practitioners, working from programs that tend to limit their initiative and flexibility. Forensic accountants are permitted a level of fluidity in their approaches and scope so they can go where they want, look at what they want, and talk with whom they want to develop the facts relative to their ongoing investigation.

NOTES

1. Jack Bologna and Paul Shaw, *Forensic Accounting Handbook* (Madison, WI: Assets Protection Publishing, 1993), p. 9.

2. Lee J. Seidler and D. R. Carmichael, eds., *Accountant's Handbook*, 6th ed., Vol. II (New York: The Ronald Press, 1981), p. 31-3. Copyright © 1981 by The Ronald Press. Reprinted by permission of John Wiley & Sons, Inc.

3. Bologna and Shaw, Forensic *Accounting Handbook*, p. 9.

4. Seidler and Carmichael, *Accountant's Handbook*, p. 31-6.

5. *Black's Law Dictionary*, 6th ed. (St. Paul, MN: West Publishing, 1990), p. 545.

6. Ibid.

7. Ibid.

8. G. Jack Bologna, Robert J. Linquist, and Joseph T. Wells, *The Accountant's Handbook of Fraud & Commercial Crime* (New York: John Wiley & Sons, 1993), p. 164. Copyright © 1993 by John Wiley & Sons. Reprinted by permission of John Wiley & Sons, Inc.

9. *Black's Law Dictionary*, p. 1421.

CHAPTER 6

"OFF-BOOK" ACCOUNTING AND FINANCIAL FRAUD

Dishonesty, cowardice and duplicity are never impulsive.

George A. Knight

DEFINITIONS

There is no standard definition for "off-book" fraud. The best definitions seen are quoted in part below:

> Off-book refers to those schemes in which the funds used for illegal payments or transfers are not drawn from regular, known bank accounts. The payments do not appear anywhere on the books and records. In relatively small amounts, such payments may come directly from the pocket of the payer, from her or his personal accounts, or may be borrowed from other ventures. In larger schemes, the funds are usually generated by unrecorded sales or by failing to record legitimate rebates from suppliers. Off-book schemes are often employed by businesses with significant cash sales. . . . The principal advantage of off-book schemes is their secrecy[1]

> Off-book frauds are those that occur outside the accounting environment, and where no audit trail is likely to exist. Examples include bribery and kickbacks. If an employee received a bribe for selecting a certain vendor, that payment would be made by the vendor and therefore would not be reflected in the books of the affected company. These frauds are detected in an indirect manner (other vendor complaints, lifestyle of the person receiving the bribes, etc.). If it is suspected that an employee is receiving illicit payments, this would ideally be proven by examining the employee's personal finances.[2]

CLASSIFICATIONS OF BUSINESS

For our purposes, businesses can be categorized with respect to off-book fraud risk as either Type A, Type B, or Type C.

Type A

A Type A company has most, if not all, of the desired theoretical accounting, control, and record strengths apparently in place. However, it has both organizational and control deficiencies in its operating environment. If such deficiencies are identified by a potential wrongdoer, the situation can be manipulated to his or her advantage. Such wrongdoing can result in the perpetration of either on-book or off-book frauds. These can be either (1) one time "hit-and-rum" frauds; (2) ongoing fraud, continuing day-to-day, week-to-week, or month-to-month; or (3) fraud occurring on a time-to-time basis, when the circumstances permit. The last one enables the opportunist to take advantage of a deficiency, usually organizational (e.g., someone performing his or her own duties and those of a person who is absent that day). The risk of detection of such wrongdoing will vary materially from company to company depending on a variety of organizational, procedural, and review criteria.

Type B

A Type B company has very general procedural control, and record criteria with a high degree of latitude, particularly to the owner(s) in a closely held business and to senior and middle management in a more broadly held business. The risk of either on-book or off-book fraud is substantially increased over that of a Type A company.

Type C

A Type C company has little or no formal procedures, weak to nonexistent controls, and very informal records. These are usually limited to a poorly kept general ledger, cash register tapes, bank statements and related documents (e.g., canceled checks, debit and credit memoranda, and deposit slips), and possibly informal transaction information (e.g., slips of paper, informal notes, and so on). Often such casualness with the records is deliberate. The risk of on-book or off-book fraud is substantially increased over that of a Type B company.

PERSPECTIVE OF FRAUD

The term *off-book* refers to the use of funds for illegal payments or transfers that are not drawn from regular, known bank accounts of the business or individual. In some cases, fixed assets (e.g., automobiles, boats, housing, or jewelry), not cash, are used to complete the illegal transaction, with such assets having been acquired at some time in the past for off-book cash. Off-book schemes are often employed by businesses, legitimate or illegitimate, that have significant cash sales. Examples of legitimate businesses using off-book schemes include

1. Restaurant, bar, or show bar (e.g., one with an admission charge) where the owner(s) is able to accumulate an untraceable cash hoard through skimming (part of the proceeds) from the whole or diversion (the total proceeds) from a specific part of the business (e.g., bar receipts or admission fees).
2. Retail enterprise, where inventory is misappropriated and the theft written down as normal shrinkage. The inventory is then sold to generate cash proceeds.
3. Manufacturing enterprise, where collusion among responsible persons enables reclassifying good inventory, raw materials, and/or finished goods as scrap. Asset value is charged off due to the reclassification. Then the assets that have been misappropriated are sold, generating cash proceeds.

The most frequently thought of illegitimate businesses that can be expected to generate large amounts of unrecorded cash are

1. Prostitution.
2. Bootlegging, now primarily limited to those areas that are legally dry; that is, certain counties in certain states.
3. Drugs of any type (e.g., marijuana, cocaine, crack, and so on).
4. Organized but unlicensed gambling of any type (e.g., betting pools, particularly on sporting events of all types).
5. Hijacking, truck and car theft, and "chop shop" operations.

Remember that the type of scheme employed—on-book or off-book—depends primarily on the source and type of funds available. If the funds used are generated and recorded by a legitimate business, then they must be deposited in regular bank accounts. Whether used for legitimate expenses or misappropriated, some level of audit trail will exist. On the other hand, a payer who has the capability to generate cash or other unrecorded income (e.g., assets of some type—inventory or fixed assets) may elect to be involved in an off-book arrangement without leaving an audit trail.

MAKING ILLEGAL PAYMENTS AND TRANSFERS

Some of the more traditional methods of concealing transactions are discussed in this section.

Cash Payments. The most favored method of illicit payments is by cash. Small amounts are hard to trace. Larger amounts are more difficult to both accumulate and then dispose of after a transaction has been completed.

Checks and Other Financial Instruments. Money orders, cashier's checks, or traveler's checks can provide the payer with an audit trail in the form of a copy of the instrument or a record of the check numbers, in the case of traveler's checks. Purchasers can use a false name when purchasing such instruments for cash. The use of a check drawn against a business bank account would leave an audit trail. Whatever the nature of the instrument, payment can be made directly, through an intermediary, or through a series of persons, entities, or accounts.

Hidden Interests.   Instead of using cash or cash items, the payer may make payments by investing funds in some joint venture or projected profit-making enterprise on behalf of the recipient. Such action may be concealed through a strawman or nominee, be hidden in a trust or other business entity, or be part of a parole (verbal) agreement between the two parties. Such arrangements are difficult to detect, and, even if discovered, proof of corrupt intent may be hard to demonstrate, particularly if there is some evidence of payment for interest in subject assets.

Loans.   A number of payoffs may be called loans. For example, a previously made direct payment may be described by both the payer and the beneficiary as a loan. However, no repayment is expected by the payer.

Also, the payer can guarantee a legitimate loan made by a financial institution to the beneficiary. Upon default by the borrower (beneficiary), the payer is called upon to repay the loan. On the surface it appears to be a legitimate situation when, in fact, it is not.

In a third scheme, the payer may make an actual loan to the recipient but at an interest rate and with terms that are not standard (that is, interest-free or below prime rate interest and all prinicpal repayment deferred to a "bullet" at the end of the loan term). The conditions of the loan clearly indicate that something was done earlier by the recipient for benefit of the payer. An example of this occurred not too long ago when the treasurer of a large state deposited state funds into a bank at either zero interest or a below-market interest rate. This was obviously quite profitable for the bank. For this accommodation, the bank made a loan to a trucking company owned by the treasurer that was located in an adjacent state. The company, however, was not credit-worthy. The loan was made at below prime rate and the bulk of the principal repayment was deferred to the end of the three-year term. Before the end of the loan term, the trucking company failed. Even with the loan charge-off, the arrangement as described was still quite profitable for the bank.

Transfers at Other than Fair Market Value.   This covers situations where either an overvaluation or undervaluation of an asset (e.g., property, car, boat, airplane, jewelry, and so on) is involved. The payer may sell, lease, or rent the subject property to the recipient at far less than its actual related value in the marketplace. In the reverse scenario, the payer may buy, lease, or rent the subject property from the beneficiary at far more than its actual related value in the marketplace. A variation on this technique is the so-called phantom sale. The recipient "sells" an asset to the payer while, in fact, retaining title or at least the use of the asset.

Payment of Bills.   The beneficiary's rent or mortgage payment, transportation (e.g., car purchase or lease payment, airfare, limousine, and so on), vacation (e.g., hotel bills, condominium rental, cruises, and so on), and entertainment expenses may be paid by the payer either directly by cash or check or by credit card. Such payments may expand beyond the beneficiary to also include some expenses incurred by one or more other persons (e.g., friend, family, or companion).

Promises of Subsequent Employment.   This is where the payer agrees to provide employment to the recipient and/or friend, family member, or companion. Such employment will be at an inflated salary and out of line with the actual duties performed or duties assumed. When the payer has received the service desired from the recipient, the employment arrangement may or may not be canceled, depending on the nature of the ongoing relationship between payer and recipient.

With respect to payments of the types indicated, keep in mind that, if funds to be paid out are restricted to regular business receipts, they must be deposited in regular accounts and used to pay legitimate business expenses. Illicit payments would come out of the same accounts but would leave an audit trail. When a payer can generate cash or other negotiable assets in other ways, this would set the stage for an off-book arrangement. No audit trail would exist from such arrangements.

HOW TO APPROACH PROVING ILLICIT TRANSFERS

Quite simply, there are only two ways to identify and trace illicit funds: from the point of payment and from the point of receipt. The forensic accountant must make the choice on how to proceed. He or she may select either one or both of the indicated approaches, depending on the circumstances, either identified or assumed. Is it known or suspected that one person is obtaining funds or assets from one or many sources or making payment of funds or assets to one or many recipients? What is the size and complexity of the organization(s) involved? What is the frequency of the payments?

Funds or assets that may be impossible to find from the payer's end may be relatively easy to identify among the recipient's accounts. The forensic accountant will attempt to choose the method that appears to be the most logical based on what is known. The latter option is elected when the known or probably scenario warrants. "As a general proposition, suspected on-book schemes are best approached from the point-of-payment. Off-book or other case schemes are easiest caught at the suspected point of receipt."[3] Based on the preceding, the forensic accountant should adopt these steps in initiating an off-book fraud review:

1. Summarize known data or suspected scenarios for the projected off-book fraud scenario.

2. Develop a business and/or personal profile on all individuals known or suspected to be involved.
3. Develop a fraud review plan with the objective of proving the suspected or known off-book payments.

Step #1 is a simple accumulation of known data or suspected scenarios for the projected off-book fraud scenario. The objectives are to determine that there is a valid reason to proceed and identify the major "holes" in the projected scenario so they will be dealt with in step #3.

Step #2 should be "alive." That means, names of individuals or businesses will be added or deleted as found to be appropriate. The initial, or phase 1, review of any individual(s) or business(es) should be expanded where the facts or assumptions warrant such action.

Step #3, built on the foundation of data available, known or suspected, from steps #1 and #2, should also be considered to be "alive." As with any fraud audit program, the fraud review plan developed under this step must contract or expand based on the information being developed during the reviews performed.

Consider steps #1 and #2 as the "familiarization" phase of the undertaking. Step #3 then becomes the program development and "review and evaluation" phases of the undertaking.

The Business Profile

To establish the business profile, it is necessary to determine the nature of the business, how it is organized (e.g., entrepeneurship, partnership—limited or general—or corporation), and its type of ownership (e.g., privately held, closely held, traded on a market). Identify the key management personnel associated with the business. What are their specific areas of authority and responsibility? Their educational and experience credentials? Their unique expertise (e.g., doctor, lawyer, accountant, economist, auditor, security specialist, or computer—management, operations, programmer, or analyst)?

Which management and support personnel are involved with the specific activity, function, entity, or support environment where the suspected fraudulent transactions have taken place? Such review undertaking can go as far down in the organization as deemed appropriate. Determine all personnel functioning as the chief financial officers and comptroller (controller) and their specific duties, activities, authority, and responsibilities. For a smaller company, this would cover all bookkeeping and other accounting personnel (e.g., accounts payable clerk, cashier, and so on).

Ascertain the primary and secondary accounting records maintained by the company and determine whether they are manual or computerized. Then review and evaluate all procedures, practices, and related internal control and check requirements to determine levels of risk in those specific areas of known or possible wrongdoing. If any risk environment, based on this review, is deemed as being too loosely controlled, these review and evaluation efforts should be expanded.

Where appropriate, determine any outside accountants, outside tax pre-parer, outside consultants, manufacturers/sales representatives who are not full-time employees, and independent contractors of whatever type and nature. (Note: Historically, such personnel have often been found to be involved in payoffs.)

Determine all bank accounts. How are they used? Who performs reconcilia-tions, and are they current? Are differences followed up and cleared properly?

Identify primary competitors, as they will often provide tips or leads for possible irregular business practices, such as filing of false claims, kickbacks, and so on.

Establish the money-flow pattern within the company for the suspected transaction(s). What are all the sources of funds? What are all the means of disbursing funds? How are the receipts, expenses, and disbursements docu-mented? How are the related records maintained?

This review, properly performed, will result in developing information normally shown on a Statement of Source and Application of Funds.

Sources of Information for the Business Profile

Stock Exchanges.   Obtain Form S-1, Perspective, if a listed company.

Business Classification and Licenses.   Check with appropriate state, county, and city/township offices.

Owners, Management, Employees, Outsiders Involved with Busi-ness.   Interview them as appropriate. Do not be reluctant to conduct second or even third interviews with anyone potentially involved in known or suspected wrongdoing when facts indicate such action is appropriate.

Suppliers, Customers, and Competitors.   Any of these can provide tips and leads for questionable business conduct or ethics. This may include information on bribes paid by suppliers to obtain business, kickbacks to custom-ers to obtain business, or kickbacks from customers to obtain "special" pur-chase pricing when not routinely being offered by business.

Financial Organizations.   This would include depository institutions (i.e., commerical banks, savings and loans, and credit unions), insurance compa-nies, and finance firms (e.g., Household International, and so on). Obtain and review copies of credit applications, financial statements, and loan files. Also obtain details of all demand deposit accounts, with special reference to how each is used (e.g., general deposits, concentration account for several bank accounts, and so on), and all investment accounts (e.g., where surplus funds may be invested for short periods when not immediately needed by the business).

Business Reporting Companies.   Obtain information from Dun & Bradstreet, Moody's, Standard & Poor's, local credit bureaus, and the Better Business Bureau in any city where the firm operates.

Any Other Sources of Data.   Public filings and state records may also provide basic information as to the company's businesses, principals, and organization. Federal or state records will provide information on income tax or other tax problems (e.g., social security, workers' compensation, and so on). Determine whether there are any legal records of any litigation pending against the company or by the company against others. Contact the telephone company for any telephone toll records. Check with UPS or similar mail and package companies to establish pick-ups and deliveries.

The Personal Profile

Determine the role in the business of each suspect. Ascertain how each person is involved in the subject wrongdoing by the nature of his or her position (e.g., duties and activities, authority, and responsibility). Identify their regular suppliers and customers.

Determine their bank accounts and brokerage accounts. How much do they have in them? What is the volume of activity? What are the sources and disbursement of funds?

Establish their asset holdings (e.g., automobiles, boats, aircraft, and real estate holdings other than primary housing). How were they acquired? What did they cost? If they have been disposed of, what and where are the proceeds from such action?

Obtain additional information, such as

1. Telephone records.
2. Better Business Bureau records.
3. Credit bureau records.
4. Liens, if any, filed against them.
5. Police or related records, past and present. This includes local and state police, as well as federal (e.g., Alcohol, Tobacco & Firearms of the Treasury Department; Drug Enforcement Agency; FBI).
6. Any current or past problems with federal or state tax authorities.
7. Lifestyle background check (e.g., using properly trained security personnel).

Focus on Identifying Off-Book Payments

Based on my own experience and that of numerous others involved in the field of fraud examination, in general, and forensic accounting, specifically, it is a recognized fact that both identifying and tracing off-book payments are routinely more difficult than for on-book fraud scenarios. For such off-book actions to be successful, both the sources and uses (applications) of those funds must be identifed. As stated earlier, the focus must be on the point(s) of receipt. It does not matter whether the point(s) of receipt are identified and traced through sound examination techniques or by tips or leads that have been properly followed up to prove or disprove the implications or facts. The source of off-book funds may be located through a number of approaches.

Direct or Indirect Evidence of Unrecorded Sales on the Suspect Company's Books and Records.
Look for evidence of transactions, focusing on costs and expenses that do not appear to be related to the known sales or business activities of the company. For example,

1. Direct charges to cost of goods sold for items purchased in the company name but shipped to one or more noncompany addresses. No sales invoices relative to those goods could be identified.
2. Shipping documents indicating deliveries to an unlisted customer (e.g., not on the company's customer list) or in the name of a fictitious customer (determined by follow-up). Inventory credited and cost of goods sold debited but no sales transaction recorded (e.g., debit to cash and/or accounts receivable and credit to sales).
3. Unexplained adjustments reducing inventory value and an attempt to hide the offsetting charge relative thereto (e.g., credit to inventory with debit to sales).
4. Rental on a warehouse in another area that is not identified as a storage facility. Some of the transactions under #1 may involve such facility.
5. Commisions paid to one or more manufacturers representatives, or sales agents, in other areas of the country, with no sales recorded in the names of those representatives or agents. Some of the transactions under #1 may be involved. This type of fraud can occur at a service firm as well as at a manufacturing or distribution company.

Evaluation of the Cost of Goods Sold to Sales Ratio.
There should be a historical pattern between the cost of goods sold and sales, the net figure being known as either gross margin or gross profit. This would be true whether the company is a manufacturing, distribution, retail, or service organization.

Applying the same principal of comparative analysis can also prove valuable to utilities (e.g., gas, electric, and water), telephone, and, in either manufacturing or distribution, transportation costs in and out. For example, what if the records indicate far more goods have been ordered than have been accounted for as having been sold or are currently in inventory? The obvious question is, what has happened to the unaccounted for inventory?

Use of the Marketplace.
Competitors may identify customers of the firm not indicated in its records. Customers have been able to identify situations where they were directed to make payments to a person or other firm and not the company for goods shipped to them from it, and situations where, during bank reconciliations, they identified payments to the company diverted to another company or person for an unknown reason.

Recognition of the Risk of Creative Accounting.   It should be understood that many off-book transactions, where there is some link to on-book assets (e.g., stealing inventory and charging it off to "shrinkage" in a retail environment), involve hiding the on-book portion of the transaction, as best as it can be done, through creative accounting. This involves passing an amount through one or more supplemental steps before it finally reaches the account of final recordation. Often this involves passing the amount through one or more accounts of the following types, which are "temporary holding" or "pass-through" accounts for the intended purpose:

1. Suspense.
2. Deferred—asset or liability.
3. Contingent.
4. Contra, offsetting debit and credit accounts.
5. Inter-unit.
6. Intra-unit.

Perform Reviews from Point of Receipt

The initial focus should be on the suspected recipient. This is particularly true when the person(s) or business(es) making payments is not known, but where it is known or assumed that some, if not most or even all, payments are in cash and are off-book transactions.

Identify Assets Held by Suspect
Both the asset and its value should be determined. Such review would include but is not limited to

1. Residence.
2. Rental real estate—consumer or commercial.
3. Second home.
4. Bank accounts.
5. Brokerage accounts—stock, bonds, commodities.
6. Automobiles.
7. Home furnishings.
8. Boats.
9. Aircraft.
10. Recreational vehicles.
11. Collectibles.
12. Loan receivable.
13. Jewelry.
14. Cash value of insurance.
15. Pension.
16. Profit-sharing plans.
17. Personal property.
18. Other assets not listed.

Relative to each of these assets, it is necessary to determine the answers to *who, what, when, where, why,* and *how* acquired and the related *cost*?

- *Who* was the seller?
- *What* is the description (nature) of each asset?
- *What* was the source of funds to acquire each asset?

- *What* documentation exists of each transaction?
- *When* did each transaction occur?
- *Where* is the documentation on the transaction located?
- *Where* is the asset located and recorded (e.g., individual or business asset)?
- *Why* is it classified as a business asset if that is how its accounting is handled? *Why* is it not classified as a business asset if such handling seems appropriate?
- *How* much did the asset cost?
- *How* was it paid for (that is, cash, check, cashier's check, money order, cash equivalent [script], hard asset swap [hard metals—gold, silver, platinum—for asset]).

Identify Actual or Contingent Liabilities of Suspect

1. Mortgages (e.g., first, second, and terms).
2. Bank or brokerage lines of credit.
3. Borrowing against cash surrender value of insurance.
4. Other loans.
5. Guarantees given on debt of others (that is, businesses or individuals—nature of guarantees to place reasonable value on contingent liability).
6. Credit cards and installment purchases.
7. Alimony and child support.
8. Taxes.
9. Other liabilities.

Again, ask the *who, what, when, where, why,* and *how* questions, such as

- *Who* is the creditor or lender for each liability?
- *What* was the original amount of each liability?
- *What* is the current balance open? (Note: Identify amount currently due on each liability).
- *What* was the purpose for incurring the debt?
- *What* security, if any, was given to support debt? (Note: Get details as to collateral, guarantees, and so on.)
- *What* documentation exists for the debt?
- *When* was each liability incurred?
- *Where* were the funds borrowed deposited or used?
- *Why* was each liability incurred?
- *How* long is the debt term for each liability?
- *How* much of each debt is currently due?
- *How* is the debt being managed? (For example, is it current or past due (how much and how many months?) Has any portion thereof been charged off? If so, identify the amount and when that action was taken. Was the charge-off on the books of both the borrower and the creditor or only one, which may be a tax-avoidance handling?

Obviously, the offset to the liability should be assets. Where are they recorded? Are they on the books of the business? (Note: A business may be used to purchase an asset but the asset is not recorded as a business asset. Rather, possession is taken by a principal of the firm or even an outsider.) For any debt, even trade payables, the forensic accountant should diligently attempt to search out and identify the asset acquired. So, consider liability identification only phase one of a two-phase review; the asset identification or how the debt proceeds were used, if to reduce other debt, should be determined by review.

Determine All Sources of Income

Obviously, this is with respect to the relevant time period (e.g., the period for which such review is being undertaken). Some categories of income to determine are

1. Salary or wages.
2. Commission and fees.
3. Profit sharing or bonuses. This would include stock convertible to cash, assets to be used as cash for payment or converted to cash by sale, as well as cash received directly.
4. Rental income.
5. Repayments of loans—interest or principal, or both.
6. Interest or dividends on bank accounts and investments.
7. Revenues from sale of assets.
8. Insurance proceeds, excluding loans.
9. Disability payments.
10. Court settlements and awards.
11. Out-of-court settlements.
12. Inheritances.
13. Other.

For purposes of this undertaking, loans should not be considered as income. Instead, they should be treated as an asset that, if properly recorded, would be offset by a corresponding liability. For each item of income identified, inquire as to

- *Who* made the payment to the subject?
- *What* was the income amount in the subject period?
- *What* legal support, if any, is there for the payment (e.g., W-2, 1099 IRS forms, and so on)?
- *When* was the income received?
- *Where* was the income recorded on the books of account, if properly indicated therein? If deposited into a bank account, identify it and the date when deposited.
- *Why* was payment made to the subject (that is, reason for income)?
- *How* was the income spent? If any of it remains, so identify.

Summarize the Significant Expenses

This would be for the same period used in developing the information above. For purposes of this effort, an expense would be any payment made for consumables for either personal or business reasons. Where offset by a liability, such amounts should not be included, as no disbursement occurred in the period. The debt would be represented by a payable at the end of the review period. Some common expense categories are interest paid out, rental and mortgage payments, utilities, transportation costs, insurance payments, credit card payments, travel and entertainment, health-related expenses, and other. For each expense category, ascertain the following:

- *Who* received the payment?
- *What* was the total amount of the expense?
- *When* was payment made?
- *Where* was the payment made or sent?
- *Why* was payment made?
- *How* was payment made (e.g., cash, check, cashier's check, letter of credit, and so on)?

Establish the Personal Profile

Follow the general criteria discussed earlier in this chapter, augmenting, as deemed appropriate, for each of the following:

1. Extramarital affairs.
2. Drug, alcohol, or gambling addiction or debts.
3. Debts (e.g., loan sharks, guaranteed loans that have been called, other debts).
4. Extraordinary medical expenses.
5. Alimony and child support payments.
6. Regular travel and entertainment expenses.

Examine Bank Account Records

Banks are potentially the most useful single source for information about the suspect, once you have identified him or her through other efforts. Once you have authorization or a subpoena, the bank will provide you with the following on both open or closed accounts:

1. Account signature cards.
2. Monthly account statements (copies).
3. Transaction data (e.g., copies of checks, deposit slips, debit or credit memorandum [DMs = debits, CMs = credits], wire/money transfers, both in or out, and so on).
4. Certificates of deposit.
5. Year-end tax summaries.

The information developed should be compared to any ledgers, registers, or account records relative thereto, as maintained by the suspect.

Keep in mind that the bank is required by the Bank Secrecy Act to keep certain records of all customers' transactions. A reference to that act will indicate those specific requirements. In addition to transaction records, the banks must retain a record of all extensions of credit over $5,000 as well as each transfer of $10,000 or more that is sent ouside the United States.

Other Key Records for Review

Other records include tax returns, including supporting schedules; credit reporting agency records; telephone toll records; credit card account records; and court records of any lien(s) filed against the suspect.

Summary

There is no mystique to proving illicit transfers. It merely requires that the forensic accountant determine his objective, establish a plan to accomplish it, and exercise due diligence, curiosity, and imagination when implementing the plan.

THE NET WORTH METHOD (OR COMPARATIVE NET WORTH ANALYSIS)

The net worth method is used when the objective is to prove illicit income circumstantially. This method should not be used by the forensic accountant until he or she is satisfied that there are no books of account or, if such records do, in fact, exist, they are not complete and reliable in that they do not properly represent the transactions affecting the subject for the review period. In either of those cases, this approach is very useful. It should show, circumstantially, the suspect's transactions and ending assets and liabilities for any review period. The technique has proved most useful when the subject is receiving currency or other payments that cannot be traced directly. The higher the percentage of such illicit income to total income, the more valuable the net worth method will prove to be. Such evidence can also prove useful to corroborate testimony given by others concerning hidden illicit payments.

The two basic methods of net worth computation are (1) the asset method and (2) the expenditures method, also known as the sources and applications of funds method. The forensic accountant would use the asset method when the suspect has invested some or all of the illegal funds in such a manner as to accumulate wealth and from it acquire assets. This, of course, would result in net worth increasing year to year.

The forensic accountant would use the expenditures method when the suspect is, on an ongoing basis, spending the illegally obtained gains on high-living, travel, and entertainment. By spending instead of investing, net worth is, of course, not increased.

Both methods begin by putting together a financial profile of the suspect as of one or more selected dates and of the transactions relative to the events between two selected dates. This would require identification of all material assets and liabilities, all sources of income, other sources of funds (e.g., loans, proceeds from sales of assets, and so on), sales of assets, and expenses incurred. For the period, the forensic accountant would determine the increase or decrease in assets held or liabilities of the suspect. Then the legitimate income would be determined. The difference between total income and legitimate income would be the income from undisclosed sources. Then the legitimate expenses would be determined. The difference between total expenses and legitimate expenses would be the irregular expenses. This format is used to develop the information necessary for determining changes in net worth for a given period.

It is important to consider the following when preparing the comparative net worth analysis:

1. Assets, regardless of when acquired, should be valued at cost, not fair market value or depreciated value.
2. Total funds available from legitimate sources should be determined by documents when possible, or estimated if necessary. Such estimates should be on the generous side.
3. Living expenses should be determined or estimated. The costs for food should be eliminated and other expenses estimated on the low side. Doubts should always be resolved in favor of the suspect.
4. After completing the exercise, interview the suspect. The purpose should be to identify all alleged sources of funds as well as to negate defenses that may be raised later.

Computing the Comparative Net Worth by the Asset Method

First, select a "beginning point" for the analysis. If there is a reasonable idea as to when the suspect became involved in illegal activities, try to select a date approximately one year before such date. For analysis purposes, that will be referred to as the "first year."

Based on data developed, compute the suspect's net worth at the end of the first year. This would be based on the cost of all assets held at the end of the first year. This is illustrated below:

Assets at Cost		Liabilities	
Cash on deposit	$ 10,000	Automobile loan	$ 22,000
Stocks and bonds	30,000	Mortgage	90,000
Condominium	160,000		
Automobile	35,000		
	$235,000		$112,000

Totals	
Assets	$235,000
Less: Liabilities	112,000
Net worth	$123,000

Compute the suspect's net worth at the end of the second year following the same approach.

Assets at Cost		Liabilities	
Cash on deposit	$ 25,000	Automobile loan	$10,000
Stocks and bonds	60,000	Mortgage	66,000
Condominium	160,000		
Automobile	35,000		
	$280,000		$76,000
Totals			
Assets	$280,000		
Less: Liabilities	76,000		
Net worth	$204,000		

Determine the suspect's known income and expenses for the second year.

Income		Expenses	
Salary	$52,000	Mortgage payments	$27,000
Bonus	10,000	Automobile loan payments	13,000
		Living expenses	5,000
	$62,000		$45,000
Totals			
Income	$62,000		
Less: expenses	45,000		
Net asset increase	$17,000		

Add the net asset increase to the net worth determined at the end of the first year. (Note: Had there been a net asset decrease in the second year, it would have been deducted from the net worth determined at the end of the first year.)

Net worth at end of first year	$123,000
Net asset increase during second year	17,000
Calculated net worth at end of second year	$140,000

Compare calculated net worth at end of second year to computed net worth at same date.

Computed net worth at end of second year	$204,000
Calculated net worth at end of second year	140,000
Net worth increase (unexplained)	$ 64,000

The unexplained increase in net worth identified above requires follow-up review and investigation.

Repeat the approach, as described, for each year of the review period. In some instances, it may be warranted to reduce the focus and perform such reviews monthly, quarterly, or semi-annually rather than annually. The principles for such reduced period reviews do not change from those described herein.

Asset Method Formula

$$\text{Assets} - \text{Liabilities} = \text{Net worth} \qquad (1)$$

$$\text{Prior year's net worth} + \text{Current year's income} - \text{Current year's expense} = \text{Computed net worth at end of current year} \qquad (2)$$

Calculated net worth from records and other data is compared to computed net worth, calculated with equation (2), to identify any difference. Such difference represents funds from unknown sources.

Computing the Comparative Net Worth Using the Expenditures Method

Based on the best information available, develop the suspect's known expenditures for the subject period (that is, a year or lesser period). This would include the use or application for any purpose, of funds on deposit or generated through sale of assets. This would include deposits to bank accounts; purchases of assets; payment of loan, credit card, and other debt; and all living, travel, and entertainment expenses.

To the degree possible, identify all sources of funds available to the suspect during the review period. To that total add the beginning cash on hand. This is the "total funds to be accounted for."

The difference between the amount of the suspect's known income and the identified expenditures is the net amount that is attributed to having come from unidentified sources. In summarizing this information, it is usual to identify application of funds before identifying sources of funds. Any difference would be the funds from unknown sources. A hypothetical comparison for a two-year period is shown on the following schedule:

Example of Use of Expenditures Method

Application of Funds:	Year 1	Year 2
Increase in bank balance	$ 9,700	$ 32,000
Downpayment on residence	12,000	—
Closing costs on residence	3,000	—
Purchase of automobile	12,000	—
Rent payments (five months)	4,000	—
Mortgage payments	6,300	10,800
Credit card payments	9,000	33,000
Other expenses (including living)	12,000	36,200
Total	$68,000	$112,000
Known Sources of Funds:		
Cash on hand	$ 4,000	$ —
Salary	52,000	54,000
Bonus	10,000	10,000
Interest and dividends	2,000	3,000
Loan proceeds	—	8,000
Total	$68,000	$75,000
Net funds from unknown or illegal sources	$ –0–	$37,000

Expenditures Method Formula

$$\underset{\text{(Application of funds)}}{\text{Expenditures}} - \underset{\text{of funds}}{\text{Known sources}} = \underset{\text{unknown sources}}{\text{Funds from}}$$

MONEY LAUNDERING

Definitions

Money Laundering/Laundering

Term used to describe investment or other transfer of money flowing from racketeering, drug transactions, and other illegal sources into legitimate channels so that its original source cannot be traced. Money laundering is a federal crime.[4]

Money Laundering Control Act of 1986
Refer to Bank Secrecy Act of 1970.

Bank Secrecy Act of 1970

Bank Secrecy Act is the common term for an act passed and signed into law in 1970 under the actual name Currency and Foreign Transactions Reporting Act. The original bill, [was] passed in 1970, and recodified in 1982, without substantive changes by the Money and Finance Act. The act was amended in 1984 with substantive changes. Additional substantive amendments were enacted on October 27, 1986, as part of the Money Laundering Control Act of 1986. The Congress, the executive branch of the federal government, the courts, and the financial community commonly refer to the bill as the Bank Secrecy Act.[5]

In October 1984, significant changes were made to the Bank Secrecy Act as a result of the passage of the Reagan Administration's Comprehensive Crime Package. These changes included:

- Rewards may be paid to individuals who provide information leading to the recovery of more than $50,000 in fines, civil penalties, or forfeitures under the various provisions of the Bank Secrecy Act.
- It is a crime to attempt to transport or ship currency or monetary instruments out of the United States illegally.
- Customs officers may conduct outbound border searches for monetary instruments without search warrants, based on reasonable cause to believe that these instruments are being transported in violation of the law.
- A Bank Secrecy Act offense may be the basis for issuing a court-ordered wiretap.
- Bank Secrecy Act offenses may be the basis for a Racketeer Influenced and Corrupt Organizations Act (RICO) charge.
- All criminal violations of Title 31 are felonies.
- Civil penalties have been increased from not less than $1,000 to not more than $10,000 for each offense.
- Currency and monetary instruments in excess of $10,000 being transported or shipped out of or into the United States must be reported on Customs Form 4790.

On October 27, 1986, the Anti-Drug Abuse Act of 1986 was enacted into law. Part of this bill is the Money Laundering Control Act of 1986. The Money Laundering Control Act of 1986 amended the Bank Secrecy Act, the Right to Financial Privacy Act, the Federal Deposit Insurance Act, the National Housing Act, and the Federal Credit Union Act. It also creates a new offense for laundering monetary instruments. All of the provisions have an impact on financial institutions and affect the Bank Secrecy Act.[6]

The Basics of Money Laundering

A forensic accountant who is attempting to trace net funds from unknown sources may identify an apparently legitimate source(s):

1. A cash based retail business (e.g., liquor store, convenient food store, and so on).
2. A number of interrelated businesses or properties. This permits moving money around several times and has the net effect of a straw man type of real estate transaction. In that situation, values increase with every movement. In the interrelated businesses, an amount increases with every movement without anyone questioning such increases. Multicompany movements complicate the audit trail so that such increases are not routinely identified.
3. Offshore loans and investment.

These are the realms of money laundering.

The forensic accountant should be aware of the distinctions between money-hiding and money-laundering schemes. The former merely conceals the existence or the source of the subject funds, or both. The latter adds to that an attempt to provide an apparent legitimate explanation for the existence of the subject funds. While both are sometimes called money laundering, only the latter actually meets the definition requirements.

Money-Hiding Methods

Some of the more common money-hiding schemes are discussed below.

1. Illegally acquired funds may be hoarded, spent to acquire only saleable assets (e.g., property, jewelry, stocks and bonds, commodities, and so on), or depositied as inconspicuously as possible.

2. Money is wired through two or more financial institutions.

3. Fictitious persons or businesses are established to enable opening bank accounts in those names. Such schemes would go so far as to obtain social security or tax identification numbers. Such accounts can be used to move large amounts for short periods. They are then closed and replaced by new accounts set up in the same manner.

4. The money launderer may open an account under the guise of a business exempt from reporting requirements. These businesses include restaurants, drugstores, and convenience food stores, all businesses that traditionally generate a high percentage of cash as a percentage of total sales.

5. The individual may offer bribes or otherwise corrupt bank officials so they do not comply with Bank Secrecy Act requirements of reporting certain specific transactions.

6. The individual may smuggle the illicit currency directly out of the country, often by private aircraft. The clean funds can return to the United States later through banks.

Money-Laundering Methods

Most experts consider all money-laundering schemes to be some form of the following three basic schemes.

Using a Legitimate Business as a Front.   That enables the concealment and comingling of illicit dollars.

Manipulating Buy-Sell Transactions.   Real estate transactions are a good indication of how to accomplish this. A buyer and seller agree to convey property worth $3 million at current market prices. Of this amount, only $2 million will be recorded as the transaction price. The other $1 million will be paid ''under the table.''

Off-Shore Transactions. This requires getting the "dirty" money out of the country by whatever means. This may be through wire-money transfers, using a bank at each end—a bank in the United States and a company outside the United States passing the funds into their account at their designated bank—or by getting the funds out of the country in some other way. Once that is accomplished, it may be possible to bring the money back in directly to another participating business, or through two or more other banks before it is then returned to the United States. The funds have then been laundered and the incoming money is considered "clean."

Federal Reporting Requirements

Following the criteria of the Money Laundering Control Act of 1986, 18 USC 1956, the forensic accountant should carefully examine the following forms for any person or business that is suspected of laundering money.

Currency Transaction Reports (CTR), IRS Form 4789. The Bank Secrecy Act and U.S. Treasury Department regulations require domestic financial institutions to report all currency transactions of $10,000 or more on IRS Form 4789 within 15 days of the actual transaction.

Report of International Monetary Instruments, Customs Form 4790 (CMIR). This form is used for any act of physically transporting, mailing, or shipping currency or other defined monetary instruments in an aggregate amount in excess of $10,000 outside the United States. The form must be filed with the Customs Service.

Report of Cash Payments over $10,000 Received in a Trade of Business, IRS Form 8300. Any person in a trade or business who, in the conduct of such business, receives more than $10,000 in a single or related transaction must file a Form 8300 within 15 days with the IRS. Financial institutions that are required to file a CTR (Form 4789) and certain businesses, such as stockbrokers and currency exchanges, are exempted.

Boat, aircraft, and automobile dealers, jewelers, pawn-brokers, and other businessess that are considered to be attractive to the criminal element are covered. Casinos are treated differently in that they file Form 8362. Nevada casinos, which make equivalent reports to Nevada state authorities, are exempt.

Foreign Bank Account Reports, Treasury Form 90-22.1 (FBAR). U.S. citizens and resident aliens are required to report annually a financial interest in or signature authority over a foreign financial account with a balance that reaches $10,000 or more.

Money-Laundering Examination Techniques

The forensic accountant uses the traditional audit tools of ratio analysis, sampling techniques, and flow-chart techniques. (Note: Short-form techniques such as TFA, SEADOC, and so on, are not acceptable. It is necessary to use the old approach of step-by-step analysis when investigating a possible or known criminal review where the intent is to prove illegal activities and transactions.) Such reviews may be supplemented by specific transaction determinations, such as manipulated buy-sell transactions and offshore transactions.

Such reviews may begin with tips or leads, or may result from deficiencies identified in procedures and practices (e.g., by internal auditing at a bank, and so on). Seeking out the who, what, when, where, why, and how of possible money laundering is not an area for inexperienced personnel. In addition to routine reviews and questions of selected transactions, experience is necessary for application of proper curiosity, evaluations of controls in practices and procedures, and evaluations of both personnel and records. If starting outside a disciplined business environment (e.g., bank, and so on), then the development of financial data is essential. The question is then, where does the information developed indicate you should go? Money laundering is a complex, not a simple, problem!

NOTES

1. Joseph T. Wells, *Fraud Examination: Investigative and Audit Procedures* (New York: Quorom Books, 1992), p. 196. Reprinted with permission of Greenwood Publishing Group, Inc. Westport, CT.

2. G. Jack Bologna, Robert J. Linquist, and Joseph T. Wells, *The Accountant's Handbook of Fraud & Commercial Crime* (New York: John Wiley & Sons, 1993), p. 122. Copyright © 1993. Reprinted by permission of John Wiley & Sons, Inc.

3. Wells, *Fraud Examination,* p. 200.

4. *Black's Law Dictionary,* 6th ed. (St. Paul, MN: West Publishing, 1990), p. 884.

5. Jeffrey L. Seglin, *Bank Administration Manual,* 3rd ed. (Rolling Meadows, IL: Bank Administration Institute, 1988), p. 47.

6. Ibid., pp. 50–51.

CHAPTER 7

COMPUTERS AND COMPUTER FRAUD

There is no such thing as a safe computer system.

Anonymous hacker

COMPUTER FRAUD

> A crime in which a computer is used as a means or instrument to commit or abet a crime, or a crime in which a computer itself is the victim. . . . Computer-related crime can be looked at as a phenomenon brought about by advances in information-process technologies. . . . Computer-related crime today is an occupational crime; that is, it is committed mainly by people with the requisite skills, knowledge, and access. Access can be gained more easily by organizational insiders (employees) than by outsiders (intruders, hackers). Therefore insiders represent a greater potential computer crime threat than do outsiders. . . .[1]

Additional definitions relative to computers are given later in this chapter.

COMPUTER AS A FORENSIC ACCOUNTING TOOL

Business use of the computer could be classified in three ways: no use, limited use, or broad use.

It is probable that a business classified under no use has a very loose accounting, administrative, and operational environment. Therefore, the exposures to both on-book and off-book fraud can be expected to be high. Such a business environment will not be considered further in this chapter.

On the other hand, a business classified under limited use could be expected to be using the computer for general ledger, cash receipts, accounts receivable, and, possibly, accounts payable. It may also be using the computer to maintain records on cash disbursements, although these are often manual, or inventory, although this is often based on "sight need" (e.g., a small pharmacy noticing open shelf space and then reordering the sold-out item) or perpetual inventory-taking control (e.g., adjusting the records to the counts just made of a specific classification or category). While the exposure to off-book fraud, if proper procedures, practices, and controls are in place, should be reduced, the reality of on-book fraud should be fully recognized.

Finally, the large business, classified under broad use, would be widely using the computer, probably on a mix of paper trail, partial paper trail and partial non–paper trail, and entirely non–paper trail. As under limited use, the risk of off-book fraud should have been reduced to a "range of risks" considered acceptable to management. However, because of the size and complexity of the business, the potential variation of systems and program approaches, and the ongoing changes to activities, functions, duties, and work-tasks, and the people to perform them, as well as changes in products and services offered, the day-to-day risks of on-book computer fraud are a business reality. The best for which management can strive is to hold such risks, threats, and vulnerabilities to an acceptable range.

Under either the limited or broad use computer environment, the forensic accountant, or a qualified associate, should

1. Review and evaluate the software used, whether developed internally or purchased from an outside software vendor. Such review should not only determine what specific software is intended to do but the level of controls built in so as to identify the perceived range of risks relative to the input, processing, and output resulting from its use.
2. If available, review the "tests" conducted on the software before it was adopted into regular use and evaluate their adequacy.
3. Where software is developed internally, ascertain the documentation standards and assess their adequacy. For all software, evaluate the adequacy of the maintenance changes made to software.
4. If available, review the "tests" conducted on the software after maintenance changes thereto and evaluate their adequacy.
5. Review and evaluate the effectiveness of "access controls" for any systems or programs.
6. Review records of historical problems involving the computer (e.g., malicious mischief, manipulation of data, input of fraudulent data and duplications of input, and so on).

Only after the preceding reviews can the forensic accountant accept the computer system, its data, and reports as being meaningful and relatively reliable. From that point, the computer can be used as a meaningful review tool.

Forensic accountants must not limit themselves to the usual audit—internal or external—data when analyzing any account of the general ledger. This includes any primary (main), secondary (sub), or tertiary (customer, creditor, or vendor) accounts. The routine computer-prepared information obtained on any account usually consists of a trial balance at the beginning of review month; depending on the level of activity, either daily or entire period listing(s) of transactions; and a trial balance at the end of review month.

The forensic accountant should think in three-month periods. These may or may not be calendar quarters, depending on the concerns of the forensic accountant. The data obtained would consist of

1. Trial balance at the beginning and end of each month of the selected three-month review period (that is, a total of four trial balances).
2. A computer-prepared comparative analysis of trend information indicated by the four trial balances.
3. Activity reports such as
   a. Daily, for each business day in review period.
   b. Monthly, for each month in review period.
   c. Alphabetically (e.g., vendor/customer) or account number order, each month and overall review period.
   d. In declining value, daily or monthly, or for overall review period.
   e. Where applicable (e.g., purchasing, expense account analysis, and so on), by vendor either by date of transactions (earliest to most recent) or in declining amount.
4. "Opposite" activity reports (Note: "Opposite," as used here, refers to entries that are the reverse of what would normally be expected.) At the primary or secondary account level:
   a. Debits to any "net worth" or "income" accounts.
   b. "Credit Memorandum" or "Adjustment" credits to accounts receivable or loan receivable, any class of inventory (e.g., raw materials, work-in-process, or finished goods), or expense accounts.
   c. "Debit Memorandum" or "Adjustment" debits to accounts payable, other current and long-term liabilities, or reserves.
5. Pass-through, clearing, suspense, inter-unit and intra-unit accounts:
   a. Daily, monthly, and period activity reports.
   b. Information under (a) sorted as to person/firm/account number affected or declining amount order.
   c. "Criss-cross" transaction identification. This involves a "matching" process whereby entries any Thursday or Friday of one week are matched by the computer against reversing entries the following Monday, Tuesday, or Wednesday. The test of records indicated as #2 and #3 covers a full-week. Such tests can be changed to any combination involving the records under #1 and #4, in either direction depending on perceived need. (NOTE: This is an expensive computer "matching" report and should only be used when there is apparent justification for incurring such cost. If it is to be used, first try it out, selecting one week from one month of the review period. If found to be worthwhile, expand to one week for each month in review period. If still found to be worthwhile, expand to entire three-month review period. Preferred week for testing is one where a month-end occurs during it.)

Summary

Fraud perpetrators, being aware of what the routine reviews of managment and the auditors are, tend to try and use the month-end to their advantage. For example, if a fraud perpetrator wanted to pass the same invoice through accounts payable twice, it would not surprise me to find the first pass through occurring in the last week of month one and the second pass through occurring in the first week of month two.

The forensic accountant should never underrate the intelligence of fraud perpetrators and should recognize that if they know the routine procedures of internal and/or external auditors, especially as to how they test and review activities and balances in a particular account, then they will perpetrate their fraud scheme so as to minimize possible discovery working against such review approaches.

The forensic accountant, applying such logic, revises traditional approaches, so as to maximize the potential of computer-developed activity and trial balance reports providing red flags of possible wrongdoing they would pursue further.

The computer is not only the primary data source for businesses classified as broad use but a useful source for businesses classified as limited use, as described earlier in this text. Generally speaking, the complexity and overall size of a business will usually be matched by the complexity and overall size of its computer environment. If the forensic accountant is not himself a computer expert, such skills should be used part-time or full-time, as needed, to assist in determining what data should be reviewed and how they can best be processed for review or analysis, or both.

COMPUTER FRAUD:

The Reality

Computer fraud is the fastest growing area of fraud. By the end of this decade, it is projected that this will become the largest single area of fraudulent activity; passing the bribery of political officials, at all levels of government. Average discovered computer fraud is currently running at $620,000+ with such fraud, on average, being ongoing for between 12 and 30 months from first incident of fraud until discovery. It is estimated that as little as 1 percent of such fraud is discovered, from the U.S. Department of Defense, to 2 percent, from the F.B.I., to 15 percent, from other organizations or persons projecting such discovery. It is the author's estimate that the number is probably between 5 and 10 percent. It is important to note that of all discovery computer fraud, only 1 out of 5 is ever reported to law-enforcement or regulatory authorities. Of every reported computer fraud situation, only 2 out of 9 is every prosecuted. Of those prosecuted, only 1 out of 3 results in a conviction. If one starts with the U.S. Department of Defense discovery estimate, then 1 out of 500 incidents is ever reported to law-enforcement or regulatory authorities and only 1 out of 2,250 ever goes to trial with only 1 out of every 6,750 incidents ever resulting in a conviction. The problem is serious and is projected to get worse even with the federal computer abuse and intrusion laws now existing.

A general profile has been developed of the computer criminal. He is a white male, age 19 to 30 years old, who is usually married (with or without children) and has some church affiliation. He has provided 2 to 12 years of service and is earning $40,000 +. He has a college degree only 20 to 40 percent of the time and no previous criminal record. He identifies with his own technology far more than with his employer's business and is employed in the data processing or accounting field. He is bright, creative, and energetic; outwardly self-confident, and willing to accept challenge; adventurous; and highly motivated. However, he feels desperate because of economic problems resulting from high living, expensive tastes, family sickness, gambling, or drug or alcohol abuse. In addition, he feels exploited by his employer and wants to get even, though he does not intend to hurt other people-just a cold, indifferent, impersonal, and exploitative employer. He sees himself as a "borrower," not a "thief."

The most common computer-related crimes involve phony vendor, supplier, or contractor invoices; phoney governmental benefit claims; phoney fringe benefit claims; phony refund or credit claims; phony payroll claims; and phony expense claims. Such crimes frequently involve a data entry clerk in accounts payable, payroll, or the benefits sections acting either alone or in collusion with an insider or outsider, depending on how effective the internal controls are in any environment.

Fraud can be classified in three ways: simple, which involves one person, either an insider or outsider, and covers some 75 percent of computer fraud; compound, which involves two or more persons, all either insiders or outsiders; and complex, which involves one or more persons inside in collusion with one or more persons outside.

Most fraud is "input" in nature. That is, the nature of the fraud is such that the fraud perpetrator does not require programming skills.

Auditing Techniques

The two basic approaches to auditing in the computer environment are audit around and audit through. The audit around approach provides checks to determine whether data input match data output. Dollar totals and hash totals are compared at both entry and output stages. The approach disregards the reality that data can be manipulated while they are being processed through a computer and focuses on input and output comparisons.

The more acceptable approach for auditing computerized accounting systems is the audit through approach. In this mode, the auditor must understand programming logic. The logic used in accounting application programs is based on a chain of events that routinely take place in a given type of business transaction and on general rules and standard operating procedures/policies (SOP).

It must be understood that in environments where computers are utilized for accounting, and particularly for on-line and distributed systems, the chance of error is magnified by the complexity of the systems. Provision is made in the system's programming (e.g., suspense accounts, unclassified expenditures, unknown vendors, unknown payees, unresolved differences, payables and receivable suspense accounts, inventory variation accounts, inter-unit and intra-unit clearing accounts, and so on) to accomodate for errors of a regular nature (e.g., those that occur due to unintentional human acts). Since data can be processed faster than related corrective actions can take place, at any point in time, there are always amounts, represented by assets either bought, sold, or disposed of, for which accounting can't be fully made in the accounts to which they will ultimately be recorded.

Nature and Extent of Computer-Related Crimes

Obviously, crimes such as embezzlement and employee theft of funds and inventory existed long before computers existed in the business arena. Accountants have long attempted to discourage such crimes by requiring a separation of duties between persons handling cash or other assets and persons making entries in the books of account. By this separation, accessibility to assets and accountability for recording transactions were divided. This was done on the principle that forcing persons to conspire to commit a theft of assets would reduce the likelihood of theft.

In the pre-computer era, all systems of record keeping had various types of paper trail. This was accomplished by requiring all business transactions to be entered in journals and supported by source documents, such as purchase orders, receiving reports, vendor invoices, disbursement vouchers, canceled checks, and sales receipts. Even with these control measures, employee theft, fraud, and embezzlement were an ongoing risk of doing business. The accounting systems were not designed to be foolproof and controls were not intended to accomplish zero defects. Therefore, wrongdoers still could find ways to circumvent or override controls.

Fraud continued into the computer era. I, for one, am of the school of thinking that such crimes as fraud, theft, and embezzlement are even more likely now that the tradional accounting controls have been reduced in their overall effectiveness. In today's computer environment, paper audit trails have often been replaced, in full or in part, by nonpaper (e.g., electronic) audit trails, which are more difficult to verify through normal audit procedures and techniques. The broader number of people who are allowed to introduce data into the system makes it increasingly difficult to control input. Speed of processing receivables is considered more important than the reduction in effectiveness of controls. I, for one, am a strong proponent of more intensive internal auditing for all firms, regardless of size, when part or all of the accounting systems are computerized.

I have been greatly surprised that some well-known writers on fraud contend that there is little reliable data supporting the claim that crime involving computers is more prevalent than before computers. They do acknowledge that individual losses from computer fraud are higher than for noncomputer fraud. They also acknowledge that the risk or threat of loss is greater in the computer environment than in the noncomputer environment. Refer to earlier computer fraud discovery estimates to see how little computer fraud is discovered of total of such wrongdoing.

Those statistics do not even consider the risk of "malicious mischief" to destroy records, which may be for revenge or to attempt to cover up or hide a fraudulent activity.

Computer break-ins by outsiders (e.g., hackers, industrial sabotage, and so on) certainly represent a far higher risk than was or is the risk of break-in to any business to get to its noncomputer business records.

Never forget that currently, the average discovered computer fraud loss is $620,000+ as opposed to $100,000 for noncomputer fraud. The average discovered computer fraud has been operational for 12 to 30 months, far longer than for noncomputer fraud.

I contend that the facts clearly indicate the fraud risks in the computer environment are higher and, therefore, the review frequency and scope of review by auditors must be broader to offset those higher risks, threats, and vulnerabilities. How should the auditors expand their scope of their computer-related audit reviews? Consider the following: First, increase "testing" of operating programs against a "master" program (e.g., originally documented program plus authorized maintenance changes). Any differences should be followed up and explained and the impact on internal controls in the program evaluated. Second, pass a "test-deck" through against a program, after a cut-off has been established, to see if the data are recorded as projected. Once the print-out is obtained, run the deck through again to bring program-related data back to their original status at cut-off.

A third method would be to conduct "tests" deliberately designed to determine if the controls built into the programs do, in fact, provide the level of safeguard intended. Such tests may be to overload a specific field, to reclassify certain data from the category to which it should be recorded into another category (category can also refer to a main or subaccount in the accounting system), or even to try to force a glitch in the program, or such other "test" as can be expected to provide reasonable comfort and confidence as to something the program is supposed to do or should not do. A "glitch" is defined as

> Temporary or random hardware malfunction. It's possible that a bug (permanent error) in a program may cause the hardware to appear as if it had a glitch in it and vice versa. At times it can be extremely difficult to determine whether a problem lies within the hardware or the software.[3]

Finally, any other periodic "test" can be performed by auditors to give them comfort and confidence relative to any known risk, threat, or vulnerability in the computer environment.

Computer Fraud Laws

The forensic accountant must have reasonable knowledge of all laws, state and federal, dealing with any aspect of computers. It should be understood that, to date, all such laws have been reactive to problems involving computers and computing. Accordingly, there are still a number of computer-related problems that are not covered, or are ineffectively covered by law but, hopefully, will be dealt with in future laws or revisions of present laws. Selected federal laws of possible interest are

1. Fraud in Connection with Federal Interest Computers (Title 18, U.S.C. Section 1030).
2. The Electronic Funds Transfer Act (Title 15, U.S.C. Section 1693n).
3. The Counterfeit Access Device and Computer Fraud and Abuse Act of 1984 (Title 18, U.S.C. Section 1030) (this is related to #1 above).
4. Computer Fraud and Abuse Act of 1986 (Public Law 99-474).
5. Electronic Communications Privacy Act of 1986 (Public Law 99-508).
6. Small Business Computer Crime Prevention Act of 1984 (Public Law 98-362).
7. Computer Security Act (Public Law 100-325).

Both federal and state legislatures have moved very quickly to make many types of computer frauds and abuses a criminal offense. The laws cover such things as hardware theft, hardware destruction, misappropriation of software, unauthorized accessing of computers, and actions involving data communications facilities to either steal data or money or to afflict some mischief.

As used in the laws, a "federal interest" computer means a federal government–owned or used computer, a computer owned or used by a financial institution, or one of a group of computers (i.e., two or more) used in committing an offense when not all of the computers are located in the same state. The elements of fraud involving a "federal interest" computer include (*a*) unauthorized access, (*b*) exceeding one's authority, (*c*) an intent to defraud, and (*d*) obtaining anything of value. While not clearly stated, software, as a thing of value, would seem be included under (*d*).

Primary Categories of Computer Fraud

Input Tampering

Input tampering involves the entry of false or fraudulent data into a computer. The data may have been altered or may be a fraudulent document (e.g., amounts raised or lowered, information thereon fabricated, or forged signature approval for entry). The primary reasons for entering such information are to overstate assets or revenues or understate liabilities and expenses. Secondarily, such input is entered to commit a fraud to the benefit of the fraud perpetrators. For example, an accounts payable clerk adds a false vendor's name to the vendors master file and then submits invoices from that vendor. Payments made on those invoices will then be misappropriated by the fraud perpetrator. In another example, an inventory supervisor may reclassify specific inventory as "scrap," even though it is not, for the purpose of misappropriating that inventory.

Input fraud is the most common computer-related crime and, not surprisingly, the easiest to prevent with effective supervision and control. The controls would include separation of duties, control totals, audit controls, and access controls.

Throughput Tampering

Throughput tampering scams are usually accomplished by altering computer instructions and, therefore, require some, although maybe quite limited, programming knowledge. Some of the scams are "french round-offs" or "salami slicing" (an example is provided as Case 1 in the next section). Based on information developed, there are fewer throughput scams than input scams.

Output Tampering

Output tampering involves the electronic theft of important company information (e.g., customer mailing lists, strategic plans or budgets, merger and acquisition plans, research and development results, formulas, and so on). This type of fraud seems to be increasing, particularly among high-technology manufacturers and software developers. Such theft has become easier with the advent of the microcomputer, because information can now be copied onto a disk or stolen over communication lines.

COMPUTER FRAUD CASES

To illustrate types of computer fraud, the following three examples have been selected.

Case 1: Fiction Regarding Materiality

This is a fraud situation known as either "a french round-off" or "salami slicing." It involves only a fraction of a cent being misappropriated from certain accounts.

A major bank went to daily interest calculations on savings accounts to meet competition. In setting up the program, they set up the following categories:

1. *Full Cent:* No adjustment necessary.
2. *Round Up:* Where an individual account had a fraction of a cent from $0.0050 to $0.0099, it would be rounded up to the next full cent, the difference to actual being accumulated with other similar account adjustments in a "suspense" account that, at the end of the run, would be cleared and charged to an interest expense account.
3. *Round Down:* Same as for #2 except fraction of a cent was $0.0001 to $0.0049. In such cases, the account would be rounded down to next lower full cent, the difference to actual being accumulated with other similar account adjustments in a "suspense" account that, at the end of the run, would be cleared and credited to an interest income account.

As management wanted to see the preceding adjustments shown broad, they had separate interest income and interest expense accounts opened just to record the round-up and round-down amounts from the entries described above.

When this changeover was announced as "in the works," the fraud perpetrators, a computer room operator and a new accounts clerk, decided to try to misappropriate from the "interest income" portion of the indicated adjustments. Their first step was to have the new accounts clerk open five new savings accounts with the minimum required used to open each. Then, after the test of the new program but before its first actual run, the computer room operator put a loop in the program redirecting the total daily interest income developed from the run, from the suspense account used to accumulate the fractions of a cent, into one of the five new accounts he and his compatriate had opened. They used each account only once a week.

The scheme worked just as planned. The total interest income accumulated each day ran from $1,200 to $1,800. The fraud perpetrators were free to draw down the manipulated interest income from one of their savings accounts the day following the credit, of a misappropriated amount, to the subject account.

Three auditors, two internal and one external, checked the program results and each assumed that the interest expense figure developed was a net figure. None checked to find out that management had wanted the interest income and expense, resulting from the daily run, to be shown separately.

Just under four months into the scheme, a fourth auditor reviewing the situation made the same assumption, but he noted the unused interest income subaccount on the bank's chart of accounts and wanted it closed, the logic being a bank rule that any main or subaccount on the chart of accounts that has not been used for more than three months should be closed. He asked computer operations to do this, and they indicated they could not. They sent the auditor to EDP Systems Planning and Development. It happened that he was sent to the programmer/analyst who had developed the program used for the purpose described. He could not believe the interest income account was not being used. He showed the auditor notes on management wanting the interest shown broad. He showed the auditor, in the program documentation, that it had been set up as requested by management. In the maintenance changes, they could find nothing to change the initial criteria for using the interest income account.

Together with an EDP auditor, they checked the prior day's run and found the funds were redirected from the suspense account holding interest income into a savings account. They then checked back each day for two weeks and found a similar redirection of that amount into a total of five savings accounts. The auditors then took over and checked the situation back to the first day the new program was run. They found the same redirection of the interest income into the five savings accounts.

The EDP auditors, through various tests and interviews identified the computer room operator who had put the loop into the program resulting in the redirection of the interest income. The security personnel, through review of account records and documents, various lifestyle checks and interviews, identified the new accounts clerk who was responsible for opening the five new savings accounts through which the diverted interest income amounts were being misappropriated. The program was corrected and funds in the five accounts reclaimed by the bank, under signed authority of the two fraud perpetrators. Management then directed the interest income subaccount be closed and all round-up and round-down amounts closed into an interest expense account, regardless of whether it had a net debit or credit balance.

In the less than a four-month period that the fraud had been ongoing, the total amount misappropriated was just under $200,000. This was developed using the "french round-off" (or "salami slicing") scheme where the maximum amount per day for any account was $^{49}/_{100}$ of 1 cent and the minimum amount per day for any account was $^{1}/_{100}$ of 1 cent, with an average of $^{25}/_{100}$ of 1 cent. To reach $200,000 a total of 80 million accounts, in aggregate, had interest income, for this program's purposes, at the indicated average rate. Using a 20-day work month, this works out to nearly 1 million accounts per day involving only the round-down calculation, as described.

The volume of data processed in computer systems tends, in my mind, to no longer let the auditor or forensic accountant hide behind the traditional shield of "materiality."

This situation is diagrammed in Figure 7–1.

Case 2: Separation of Duties—A Meaningful Control

In a large medical partnership, a clerk was assigned responsibility for handling both payroll and expense account reimbursements for all doctors. Salaries were paid to the doctors monthly, usually by electronic transfer to the bank and account they specified. The doctors could have their expenses chargeable to the partnership included as an adjustment to their salary payment, or they could receive a separate check for them. If the latter option was selected, sometimes the checks would be computer prepared and, on other occasions, manually prepared. The clerk would receive expense claims directly from the doctors. She went out of her way to have them processed and made part of that doctor's monthly salary and expense reimbursement payment. When that was accomplished, she could reintroduce the expense claims into the system and obtain a check for just the expense element. The doctors having received expense reimbursement with their salaries were satisfied. The clerk could then take the separate expense reimbursement checks, endorse them, and deposit them into an account she controlled in a false name. She did not issue two checks for the same expenses. Therefore, when a doctor's expenses were reimbursed by check, she did not draw a second check for misappropriation by her.

No programming skills were required by the clerk. Those that she paid twice, once to the doctor and once to herself, were done by using the computerized payroll system and the separate computerized expense reimbursement system. Since they were not routinely matched, the fraud was not detected for a long period of time. It was discovered when a doctor complained to the chief accountant about the amount of one reimbursement. He assigned a clerk to follow up and find out what was wrong. His clerk found it in the computerized expense reimbursement system but did not inform the chief accountant, as he was pulled off on another matter. As it happened, the reimbursement amount in that instance was correct. When the doctor called on the matter again, the chief accountant assigned another clerk. He checked the computerized payroll

FIGURE 7–1
Case 1 Operating Scenario

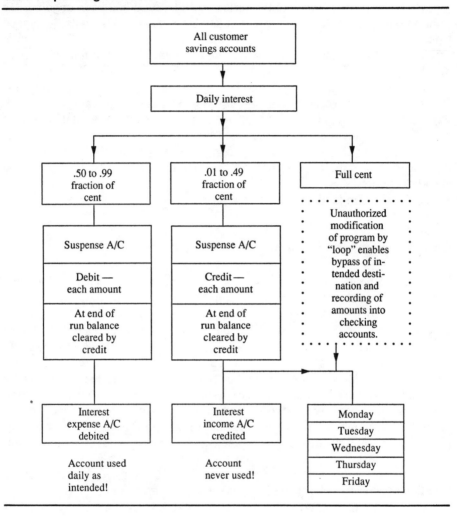

system, where $96.19 had, by clerical error, been input as $69.19. The doctor was complaining because he was underpaid by $27. Based on the second clerk's findings, a separate expense reimbursement check for $27 was drawn up and sent immediately to the doctor. When the first clerk came in and indicated the reimbursement was correct, the chief accountant matched them and found the duplicate payment of the same reported expenses. A review of the canceled checks, both made to the doctor, indicated readily a difference in signature. The auditors were called in and through follow-up identified what had happened. Further testing revealed that such duplicate payment of doctors' expenses was a relatively regular, not unusual, practice. The audit quickly identified the fraud perpetrator and the total amount of the fraud, which had been ongoing for roughly a year before discovery.

The computer was merely used as a tool to record the duplicate payment of the doctors' expenses. Had that clerk's job been separated so she handled either payroll or the expense reimbursement, but not both, this fraud could not have occurred without collusion of the personnel handling the two different functions. Forcing collusion for a fraud to be perpetrated is one of the best controls that can routinely be established in vitually any situation.

Case 3: Don't Blame the Computer—A Human Did It!

A small company purchased a general ledger computer software package. One of the controls supposedly built in was the ability of the software to check all purchase invoices to prevent duplicate payments of accounts payable. A file of all paid invoices was maintained and all new invoices checked by reference to the supplier's name, the invoice number and date, the amount on the invoice, and an identifying code.

An accounts payable clerk who had used the same software package at a prior employer's knew that the software had the capability to consolidate invoices from different units of a company and pay the total. The feature enabled payment with only code 1, company name. Where appropriate, it could break down a company as to code 2, division (e.g., manufacturing, sales, and so on); code 3, location, other than head office; and codes 4 through 9, as designed by vendor or desired for use by the payee firm. The clerk knew that an original invoice could be paid with only code 1, but the same invoice could be paid a second time if any one of codes 2 through 9 was filled in (e.g., code 1 was shown on the computer in two field spaces as "10"; if code 2 was added, it would show on the computer as "12"). The accounts payable clerk would make up duplicates of the documentation on invoices selected from vendors with whom the firm did a lot of business to reduce the possibility of discovery. He would then process the original invoice with code 1 only. The payment check would be prepared by the computer and mailed to the vendor. Then, usually several days later, he would process the duplicate documents changing the mailing address and code used. The computer would not match it as a duplicate. The computer would then prepare the check and mail it as directed, to an address designated by the fraud perpetrator at a mail box he had rented at a Pak Mail, Mail Room Plus, etc., type of business. He would pick up the checks and deposit them into a checking account he had opened under a fictitious name. He could draw down the proceeds as and when he wished. As soon as the checks were drawn on the fraudulent payments, he would destroy the duplicate documents so the vendor file showed only the original documents.

Then, a check was returned because the postage meter had not put postage on the envelope. A call to the vendor identified that they had already received payment on the invoice. When the accounts payable clerk could not explain the duplicate payment, the president called in the public accountants to check into the accounts payable system and all payments for the last year. This disclosed the fraud. When confronted with the evidence, the fraud perpetrator confessed to his actions. Again, the computer was merely used as a tool to perpetrate the fraud.

This is a situation where a program or system has unused features. When they exist, they represent a "window of vulnerability" to fraud, as in this incident. Features built into a program, whether developed or purchased, should be eliminated or "blocked" through some programming effort to reduce or eliminate such vulnerability. Computer security and data integrity are a day-to-day accounting, administrative, and opeational problem. The risks, threats, and vulnerabilities must be recognized and dealt with as appropriate. It is a complex not simple problem!

DEFINITIONS

Computer

General-purpose machine that processes data according to a set of instructions that are stored internally either temporarily or permanently. The computer and all the equipment attached to it are called hardware. The instructions that tell it what to do are called software. A set of instructions that perform a particular task is called a program, or software program.[4]

Computer System

Complete computer made up of the CPU, memory and related electrics (main cabinet), all the peripheral devices connected to it and its operating system. Computer systems fall into ranges called microcomputers (personal computers), mini-computers and mainframes . . .[5]

Client/Server

(1) Architecture in which the client is the requesting machine (PC or workstation) and the server is the supplying machine (LAN file server, mini or mainframe) . . . . (2) Request/supply relationship between programs. Applications can be designed whether running within the same computer or in multiple computers, in which one program (the client) requests data from another program (the server).[6]

Distributed Processing

System of computers connected together by a communications network. The term is loosely used to refer to any computers with communications between them.[7]

Host

Main computer in a distributed processing environment. It typically refers to a large timesharing computer or a central computer that controls a network.[8]

LAN (Local Area Network)

Communications network that serves users within a confined geographical area. It is made up of servers, workstations, a network operating system and a communications link.[9]

Server

Computer in a network shared by multiple users.[10]

WAN (Wide Area Network)

Communications network that covers wide geographic areas, such as states and countries.[11]

NOTES

1. G. Jack Bologna and Robert J. Linquist, *Fraud Auditing and Forensic Accounting: New Tools and Techniques* (New York: John Wiley & Sons, 1987), pp. 61–62. Copyright © 1987 by John Wiley & Sons, Inc. Reprinted by permission of John Wiley & Sons, Inc.

2. Joseph T. Wells, *Fraud Examination: Investigative and Audit Procedures* (New York: Quorum Books, 1992), p. 40. Reprinted with permission of Greenwood Publishing Group, Inc., Westport, CT. Copyright © 1992 by Greenwood Publishing Group, Inc.

3. Alan Freeman, *The Computer Glossary*, 6th ed. (New York: AMACOM, 1993), p. 249.

4. Ibid., p. 95.

5. Ibid., p. 100.

6. Ibid., p. 83.

7. Ibid., p. 146.

8. Ibid., p. 266.

9. Ibid., p. 303.

10. Ibid., p. 463.

11. Ibid., p. 551.

CHAPTER 8

INVESTIGATION

When you approach a problem, strip yourself of preconceived opinions and prejudice, assemble and learn the facts of the situation, make the decision which seems to you to be the most honest and stick with it.

Chester Bowles

Predication

Predication is the totality of circumstances that would lead a reasonable, professionally trained, and prudent individual to believe a fraud has occurred, is occurring, and/or will occur. Predication is the basis upon which an examination is commenced. Fraud examinations should not be conducted without proper predication.[1]

FRAUD THEORY APPROACH

It is important, because of the broad commitment of time and resources, for each fraud examination to begin with the proposition that the case will eventually end in litigation. The theory of fraud examination is explained in some detail later in this chapter. A useful investigative checklist is provided at the end of this chapter.

ASSEMBLE THE FRAUD EXAMINATION TEAM

The internal fraud examination team, also called the CHARLES+ team, is composed of seven staff functions, augmented as needed:

C: Comptroller/chief financial officer.
H: Human resources (personnel).
A: Internal audit.
R: Risk management (insurance).
L: Law/legal.
E: Electronic data processing/MIS management. and
S: Security.
+: Covers any other needed discipline.

The primary fraud examination team members are:

Leads: Internal audit   Security

Primary support: Law

Internal audit and security would usually have the responsibility for conducting various phases of a fraud examination. Law would advise them on information they would like to have to help them in legally proving and/or prosecuting a case and dos and don'ts relative to any specific aspect of the case. The secondary team members would be the other four indicated functions on the CHARLES + team.

Internally, the team may also have participation of a management representative. Externally, the team may be supplemented by any specific skills needed for the ongoing examination. Some typical participants would be an industrial psychologist, an outside consultant with specific expertise in the area or discipline where the fraud is known or assumed to exist, a representative of the public accounting firm used by the organization, and, based on the complexity, duration, and/or amount involved, or the lack of appropriate fraud examination expertise internally, a forensic accountant.

STEPS IN FRAUD EXAMINATION

It is important that the general fraud methodology be conceived and constructed so that all cases are initially handled in a uniform fashion. First, review preliminary information that justifies the undertaking of a fraud examination. Determine the skills required on the fraud examination team, develop a preliminary timeplan for the review effort, and make specific assignments. Examine all documents, then interview neutral third party witnesses and any corroborative witnesses.

Following these review efforts, interview those suspected of some level of involvement in the fraud situation. Attempt to start with the least involved or the lowest level person(s) involved and work your way up to the most involved or the highest ranking person(s) involved. The forensic accountant should never forget that no promise or commitment should be made to obtain information except for that approved specifically or in principle by those who have such authority. This would be the appropriate law-enforcement and prosecution personnel involved.

Finally, interview conspirator/coconspirators, again starting with lowest level person and working up. As a general premise, the target is examined last. An interview or interrogation would usually be conducted even when it is felt that the subject will not offer a confession. That fact may later impeach the subject when the facts differ from what he or she stated.

DATA SOURCES

To learn more about the coconspirators or the target, it is important to develop background information on them. This could identify prior legal problems (e.g., prior felony conviction(s) in other states, any prior arrests in the state where the fraud examination is being undertaken) or personal problems (e.g., filing for personal bankruptcy, and so on).

Rather than detail the numerous sources of such information on any individual(s), it is suggested that the reader obtain a copy of Edmund J. Pankau's book *Check It Out: Everyone's Guide to Investigation* (Houston, TX: Clock & Data Press, 1990), available from Clock & Data Press, P. O. Box 131016, Houston, TX 77219 (Tel. No.: 713-880-1111).

APPROACH TO FRAUD EXAMINATION

It is important for everyone to remember that no absolute assurance can be given that fraud does or does not exist in any activity, function, product, service, facility, entity, or organization. Why? Because fraud remains concealed until identification or discovery. Identification may be the result of a tip from a source, a lead from someone involved in the fraud or benefitting from it, or a confession by a participant in the fraud. Discovery may occur because of various managerial controls, ranging from organization (e.g., separation of duties), policies (e.g., setting forth the ethics standards of the business), and procedures (e.g., indicating who does what relative to a specific activity, function, work-task, or duty and the range of internal controls built therein), to internal audit (e.g., responsible for providing management with reasonable "comfort and confidence" relative to performance and the day-to-day control of risks to levels considered acceptable to management).

It is important to keep in mind that, in the routine business environment, for any discovered fraud:

1. Auditors find only 20 to 25 percent.
2. Procedures and the internal controls therein identify some 20 to 25 percent.
3. The remaining 50 to 60 percent are discovered by tips, by leads, or accidentally.

It is important for a forensic accountant to be aware that, in complex fraud scenarios, the fraud perpetrators may actually use a "bait" fraud to conceal other ongoing frauds. Obviously, the hidden frauds are financially the most rewarding. Ironically, the discovery of a fraud will often distract the investigator from proceeding, with the result that the hidden frauds can continue from that point in time until discovery. For reasons such as this, a forensic accountant should never express any opinion that any enterprise is free of fraud.

Some years ago, while a group head in audit at a major bank, I traveled from the United States to Europe with the general auditor of another major bank. During the trip he bragged that "my bank has never had a fraud overseas." He refused to back down when I insisted there was a difference between his statement and the reality that "his bank had never discovered a fraud overseas." Some three months later, when we were both back in our offices, he telephoned me to advise that "they had discovered two major frauds [$1 million +] that had been ongoing for over a year each when found."

THEORY OF FRAUD EXAMINATION

Every fraud examination should begin with the perspective that any case developed will potentially end with litigation. The forensic accountant, in any complex fraud examination, must implement the case theory approach. This has been found to be a most valuable tool. First, analyze the available data and create a hypothesis. Then perform reviews to augment the database with the objective of proving or disproving the hypothesis. With the increased database, test the hypothesis. If the findings are positive, continue the evidence-gathering effort until the hypothesis is proven to the point at which a legal case can be made. If the findings indicate the hypothesis is not totally correct, refine and amend the hypothesis and continue the evidence-gathering effort until it is possible to draw a positive conclusion and proceed to the point at which a legal case can be made. This phase of the case theory approach can be repeated under as many different hypotheses as necessary until the case is proven or there is satisfaction that no fraud exists in the subject activity, function, product, service, or entity within the organization where the reviews are being performed.

Restated, the case theory approach begins with the assumption, based on the known fact, that a fraud may have occurred. Then the reviews, as indicated, are undertaken to prove or disprove that assumption. That is the basic objective for initiating the indicated reviews.

INVESTIGATIVE OBJECTIVES

One of the characteristics that somewhat distinguishes white-collar crime investigations from those of non–white-collar crimes is that the investigator must establish the intent as well as the underlying motives of the subject(s) by identifying the jigsaw puzzle pieces of what has been going on and building the puzzle to the point at which individual pieces that appear to be legitimate when combined with other pieces will indicate the criminal activity(ies).

ELEMENTS OF WHITE-COLLAR OFFENSES

All white-collar offenses have been found to have the following common elements:

1. *Intent:* To commit a fraudulent act.
2. *Disguise of wrongdoing:* Efforts to hide the fraudulent act by improper actions and/or misrepresentations.
3. *Carelessness of the victim:* Which may have helped the fraud perpetrator to select a specific "target."

It is necessary to prove intent in nearly all criminal fraud situations. Ironically, intent is often not self-evident. Therefore, it must be proven through a pattern of activity. Some of the more common ways to show intent would include proof that the subject

1. Did not give any legitimate reasons to explain his or her actions.
2. Repeated the wrongful actions necessary to make the fraud scheme function.
3. Made conflicting statements.
4. Made admissions relative to his or her improper actions.
5. Attempted to misdirect or otherwise slow the progress of the investigation into the offense.
6. Made knowingly false statements.

Where appropriate, the victim (the company) must establish that the wrongdoer breached his or her responsibilities for the assets whose care was entrusted to him or her.

Fraud is unique in that concealment is required. In traditional crimes, there is generally no effort to conceal the wrongdoing. The objective of concealment, of course, is to keep the victim ignorant of what has occurred.

COLLECTION, ORGANIZATION, AND ANALYSIS OF EVIDENCE

The proof in most complex white-collar cases proceeds usually through basic stages:

1. Build the circumstantial case through interviews of cooperative witnesses and the available documentation.
2. Use the circumstantial evidence to identify and turn an inside witness who can provide direct evidence against the defendants.
3. Seal the case, identify and rebut defenses, and prove intent through examination of the subject or target.[2]

QUALITIES OF FRAUD EXAMINER

Forensic accountants must be able to effectively utilize the skills from their education and training (e.g., accounting or auditing, or both). They need to solicit facts on any aspect of the case from people with whom they have contact. After evaluating the data developed, they will

1. Determine where more work is required and initiate actions to either perform it or have it performed.
2. Draw the proper conclusions from it.
3. Ascertain if the review findings provide adequate evidence for a prosecutor to use in taking appropriate legal action for the situation.

Finally, they report the results of the examination. This must be done accurately and completely.

Peter Drucker is supposed to have said that "there are only three problems in business—they are 'communications,' 'communications,' and 'communications.'" Forensic accountants must be expert in communications. Why? Because being about to deal effectively with people is essential to their doing their job properly. Some of the positive aspects of communication and interpersonal skills that forensic accountants must possess are their attitude toward others, the interest they show in others, and their establishment of rapport with others. They must be able to adjust to differing personalities and circumstances.

Forensic accountants need the ability to understand accounting and finance, internal controls, and the levels of risk that the management of the subject organization has decided to accept. This will enable the fraud examination to identify procedures, practices, and controls that result in the actual risks exceeding the desired level of those risks. Such situations may be red flags as to possible wrongdoing.

A USEFUL INVESTIGATIVE CHECKLIST

1. Review report and workpapers of last internal audit and/or public accounting review in area of concern.

2. Evaluate data accumulated prior to your participation in the fraud review effort.

3. If you do not have a sound foundation as to the activity or function where fraud review is being undertaken, perform a prefamiliarization (e.g., reading up on principles and practices in environment) and familiarization (e.g., observing actual work environment and getting to know key personnel) so you have an adequate knowledge level in the fraud review environment.

4. Determine the concerns of management: have they identified an actual fraud or do they merely have concern that a fraud activity may be in existence? This requires an understanding of "area of concern," "parties of concern," and "possible nature of fraud, including amount thought to be involved."

5. Ascertain the records needed, where they are kept, and for how long they will be needed. Determine if originals can be withdrawn from files and replaced with copies.

6. If appropriate, determine if a cut-off would be appropriate for certain records. If so, determine when such cut-off will occur.

7. Review and understand the organization in such area and specific authority and responsibility of key personnel.

8. Assemble investigative team.

9. Lay out fraud examination plan.

10. If and as appropriate, utilize outside information sources to supplement internal data (e.g., Dun & Bradstreet, Moody's, Standard & Poor's; city, county, state, and federal tax sources; Better Business Bureaus; professional associations, such as AICPA, bar association, and so on; state and federal bureaus of investigation and/or regulatory authorities for a specific industry, for example, banking; and so on). Where warranted, use outside services for lifestyle and background checks (e.g., Burns, Pinkerton, Wackenhut, and so on).

NOTES

1. Association of Certified Fraud Examiners, *Advanced Fraud Symposium: Planning the Investigation Segment* (Austin, TX: Association of Certified Fraud Examiners, 1992), p. 1.

2. Joseph T. Wells, *Fraud Examination: Investigative and Audit Procedures* (New York: Quorum Books, 1992), p. 251. Reprinted with permission of Greenwood Publishing Group, Inc., Westport, CT. Copyright © 1992 by Greenwood Publishing Group, Inc.

CHAPTER 9

GATHERING EVIDENCE

The best evidence rule deals with written documents proffered as evidence.

Association of Certified Fraud Examiners, Fraud Examiners Manual

EXAMINATION EVIDENCE—DECISIONS AND RULES

Introduction

A lot of information is gathered during most investigations. However, only a small portion will wind up as evidence.

> Evidence, then, is actually distilled information. The distillation process is one of the gathering, examination, and appraisal plus a constant testing against both the theory of the case and possible violations of law.[1]

> Every fraud examiner faces the decision of how much evidence to accumulate. Given enough time and money, perhaps more frauds could eventually be resolved. . . . In each fraud case, a tradeoff must be made between the cost and the benefits of additional searching.[2]

> The purpose of obtaining evidence is to substantiate or refute specific allegations.[3]

Information Sources

Information will come to the fraud examiner either from persons (e.g., tips, leads, or explanations of situations identified during the reviews) or things (e.g., accounting records, personnel records, reports or exception reports, computer-stored data, bank records, transaction documents, contracts, notes, miscellaneous items, and so on). Some will come without investigation or solicitation, but most will be the result of due diligence of performance in those areas.

The fraud examiners' productivity will be enhanced if they know the system of the organization, its procedures, its paper flow, disposition of documents, handling of both cash receipts and disbursements, and records retention practices.

Information Gathering

Obviously, the defense and prosecution, in any case, have specific strategies and objectives for use of information developed. The fraud investigator must understand them so that the reviews performed focus on helping achieve the indicated strategies and objectives.

Typically, the defense strategy is to control critical information and, where legally possible, control access to it. On the other hand, the prosecution strategy is simply to develop as much evidence as possible. To do this, they must have access to as much information as possible. To avoid evidence being destroyed, the prosecution must strive to obtain evidence as quickly as possible. They can call on the legal system to help them whenever possible (e.g., administrative summons, grand jury subpoenas, search warrants, consent searches, civil investigative demands, voluntary disclosures, and so on).

Objectives of Evidence

Competency of Evidence

Competency is defined as "the quality or state of being competent."[4] Competency of evidence focuses on the degree to which any specific evidence is considered to be believable. When any evidence is considered highly competent, it can also be considered to be persuasive. In such situations, its competency will not be improved if more related evidence is gathered or it had been collected on a more timely basis. "It can only be improved by selecting evidence-gathering techniques that increase one of the elements of competency which are: (1) relevance, (2) objectivity, and (3) legality."[5]

Evidence is considered to be relevant when it clearly pertains to the examination. It must logically help prove or disprove a specific fact(s) at issue.

Evidence is considered to be objective when it can readily be deemed to lend proof to a point. Some contend that evidence is objective if two or more people draw the same conclusion upon examining it.

Evidence is considered legal when it answers all of the related legal requirements. Specifically, this occurs when the evidence is rightfully admissible. "Evidence that is obtained from incompetent individuals, and evidence that is disqualified because of inadequacies on the part of examiners or others would not be legal evidence."[6]

Sufficiency of Evidence

The quality of evidence obtained determines whether it is sufficient or not. In making such determination, its nature must be considered. "For example, a small amount of direct evidence (such as eyewitness information) might be sufficient while a larger amount of indirect evidence might be insufficient."[7] Indirect evidence is that which deals with a probability of the facts or is circumstantial.

Materiality of evidence is the final aspect of sufficiency. Material evidence is evidence without which the case cannot be fully supported. Evidence is material if it supports the probability or improbability of a significant fact.[8]

Timeliness of Evidence

Timeliness refers to *when* evidence was developed. It is usually considered that evidence is more competent and persuasive when it is obtained as early as possible in the examination. Whenever possible, written documents, depositions, photographs, photocopies, microfilm, and microfiche represent preferred evidence. The reliability of some evidence can be reduced as the memories of eyewitnesses fade. There is also the risk of evidence disappearing (e.g., destroyed or misplaced documents, even perishable goods—where photographs thereof are the best retainable evidence).

TYPES OF EVIDENCE

Introduction

The four general classifications of evidence are people, documents, physical evidence, and personal observations. Each of these may be broken down into classes. For example, an auditor on a financial statement review would have some or all of the following classes of evidence:

1. *Observation:* actually seeing certain things being done.
2. *Comparative analysis:* matching actual performance to criteria in policies and procedures of the firm and of GAAP/GAAS and, as appropriate, laws, and regulations (e.g., a bank filing reports with the U.S. Treasury on cash transactions of $10,000 or more).
3. *Physical examination:* inspection or count.
4. *Confirmation:* receipt of a response from an independent third party.
5. *Documentation:* supporting all economic events recorded and all binding contracts into which the firm has entered (e.g., loan agreement with bank, leases on premises or equipment, and so on). Documentation information may be stored on computers or maintained in records retention.
6. *Interpersonal:* developing written or oral information through contact with personnel at all levels.
7. *Accuracy:* rechecking computations, verifying accuracy of data in reports and as stored in computers.

People as Evidence

People include witnesses, victims, complainants, contacts, informants (who provide leads), clients, customers, vendors, police, expert witnesses, and anyone else who can provide information of value to the case.

Such evidence can be direct, for example, an eyewitness, or indirect, for example, an expert witness. Its advantage of communicating the desired information is obvious. However, such testimony has the disadvantage of confusing, confounding, or being inconsistent with other data presented. Skilled lawyers, both for prosecution and defense, have the ability to reduce the intended credability of the person presenting the evidence or the evidence itself, or both.

Documents as Evidence

We are all aware that documents can be used to conceal fraud. They can be altered, created (counterfeits), forged, or destroyed. Properly selected documents will usually meet the three objectives of evidence discussed earlier. The key is that they should be objective, independent, and easily understood. The fraud examination must be aware of the numerous ways by which documents may be used in fraud, including

1. Enabling the fraud to be perpetrated.
2. Hiding the fraud (e.g., destruction of documents).
3. Misdirecting the fraud examiner.

The fraud examiner must be familiar with a discipline known as "questioned document examination." Persons who are specialists in questioned document examination are trained in forensic chemistry, microscopy, and photography. Accordingly, they are qualified to function as an expert witness. "They express expert opinions on such matters as (1) the authenticity of documents, (2) the author of the document, (3) alteration of documents, and (4) document preparation."[9] It is not expected that the regular fraud examiner or forensic examiner will have such skills. They do, however, need to know such expertise exists and the range of services such individuals can provide.

The "best evidence" rule deals with written documents proffered as evidence. This rule simply requires that where the contents of the document are at issue, for whatever reason, the original, if available, and not a copy thereof, must be presented at a trial. Where this is not possible, for example, the original has been destroyed or is held by an opposite party and is not subject to legal process by search warrant, then the court must be so informed of such facts. Then an authenticated copy may be substituted.

Photocopies of original business documents and other written material (e.g., writing or printed materials) are often made to preserve evidence. These are used by fraud examiners so that original records, deemed by management as needed to run a business, are not removed from the appropriate files or records. To ensure that there is no deliberate or inadvertent destruction or loss of any such documents, a certified true copy should be made and retained by the fraud examiner. While acceptable to most courts, the original documents are still preferred by them.

My approach is somewhat different than that of other fraud examiners. When I identify an original document that is, in my opinion, a key document for the case on which I am working, I take the original document. On the back or on a small piece of paper attached to it, I mark where it was found, the date and time it was removed from the file, the person told that it was being removed and replaced with a copy, and the fact a copy was put in the file and I hold the original. When the copy is placed in the file, it is marked on the back in the upper right corner, or on a small piece of paper stapled to it, that I hold the original document and when I took it. I use two rubber stamps to record this information:

1. Document held by me:
   ORIGINAL HELD
   BY W. T.
   THORNHILL
2. Date and time taken:
   TAKEN: 10/12/93
   TIME: 11:45 AM

It is necessary for me to write in the date and time following the words on the stamp.

Obviously, I only do this when it has been cleared by the attorney for whom I am working and/or company management. If I am not permitted to take the original, I mark my copy as to the date the document was found and where it was found, indicating file cabinet, draw from top, and specific folder, if applicable.

Unfortunately, on fraud examinations, I have had original documents disappear between the time when they were first seen and when I went back to retrieve them. That is why you should consider my current preferred approach, as described.

When an original is not available and a copy of a document is presented to the court, it is known as "secondary evidence." This is the same level of creditability as the recollections of a witness presented verbally. Remember that when introducing secondary evidence, one must explain why the original document is not being presented to the court. While federal courts give no preference to the type of secondary evidence, the majority of other jurisdictions do.

It is important to be aware of the "chain of custody" responsibility for evidence in the form of document or object (means or instrument) seized at a crime scene or as a result of a subpoena duces tecum (for documents), or discovered in the course of a fraud examination. Such documents should be marked, identified, inventoried, and preserved to maintain them in their original condition and to establish a clear chain of custody until they are introduced at the trial. Gaps in possession or custody, should they occur, could result in the evidence being challenged at the trial, with the other side trying to raise doubt as to their authenticity. Remember that for a seized document to be admissible as evidence, it is necessary to prove that it is, in fact, the same document seized and in the same condition as when seized.

Physical Evidence

While fraud examiners will not use physical evidence as often as documents or people, it is important that they understand such evidence can be important.

Obviously, physical evidence is of great importance to investigators dealing with crimes of violence. In many cases, such physical evidence will be subjected to forensic analysis. The fraud examiner, who has a background in accounting or auditing, should rely on the judgment of the investigative, security, and legal practitioners as to how to deal with physical evidence.

Broadly speaking, physical evidence can be classified as objects (e.g., broken locks, disconnected burglary alarm systems, and so on), substances (e.g., grease, graphite, and others), traces (e.g., paint left on tools or equipment), and impressions (e.g., cutting marks on glass, tire tracks, fingerprints, and so on). Do not underrate the importance of physical evidence to its potential value in proving a point in a nonviolent crime. Let the qualified experts guide you.

Personal Observations as Evidence

The fraud examiner must be aware of the importance of using the senses to assess certain activities and functions. It is probable that during any fraud examination, the forensic accountant will have the opportunity to exercise sight, hearing, and touch frequently, and smell and taste on occasion. The main thing is for you to see it, not merely report that someone else saw it.

Rules of Evidence

In the rules of evidence, anything perceptible by the five senses and any form or type of specified proof, such as testimony of witnesses, records, documents, facts, data, or concrete objects, may be legally presented at a trial to prove a contention and induce a belief in the mind of the court or jury.

Principles of Testimony

In the U.S. tradition, witnesses other than experts cannot generally testify as to probabilities, opinions, assumptions, impressions, generalizations, or conclusions but only as to things, people, and events they have seen, felt, tasted, smelled, or heard firsthand. Even then, those things must be legally and logically considered as relevant.

Logical relevancy simply indicates that the evidence being offered must tend to prove or disprove a fact or consequence.

Evidence can be direct of circumstantial. Direct evidence will prove a fact directly. Circumstantial evidence proves the desired fact indirectly. Therefore, indirectly, it depends on the strength of the inferences raised by the evidence.

The materiality rule requires that evidence presented must have some material (importance) value to a case or otherwise prove the point in issue.

Competency of evidence means that which is adequately sufficient, deemed reliable, and is considered relevant to the case and is presented by a qualified and capable witness. It must be remembered that competency differs from credibility. Competency is a question that arises before considering the evidence given by a witness. Credibility is one's veracity. Competency is for the judge to determine; credibility is for the jury to decide.

Judicial notice is a process by which a judge may, on his or her own motion and without the production of evidence, recognize the existence of certain facts that bear on the controversy being tried.

Cautions when Collecting Evidence

"Fraud examiners must exercise due care when gathering evidence. There are risks involved, including gathering evidence illegally (without adequate search warrants or probable cause), losing or mishandling evidence."[10] The importance of due diligence and extraordinary care by the fraud examiner in developing and accumulating evidence cannot be overly emphasized.

NOTES

1. Jack Bologna and Paul Shaw, *Forensic Accounting Handbook* (Madison, WI: Assets Protection Publishing, 1993), Chapter 5, p. 1.

2. Joseph T. Wells, *Fraud Examination: Investigative and Audit Procedures* (New York: Quorum Books, 1992), p. 154. Reprinted with permission of Greenwood Publishing Group, Inc., Westport, CT. Copyright © 1992 by Greenwood Publishing Group, Inc.

3. Ibid.

4. *Webster's Ninth New Collegiate Dictionary* (Springfield, MA: Merriam-Webster, 1986), p. 268.

5. Wells, *Fraud Examination,* p. 155.

6. Ibid.

7. Ibid.

8. Ibid., p. 156.

9. Ibid., p. 162.

10. Ibid.

CHAPTER 10

─────────

INTERVIEWING AND INTERROGATION

─────────────────────────────

Man is known by what he says and by what he does. The spoken word is potentially the largest source of the various forms of evidence available to the investigator.

Robert F. Royal

INTERVIEWING

Perspective

An interview is a data-gathering exercise. In the ordinary course of an audit examination, the objective is to learn about what is being done, why, and the specific authority, responsibility, duties, and work tasks of individuals being interviewed. When an interview is being conducted in connection with a fraud examination, its primary objective remains a data-gathering exercise, but with a focus more on specific factors relative to the possible or known fraud situation.

There is a need for victims, witnesses, and suspects to be interviewed that is routine in both public law enforcement and fraud investigation efforts conducted in the private sector. There is, however, a fundamental difference as to how the public and private sectors approach investigations. The objective in public law enforcement is to prepare a case against the interviewee and/or others, specifically for prosecution and trial. On the other hand, the private sector may have the same interest as the public sector or may merely be preparing a case to enable the Human Resources (Personnel) Department to terminate the suspect's employment and, at the same time, prepare a defense, if needed, for any legal action (e.g., unemployment, arbitration, and so on) by the discharged former employee against the firm.

Definitions

Interview
An interview is a nonaccusatory structured question-and-answer session in which specific behavior-provoking questions are asked. The questions should

be intended to obtain information. While listening to the responses to questions, the interviewer must be observing the behavior symptoms of the interviewee. Such undertaking may confirm previously identified factors or conditions as well as introduce new information that can be accepted or may require further reviews, testing, and/or interviews of others.

Interviewer

An interviewer is an individual skilled in the nature and approach to effective interviewing and capable of interpreting both verbal and physical behavior.

Interviewee

An interviewee is a person who may provide information for the ongoing review, a suspect who is currently thought to be in some way involved in the matter under review, or a witness who can provide direct or indirect evidence relative to the matter under review. It should be understood before the interview begins that the witness may or may not be providing truthful information.

Suspect

Any individual within the scope of the [matter] who has not yet been cleared by the investigation. A suspect under this definition can be either truthful or untruthful.[1]

Overview of the Interview Process

Part 1: Preparation and Strategy

The interviewer should preplan the interview. At a minimum, the general subject areas should be laid out in the desired order of questioning. At a maximum, the interviewer should lay out a broad list of specific questions to be asked. They can be supplemented during the interview based on responses received during the interview from the interviewee.

Part 2: Interviewing

This part of the undertaking looks at the nonaccusatory interview in the following ways. The interviewer must consider

1. *Fact gathering:* This is the actual heart of the undertaking. It is where most of the effort should be directed.
2. *Cognitive interviewing:* This is a method used to enhance the recollection of the interviewee.
3. *Selective interview:* This is a means by which to evaluate the information being provided by the interviewee to determine if it is or is not truthful.
4. *Neurolinguistics:* This is a method of evaluating both verbal and physiological responses by the person being interviewed. Verbally, the interviewer focuses on visual, auditory, and kinesic modes. Physiologically, the interviewer observes all aspects of what has become more commonly referred to as "body language."

It is justified to again mention that such undertaking is nonaccusatory in nature. Even so, there is a lot to be learned over and above the actual words stated by the interviewee in response to the questions of the interviewer. The effective forensic accountant, when conducting interviews, must have the skills to pick up signals, verbal and physical, sent to him by the interviewee and then to follow up on them with additional questions, or follow-up actions, as the circumstances warrant.

Interviewing, relative to a possible or known fraud situation, must never be conducted in the naive approach of only listening to the words given in response to questions. It is important to remember that the information given by the interviewee to the interviewer breaks down somewhat along the following lines, on average:

1. Verbal:

Actual statements taken literally	40%
Neurolinguistic inferences (auditory and kinesic mode) provided in statements made	20
Total verbal	60%

2. Nonverbal:

Eyes	20%
All other body language	20
Total nonverbal	40%

While the above percentages will vary, the breakdown of total information provided by the interviewee can be projected to be in the plus or minus 5 percent range of the figures shown.

Positioning

The objective of the interviewer is to be as unintimidating as possible when meeting with the interviewee. The way the two persons are seated should reflect that to the maximum degree possible. Keep the following principles in mind: If you are in the office of the interviewee, where there is a seating option, the interviewer should take the seat that is the least restrictive (e.g., as far away from the interviewee's path to the door as is possible). The overriding factor, however, is that the interviewer should not be more than three leg lengths away from the interviewee, even if they are separated by a desk. For example, the interviewer should not sit in a seat or couch some distance away from the interviewee, even though it would be the least restrictive seat in the room from the perspective of where the interviewee is seated. Either both should be in the reception area of the office or both near the desk.

If the interview is held in a conference room, let the interviewee take the seat nearest the door. Again, however, the interviewer should not be more than three leg lengths distant from the interviewee.

INTERROGATION

Perspective

Interrogation is an important tool that, if properly used, can develop information, and/or a confession(s), from wrongdoer(s) in any matter under investigation.

Definitions

Interrogation

An interrogation is an accusatory question-and-answer session between the interrogator and suspect during which the suspect will be accused of involvment in the particular incident or series of incidents.

Some attorneys prefer to call this undertaking an interview. If that is done, this should be called an accusatory interview in contrast to the regular data-gathering interview described earlier. If such distinction is not made, the meaning of the word *interview* can be confused between the two different approaches to use of the word. Most security personnel and auditors, including forensic accountants, prefer using *interview* and *interrogation* as defined in this chapter. Lawyers, on the other hand, tend to use *interview* for both undertakings.

Interrogator

An interrogator, like an interviewer, is an individual skilled in the nature and approach to effective interviewing and capable of interpreting both verbal and physical behavior.

Attitude/Approach of Interrogator

Study has shown that the greatest reasons for denials by persons being interrogated are the fear of consequences of confessing, the attitude and personality of the interrogator, and the suspect's perception of the interrogator. Therefore, this is an undertaking requiring some recognition by the interrogator of the way he is perceived by the person being interrogated. Be strong, be forceful, but do not be overbearing, overly aggressive, or nonempathic. When an interrogator is disliked by a suspect, that may culminate in distrust and denial, rather than the confession for which the undertaking is striving. The interrogator who comes across as too mechanical, matter of fact, or passive may cause a denial. In addition to the intimidation factor, the interrogator must come across as a reasonable person who has a tough job to do.

On the other hand, an interrogator who is too passive may come across to the suspect as being weak. When that happens, the suspect may exploit it through either denials or aggressive behavior. An interrogator who tries to rush the suspect into a confession may actually encourage the suspect to deny. The suspect feels he or she can win the encounter by waiting the interrogator out.

When an interrogator does not come across to the suspect as being certain of the facts, this can cause a suspect to deny. He or she would base such denial on the belief that he or she has not as yet been identified by the ongoing investigation. The suspect is assuming that incorrect statements or uncertainty by the interrogator could be because either the interrogator is not properly prepared or the investigation is not being competently performed. The suspect may also be denying because he or she believes the interrogator can be fooled.

An interrogator's reputation may result in denial by the suspect. If the interrogator is known as ruthless, rough, uncaring, or unfair, the suspect may deny everything, because he does not want to deal with such an individual. An interrogator may cause a suspect's denial by using realistic words that recreate the seriousness of the incident in the suspect's mind. A good interrogator will use rationalizations to minimize the seriousness of the suspect's actions. Finally, the interrogator should avoid long pauses or silences. These allow the suspect an opportunity to think and consider other ways by which he or she might convince the interrogator of his or her innocence. Silence rarely will enhance the likehood of a confession by the suspect.

The Accusation

This is the last step in the investigative process. The interrogator, prior to conducting the interrogation, should determine the accusations available and the ways of establishing the credibility of the investigation. It is imporant that the interrogator establish in the mind of the suspect that guilt has been fully established by the investigation. An improper approach to making the accusation will increase the probility of denial by the suspect. The interrogator should always have a Plan B should Plan A fail in making the accusation. A denial should not distract from the effort to push the interrogation to a satisfactory climax.

The Role of the Interrogator

It is important that interrogators understand they have a role to play. They should view themselves as actors in a play. The role they choose must serve to accomplish their end objective: a confession from the suspect. Interrogators must consider their dress, language, approach, and professionalism, and the anticipated impact each will have on the suspect.

Miranda Rights

In public law-enforcement cases, it should be anticipated that the suspect will invoke his rights under *Miranda*. Should that occur, it is important that the interrogation stop immediately. If not, any resulting confession will be rendered inadmissible in the courts.

Should an interrogator in the private sector read the *Miranda* warning to a person he is about to interrogate? That question should always be asked of an attorney before an interrogation is to be undertaken. If it is the intent to use a confession or other facts obtained in the interrogation in a subsequent court case, the burden of such decision should rest with an attorney, even though neither the attorney nor the interrogator are, by definition, members of the judicial or law-enforcement arms of the public sector.

If you are not working for a law-enforcement or regulatory agency, you should discourage use of the miranda warning. It is not normally required and tends to build up an unnecessary wall of resistance from the suspect being interrogated.

Positioning

In an interrogation, the objective is to be intimidating but to stop short of duress. Wherever possible, the interrogator should be between the suspect and the door. To the degree possible, he or she should be no more than two leg lengths away from the suspect. It is important in an interrogation to get the suspect into a closed conference room or office other than his or her own. Since interruption can destroy all the effort of the interrogation, up to that point in time, I use the following actions to minimize the possibility of any interruption:

1. I disconnect the telephone if it is softwired. If hardwired, I request the operator to shut off the line. If that cannot be done, I take the telephone off the hook and cover it with a coat, towel, or some other object and adjust the sound to the lowest level.
2. I have a staff accountant stationed outside the door to keep people out while the interrogation is under way. That person does not move into position until after I am in the room with the subject. Before doing this, get an attorney to confirm it is not "false imprisonment."

These techniques permit me the maximum opportunity to interrogate the suspect one-on-one with minimum possibility of interruption.

Nine General Rules for Interrogation

1. Make a Direct Positive Confirmation
Indicate that you have in the file the results of the investigation into the issue that clearly indicate the suspect's participation, if more than one are involved, or the suspect's guilt, if only one is involved.

2. Develop a Theme
In a monologue, the interrogator proposes the reasons and motives for the wrongdoing.

3. Handle Denials
Be aware that truthful suspects usually do not ask to talk, and they do not move beyond this step as their denials increase. Deceitful suspects will quite

often try to deny. If the interrogator resists the denials, the deceitful suspects will usually persist, which can provide a level of reassurance that the suspect is guilty.

4. Overcome Objections
This is a statement or reason offered by the suspect to prove he or she is not involved in the wrongdoing covered by the interrogation.

5. Procure/Retain Suspect's Attention
Do not let the suspect draw into a shell. The interrogator attempts to regain the suspect's attention by intensifying the theme. Establish physical closeness. Physical gestures of sincerity are to be used by the interrogator to establish an attitude of understanding.

6. Handle Suspect's Passive Mode
At this stage, the suspect should be less tense and may appear defeated. He or she is listening to you and may begin to cry. Intensify the theme and condense it down to one or two sentences underlying the essential elements. Begin reviewing the component elements of the wrongdoing. Maintain close physical proximity.

7. Present an Alternate Question
This consists of a question in which the suspect is offered two incriminating choices concerning some aspect of the wrongdoing, based on an assumption of guilt. For example, "did you plan this out or was it a spur-of-the-moment action?" Pick one and press it. Change to the other option if warranted.

8. Have Witness Relate Various Details of the Offense
Following acceptance of an alternative, use a statement of reinforcement, such as "[First name of suspect], I was sure that was the case all along!" Use open-ended questions to obtain details of the offense. Obtain collaboration facts only a guilty person would know.

9. Convert an Oral Confession into Writing
Options here include a third party hearing the repeated confession, the suspect writing out the confession, or a secretary taking down the confession and typing it up and then the suspect signing it.

Based on advice from a former assistant federal attorney, whenever possible, I use a tape recorder to record the confession when first given. The attorney told me words to say at the beginning of the tape, including that the suspect acknowledging his or her name and the fact the confession is being given of his or her own free will. The attorney also told me words to say at the end of the confession, again with the suspect acknowledging his or her name and confirming he or she gave the confession of his or her own free will. I prefer this to the three options given above because each gives suspects time to think, and they often do not provide as much information the second time as they did the first time they confessed.

Do's and Don'ts

Do's

1. Pay attention to the same factors indicated earlier for interviewing. Note all aspects of verbal, eye, and body responses.
2. Keep constant pressure on suspect.
3. Attempt to pressure suspect to respond with questions requiring "closed" answers until you feel you can relax pressure and encourage broader answers, hopefully leading up to a confession.

Don'ts

1. Do not threaten.
2. Do not block exit physically. If the suspect starts to leave, try to talk the suspect back but do nothing to restrict his or her departure if he or she persists.
3. Do not make promises or misstatements to obtain information from the suspect. Such action could make any confession obtained null and void, and certainly not admissible in any court.

Understand the Types of Questions and How They Are to Be Used

General Questions

General questions deal with the general subject area. They do *not* focus on any specific aspect of wrongdoing. Start with closed questions. The answers to these should be yes, no, I don't know, and so on. Move into open questions, where sentences can be used in response.

Specific Questions

Specific questions focus on specific aspects of wrongdoing. Again, start with closed questions and then convert to open questions when appropriate.

Bait Questions

Bait questions are designed to trip the suspect being interrogated. Usually such questions are developed from information obtained during the investigation or in an earlier interview involving the suspect.

SUMMARY

Persons trained in accounting and auditing should develop their skills in interviewing and interrogation one step at a time. Break each step down to the needed understanding of the art and the disciplines applicable. One approach would be as follows:

Interviewing

1. Develop interviewing approach and lay out series of questions.
2. Conduct field interviews.
3. Learn the disciplines of neurolinguistics, starting with tonal inflections, proceeding to reading eyes and, finally, other body language.

Interrogation

1. Through role playing learn how to apply the Do's and Don'ts, including establishing the proper attitude/approach to the undertaking. Follow the nine rules of interrogation. Be prepared to change approach and style when it appears that the suspect is on the verge of confessing. If that does not occur, be prepared to reactivate or initiate pressing approach.
2. Develop your interrogation style and approach, and lay out questions to be asked. Keep format loose so you can react to responses, verbal and other, from suspect. Your format should include a Plan B to be used in event Plan A does not work as expected. Apply the disciplines of neurolinguistics.
3. Evaluate what you did right and what you would change after the interrogation has been completed. Even if you obtain a confession, you will identify errors in approach and style that you will attempt to avoid or change in any future interrogation efforts.

It has been my experience that many accountants and auditors do a good job of basic interrogation. However, few of them understand neurolinguistics. Even fewer of them want to function in an adversarial mode, which is required in interrogation. I have found security personnel, particularly those with experience at the federal or state police level, are the best at extracting confessions to white-collar crime situations. The good-cop/bad-cop routine of street police dealing with violent crimes seldom works in such situations. Therefore, it is wrong to assume that all law-enforcement officers are effective at interrogation for white-collar crimes.

The next most effective interrogators are lawyers who have had prosecution experience in the federal or state attorney offices. Again, do not assume that all lawyers are effective in interrogation for white-collar crimes. Finally, the auditors and forensic accountants who are most effective at interrogation are those who have been with the federal and state law enforcement agencies (e.g., FBI, Secret Service, postal inspectors, and state police). Others without their formal training can become adept at interrogation if they work at it. It will not happen unless all of the fundamentals, disciplines, and principles indicated in this chapter are adopted in a style and approach with which the interrogator is comfortable.

NOTES

1. David E. Zulawlski and Douglas E. Wicklander, *Practical Aspects of Interview and Interrogation* (Boca Raton, FL: CRC Press, 1993), p. 5.

PART 3

PRINCIPLES OF FORENSIC ACCOUNTING

CHAPTER 11

ESSENTIAL THEORIES AND PRINCIPLES OF FRAUD

When two people meet to discuss money belonging to a third, fraud is inevitable.

Michael J. Comer

LEGAL PERSPECTIVE

Definition of Fraud

A generic term, embracing all multifarious means which human ingenuity can devise, and which are resorted to by one individual to get advantage over another by false suggestions or by suppression of truth, and includes all surprise, trick, cunning, and any unfair way by which another is cheated. . . .

As distinguished from negligence, it is always positive, intentional. It comprises all acts, omissions, and concealments involving a breach of a legal or equitable duty and resulting in damage to another. And includes anything calculated to deceive, whether it be a single act or combination of circumstances, whether the suppression of truth or the suggestion of what is false, whether it be by direct falsehood or by innuendo, by speech or by silence, by word of mouth, or by look or gesture.[1]

Types of Fraud

There are 11 types of fraud defined in *Black's Law Dictionary*.[2]

Actual or Constructive Fraud

Actual fraud consists in deceit, artifice, trick, design, some direct and active operation of the mind. . . . Constructive fraud consists in any act of commission or omission contrary to legal or equitable duty, trust, or confidence justly reposed, which is contrary to good conscience and operates to the injury of another.

Extrinsic Fraud

Fraud which is collateral to the issues tried in the case where the judgement is rendered.

Fraud in Fact or in Law

[Fraud in fact] is actual, positive, intentional fraud. Fraud disclosed by matters of fact, as distinguished from constructive fraud or fraud in law. Fraud in law is fraud in contemptation of law; fraud implied or inferred by law; fraud made out by construction of law, as distinguished from fraud found by a jury from matter of fact. . . .

Fraud in the Execution

Misrepresentation that deceives the other party as to the nature of a document evidencing the contract.

Fraud in the Factum

Misrepresentation as to the nature of a writing that a person signs with neither knowledge nor reasonable opportunity to obtain knowledge of its character or essential terms.

Fraud in the Inducement

Fraud connected with underlying transaction and not with the nature of the contract or document signed. Misrepresentation as to the terms, quality or other aspects of a contractual relation, venture or other transaction that leads a person to agree to enter into the transaction with a false impression or understanding of the risks, duties or obligations she has undertaken.

Intrinsic Fraud

That which pertains to issue involved in original action or where acts constituting fraud were, or could have been, litigated therein.

Legal or Positive Fraud

[Legal fraud] is made out by legal construction or inference, or the same thing as constructive fraud. Positive fraud is the same thing as actual fraud.

Mail and Wire Fraud

Criminal offense by using mails or interstate wires to create or in furtherance of a scheme or artifice to defraud, or for obtaining money or property by means of false or fraudulent pretenses.

Tax Fraud

Federal offense of willfully attempting to evade or defeat the payment of taxes due and owing. . . . Tax fraud falls into two categories: civil and criminal. . . . In either situation, the IRS has the burden of proving fraud.

Fraud on Court

A scheme to interfere with judicial machinery performing task of impartial adjudication, as by preventing opposing party from fairly presenting his case or defense. [This can involve] bribery of a judge or jury to fabrication of evidene by counsel and must be supported by clear, unequivocal and convincing evidence.

THEORIES IN CRIMINAL MOTIVATION

It would be simple to take the view that thieves are born dishonest and nothing that society can do will reform them. It would be equally unrealistic to assume that all criminals are socially deprived misfits who deserve nothing but understanding and compassion. Somewhere between these two extremes, the truth may be found.[3]

Organized Criminals

When the term *organized criminals* is used, the first thought of most people is *Mafia*. In fact, organized criminals long ago recognized rewards could be obtained from nonviolent crime. This includes credit frauds and investment scams, as well as laundering of funds through firms that may or may not be legitimate. Sometimes, however, to enable them to accomplish their nonviolent objectives, threats of violence against one or more other persons are required. These may be members of the public. More probable is that such threats will be against coconspirators or employees of victim organizations, or both. To put this into perspective, consider that

1. The amount of the largest bank robbery was only about 1 percent of the largest known white-collar fraud.
2. The total of white-collar fraud in banks is estimated to be 50 times greater than all crimes of violence against banks in any calendar year.

First-Time Offenders

Probably the majority of white-collar criminals, when identified, can be defined as first-time offenders. Some experts question use of that term on the basis that most criminals are not caught in this first criminal act.

It is important to understand what leads people into corporate fraud. Two well recognized criminologists, Edwin O. Sutherland and Donald R. Cressey, have examined the motivation of white-collar criminals in depth. While their research produced somewhat differing conclusions, their combined opinions provide a possible explanation of that motivation.

In his theory of "differential association," Sutherland has asserted:

> "A complete explanation of white collar crime cannot be derived from available data. The data which are at hand suggest that white collar crime has its genesis in the same general process as other criminal behavior, namely differential association. The hypothesis of differential association is that criminal behavior is learned in association with those who define such behavior favorably and in isolation from those who define it unfavorably. A person in an appropriate situation engages in such criminal behavior if and only if the weight of the favorable definitions exceeds the weight of the unfavorable definition."[4]

It should be noted that Sutherland did not contend his hypothesis covered all cases or that it should be accepted as an explanation of all white-collar crime. It does not attempt to explain the white-collar criminal acting on his or her own. On the other hand, Cressey's theories do attempt to do just that:

> "Trusted persons become trust violators when they conceive of themselves as having a financial problem which is non-shareable, are aware that this problem can be secretly resolved by violation of the position of financial trust, and are able to apply to their own conduct in that situation verbalizations which enable them to adjust their conceptions of themselves as trust persons with their conceptions of themselves as users of the entrusted funds or property."[5]

What causes a particular person to perpetrate a specific crime? How do they justify their criminal actions? The answer to both is that there may be simple reasons or some complex combination of reasons. For example, some contend that stealing from a large multinational employer is so distant that the guilt from such criminal actions can be easily rationalized and, therefore, diminished. Would they steal from a small shopkeeper or colleague? The contention is that they would not. The reality, based on my experience, is that size means nothing. For example, why do so many small stores that handle the lottery have repeated instances of part-time and full-time employees stealing the $1 scratch lottery tickets?

Sutherland suggested that the stigma of crime is lacking when certain laws are violated (e.g., evasion of income tax, computer software and video piracy, and customs duty). They are explained as acceptable crimes. However, how does the forensic accountant determine who will not perpetrate any crime, who will perpetrate only acceptable crimes, as indicated, or who will perpetrate a crime beyond the range of wrongdoing classified as acceptable? While the principles established by the criminologists are interesting, they do not, on their own, identify a person who will perpetrate a crime, white-collar or other, or, for that matter, who will not perpetrate a crime, white-collar or other.

Computer Abuse Motivation

It is interesting to note that computer technicans seem to think differently than those not involved in the field. They are often young and highly intelligent and have a seemingly inbred dislike and disregard for authority. Because their work often requires them to work around problems, they like to find shortcuts to get a job done or a problem solved. As a result, they are resentful of what they consider to be artificial barriers imposed by management or senior nonmanagement employees who have very limited knowledge of the modern computer technology environment. This is a real problem. In the real world of computers, the junior members of data processing, right out of college, often have computer technical skills that are more current and at far higher levels, particularly in specialist areas of systems planners, systems analysts, and programmers. What they often do not recognize is that they often lack an adequate knowledge base about the organization for which they work, or the maturity to apply their skills fully and effectively in a broad business of governmental environment.

> This produces two dangers: the first is that junior employees can "look down" on their managers and challenge their authority generally. More importantly, managers are unable to check the work of their subordinates in these specialist areas; honesty and accuracy have to be taken on trust.[6]

Practical Theories of Motivation

It is interesting to note that Emile Durkheim "reasoned that where a person's aspirations are balanced by opportunities, a state of contentment exists. On the contrary, he suggested that crime breeds in the gaps between opportunities and aspirations. Where aspirations cannot be fulfilled through legitimate opportunities, unconventional methods will be sought."[7]

Relative thereto, consider that "it is clearly very difficult to generalize about any aspect of human behavior and the various theories on motivation are not totally compatible nor relevant to the technical era."[8]

A security firm in England identified the following characteristics of white-collar and computer fraud perpetrators:

1. They were resentful of their employer organization.
2. Their financial expectations are not being met.
3. Their contributions are not properly recognized.
4. They have a basic disrespect not only for their superiors but also for their colleagues.
5. They have little or no respect for the property of their employer or other people.

> Frequently perpetrators were seen by management as hard workers but with limited chances of advancement: perpetrators often believed their managers were "stupid," "weak," and "amoral."[8]

> Motivation, like all aspects of human behavior, changes and is subject to external social forces. An honest person one day may be a criminal the next; having overstepped the line, he is likely to repeat his behavior. The effects that social pressures have on personal motivation cannot be quantified although research suggests that rapid changes in the structure of society and in crime run on parallel lines.[10]

Summary

It would seem that the conclusions reached above merely put the forensic accountant, and those who use the services of such individuals, on notice that business and government need to remain constantly alert to those realities in human nature that could prove to be detrimental to their specific interests. The defenses against any specific risk scenario must be designed with full recognition that people are the perpetrators of fraud. In computer fraud, the machinery is merely a tool for the fraud perpetrator. People, not machinery, systems, or controls for systems, should be the main focus to protect the interests of the organization.

BASIC THEORIES OF FRAUD

Theory of Opportunity

Consider Figure 11–1 as a way to put risk, relative to people, into perspective. This theory assumes that all people have some degree of opportunity to commit fraud. The likely targets are their employer, suppliers and customers of their employer, third parties, and governmental authorities. Such opportunity is governed by three factors: (1) the degree of access they have to premises, assets, records, and the computer systems; (2) their capability of identifying risk situations and exploiting them; and (3) the time to plan and commit the fraud. Remember, they select the time and place.

It is important to keep in mind that 75 percent of all frauds are considered simple, as described below, relative to the participant(s) involved. I use the following categories:

1. *Simple:* One person, insider or outsider.
2. *Compound:* Two or more persons in collusion, all insiders or outsiders.
3. *Complex:* One or more insiders in collusion with one or more outsiders.

First, it should be understood that most corporate frauds occur through breaches of trust by employees and others to whom access is granted. The *Computer Faud and Security Bulletin* of the Computer Security Institute found that more than 30 percent of major fraud losses could have been prevented if proper background checks had been made on potential employees and persons to whom funds had been advanced.

In addition, the majority of frauds are perpetrated by people with the lowest skill levels (e.g., data entry operators). Such frauds usually have a smaller average amount. As higher skills are involved (e.g., computer programmer/analyst), the number of frauds normally declines but the average amount of each fraud is higher.

Skill combined with rank (e.g., EDP/MIS management) creates the highest risk of fraud perpetration. Rank can intimidate subordinates so they will not

FIGURE 11–1

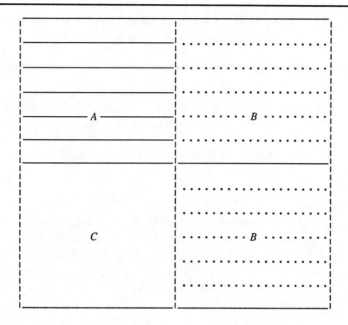

Note: Each block represents 25 percent.

Individuals in A will steal whenever they can (25 percent).
Those in B will steal whenever they think it is possible to get away with it (50 percent).
Those in C will not steal (25 percent).

report questionable practices or even known wrongful activities. The frauds normally decline in number but they are usually larger in amount.

It is interesting to note that, as a general statement, the higher the skill or rank level of the fraud perpetrator, the longer the period that such fraud will go undetected.

The forensic accountant should be aware of this reality: "In the same way that social pressures may increase the justification for crime, changes in the complexity of commerce affect criminal opportunities."[11] International communications now function with such frequency and speed that a fraud perpetrated successfully at a city in the United States could be repeated in Europe the next day and in Asia the following day. "The last decade has seen the development of the international criminal—the forger, the securities or insurance thief and commodity fraudsman, all of whom have been able to manipulate boundaries and laws to their advantage."[12]

Therefore, opportunity for fraud depends on

- *Access:* To assets, systems, and/or records.
- *Skills:* The higher the level, the higher the risk.

- *Time:* The fraud perpetrator usually selects the time and the place, looking for weaknesses in the fraud defense mechanisms.
- *Rank:* The ability to bypass controls and intimate subordinates, which may result in irregular conduct not being reported.

Theory of Concealment

When viewed from its most basic level, the perpetration of fraud is simple. Its objective is simple. It is intended to gain a dishonest advantage over the victim. To help accomplish the end objective, the fraud perpetrator will often attempt to create confusion, whether on-book or off-book fraud. Let us consider each of these.

On-Book Frauds

An on-book fraud is one that occurs within the business. Illicit payments or activities are recorded, generally in some disguised manner, in the regular books and records of the company. Even where such deliberate deception exists, an audit trail (however obscure) normally exists, although it may be difficult to identify. When, and if, identified, it will usually aid in discovery of an on-book fraud.

Off-Book Frauds

An off-book fraud normally occurs outside the accounting mainstream. Generally, for such frauds, no audit trail is likely to exist. For an off-book fraud to occur, the company usually has unrecorded vendor rebates or significant cash sales. Examples of off-book frauds include bribery (violation of the False Claims Act) and kickbacks (violation of the Anti-Kickback Law). Off-book frauds are normally proved at the point of receipt, that is, where the initial red flag (of fraud) will appear with regard to the receipt of illicit funds. An upward lifestyle change by a specific officer or employee may be a sign of something irregular going on. For example, if an employee suddenly has a new home and a new car and is taking expensive vacations (e.g., cruises, and so on), but his or her salary has not changed, it clearly warrants follow-up to determine whether there is a valid source for the indicated new wealth (e.g., inheritance, lottery, and so on). When no logical explanation for the apparent increased wealth is identified and irregularities are suspected, the prudent man principle dictates that a fraud investigation be conducted in an effort to determine the source(s) of the possible outside income. This extra effort is warranted because, as a general statement, off-book frauds have historically been found to involve larger amounts than on-book frauds.

Thefts may not be concealed for several reasons. First, concealment may not be necessary because the victim's records will not disclose the loss. However, even if uncovered, the records may be insufficient to pinpoint the fraud perpetrator (i.e., there is no audit trail). In addition, the victim may condone the loss. Also, it may be that there is no simple way to conceal the fraudulent activity(ies).

For our purposes,

1. Concealment is a key factor of most systematic fraud.
2. Misrepresentation refers to the falsification of a personal, physical, or commercial reality. It can occur during or after theft. Intent is to assist in the commission of the fraud or to conceal a fraud loss.
3. Manipulation refers to modifying an accounting record. Such documentary action before, during, or after a theft is intended to assist in commission of the fraud.

Theory of Deviations

Fraud could be considered a deviant behavior. Why? Because it is contrary to the desired rules of sociology, that is, the conduct of an individual as part of a group. Fraud perpetrators, not wanting to be discovered, attempt to hide their wrongdoing. Therefore, fraud perpetrators seek out ways in which they can conceal their guilt. As a result, to the forensic accountant, deviations from accepted procedures are often the first sign of a fraud.

Theories of Minimum and General Collusion

Remember that approximately 25 percent of fraud is other than simple. Restated, that means one out of four fraud situations involves collusion between two or more individuals.

[Collusion] usually occurs under two distinct circumstances:

* to provide the necessary opportunities, resources or skills to commit a fraud (minimum collusion)
* to share the benefits of low skill frauds among the maximum number of people (institutionalized fraud or general collusion).[13]

Minimum Collusion
Collusion can increase the opportunity for fraud. Combined skills may enable a particular wrongful act to be perpetrated. Such collusion usually is required for high level manipulative fraud. Usually such collusion is limited to the minimum number of people needed for fraud to succeed.

Maximum Collusion
In most areas of business and government, frauds involving low levels of skill are relatively commonplace. Because the employer is viewed as impersonal, it is often relatively easy to get people to cooperate on a fraudulent activity, particularly where the probability of discovery is assumed to be relatively low. Ironically, as a general statement, the more people involved in a fraud, the higher the probability the amount will not reach major proportions. For our purposes, I would define "major proportions" as six figures or more. Such fraud reemphasizes the need for sound internal check requirements being built

into the internal control systems, the premise being that no person or group of persons should have total control over any transaction or group of transactions. The advantage to the forensic accountant is that the more people involved in a fraud, the higher the probability of earlier discovery. Why? The chain of people involved in the fraud scheme is only as strong as the weakest link.

CLASSIFICATIONS OF FRAUD PERPETRATORS

Internal

A fraud perpetrator on the victim's payroll will, during the performance of his or her job responsibilities, have access to various company assets or records. The range of the assets or records will depend on his or her function within the organization.

External

All fraud perpetrator's who are not employed by the victim organization are classified as external. This includes former employees. Such persons normally will not have access to assets or records of an organization. As a result, their fraud opportunities are usually limited almost entirely to unconcealed frauds. An exception is computer hackers, or other persons equally qualified in computers, who break into computer records of the organization.

> Organized criminals are in a class by themselves and represent a risk which most companies—acting independently—are unable to counter. When organized criminal conspiracies include or involve company employees, opportunities and concealment courses are virtually unlimited and are often based on extortion.[14]

WHAT A FORENSIC ACCOUNTANT SHOULD KNOW ABOUT FRAUD

The forensic accountant should have some depth of knowledge of fraud from human, social and economic, legal, and accounting and auditing perspectives.

Human Perspective

We must accept the reality that fraud is a serious human weakness. Statistically, three out of four persons will actually steal under the right set of circumstances. All of us, however, have faced the temptation to cheat, lie, and steal at some times in our lives. How many of us can claim to never having been the perpetrator of a fraud? Remember, a lie is a form of fraud, as it misrepresents or hides something. Obviously, most if not all of us have been the victim of fraud(s).

Social and Economic Perspective

Fraud is a socially unacceptable behavior. It can destroy human relationships. It can seriously affect human interactions by damaging or destroying trust. Without such trust, human interaction and relationships suffer. It can also affect business or job relationships as well as personal relationships. Can it affect the need for economic or social survival? Yes! What kind of world will we live in without truth and honesty?

Legal Perspective

This book earlier defined fraud, with respect to both its general perspective and its various types. In one sentence, fraud is a willful misrepresentation of a material fact for the purpose of deceiving another to his or her economic detriment. Criminal law sanctions may involve the assessment of fines or incarceration. Civil law sanctions may include the reward of damages for losses sustained or punitive damages representing some multiple of such losses.

Proving fraud is basically a matter of documenting the facts in any specific situation. Evidence may consist of false entries in books of account; altered, forged, or destroyed business records and documents; books, records, and documents of independent third parties that support the amount or fact of loss; and, while less desirable than documentary evidence, verbal evidence, which can, in certain circumstances, be quite valuable in a criminal or civil legal action.

Accounting and Auditing Perspective

From such perspective, fraud is an intentional misrepresentation of a material fact in books of account or in financial statements. Such misrepresentation may be directed against organizational outsiders (e.g., shareholders or creditors) or against the organization itself (e.g., embezzlement, incompetence, misapplications of funds, or thefts) or indicate improper use of organizational assets by directors, officers, employees, or agents.

The forensic accountant must be qualified to identify and deal with any irregular conduct affecting the books of account, including the failure to record assets, liabilities, income, expenses, or investments (equity). Remember that, in the final analysis, an off-book fraud results in the misrepresentation of the results of an organization on its books. The forensic accountant must also be concerned with the integrity of reports representing the status of the books at every point in time or for any period of time.

NOTES

1. *Black's Law Dictionary,* 6th ed. (St. Paul, MN: West Publishing, 1990), p. 660.
2. Ibid., p. 661.

3. Michael J. Comer, *Corporate Fraud*, 2nd ed. (London: McGraw-Hill Book Company (UK) Ltd., 1985), p. 14.

4. Edwin O. Sutherland, "White Collar Crime," CBS (1961), as quoted in Comer, *Corporate Fraud*, p. 15.

5. Donald R. Cressey, *Other People's Money* (Newark, NJ: Patterson Smith, 1973), as quoted in Comer, *Corporate Fraud*, p. 16.

6. Comer, *Corporate Fraud*, p. 20.

7. Ibid., p. 21.

8. Ibid.

9. Ibid., pp. 21–22.

10. Ibid., p. 22.

11. Ibid., pp. 24–25.

12. Ibid.

13. Ibid., p. 28.

14. Ibid., p. 29.

CHAPTER 12

PRINCIPLES OF ACCOUNTING,FINANCIAL STATEMENTS, AND FINANCIAL ANALYSIS

Common sense does not ask an impossible chessboard, but takes the one before it and plays the game.

Wendell Phillips

KEYSTONE OF FORENSIC ACCOUNTING SKILLS

The field of accounting, and its related subjects (e.g., financial analysis, financial statement analysis, and so on), is the keystone of the required knowledge and skills of the forensic accountant. Merely having a good knowledge and understanding of accounting and related subjects is just not adequate. The forensic accountant must be very highly qualified, as to both education and experience, in matters relating to accounting. Since most accountants have areas of specific expertise (e.g., budgeting, financial analysis, general accounting, tax accounting, and so on), forensic accountants must know where they could be considered as expert and where they are merely competent or good. In those latter areas, they must have contacts who can assist and advise them. Therefore, in appropriate perspective, forensic accountants, through their own expertise and by using others who have an expert level of skills in those areas where utilized, can provide expert advisory and consulting advice and work relative to all aspects of accounting. This advisory and consulting advice and work can be provided to management, practitioners of the legal profession (either defense or prosecution), and courts.

ACCOUNTING DEFINED

Accounting has been defined by a number of organizations. The American Institute of Certified Public Accountants (AICPA) stated:

> Accounting is the art of recording, classifying, and summarizing in a significant manner and in terms of money, transactions and events which are, in part at least, of a financial character, and intepreting the results thereof.[1]

The American Accounting Association (AAA) defined accounting as "the process of identifying, measuring, and communicating economic information to permit informed judgments and decisions by users of the information."[2] A stated objective of accounting was given as the "Measurement and communication of data revealing past, present, and prospective socio-economic activities."[3] That document continued by stating the purpose of accounting to be "to improve control methods and decision making at all levels of socio-economic activities."[4]

The Financial Accounting Standards Board (FASB) has defined its area of concern, indicating that

> Financial reporting included not only financial statements but also other means of communicating information that relates, directly or indirectly to the information provided by the accounting system—that is, information about an enterprise's resources, obligations, earnings, etc..[5]

Relative to the intended use of accounting information, the FASB states that

> Financial reporting is not an end in itself but is intended to provide information that is useful in making business and economic decisions—for making reasoned choices among alternative uses of scarce resources in the conduct of business and economic activities.[6]

FRAMEWORK OF ACCOUNTING

The AICPA's Special Committee on Research Programs establishes three basic terms:

> *Postulates* are few in number and are the basic assumptions on which *principles* rest. They necessarily are derived from the economic and political environment and from the modes of thought and customs of all segments of the business community. The profession, however, should make clear their understanding and interpretation of what they are, to provide a meaningful foundation for the formulation of principles and the development of *rules* or other guides for the application of principles in specific situations. . . .[7]

The AICPA study group set forth the terminology that became the basis for the current framework of accounting.

> To serve users' needs, the accounting process should consist of an interrelated and compatible system of *objectives, standards* or *principles,* and *practices* or *procedures. Objectives* should identify the goals and purposes of accounting. *Standards* should follow logically from *objectives,* and should provide *guidelines* for the formulation of accounting *practices* compatible with the desired goals. All three levels of the system should be linked rationally to the needs of users.[8]

The FASB has adapted this system for its conceptual framework:

Objectives. The objectives underlie the other phases of the conceptual framework and stem largely from the needs of those for whom the information is intended.

Qualitative Characteristics. Qualitative characteristics are the criteria the FASB will use in selecting and evaluating financial accounting and reporting policies.

Elements. Elements of financial statements are the building blocks with which financial statements are constructed—the classes of items of which financial statements are composed. There are eight elements: assets, liabilities, owner's equity, revenues, expenses, gains, losses, and comprehensive income.

Recognition and Measurements. To be formally incorporated in a particular set of financial statements, an item must not only qualify as an asset, liability, revenue, expense, or other element, but also must meet criteria for recognition and have a relevant attribute (or surrogate for it) that is capable of reasonably reliable measurement or estimate.

Reporting or Display. Display of information provided by financial reporting depends on elements, recognition, and measurement and is closely related to other aspects of display, such as displays of comprehensive income and its components and displays showing funds flow and liquidity information. It concerns what information should be provided, who should provide it, and where it should be displayed.

ELEMENTS OF ACCOUNTING

The AAA committee[9] describes the elements of the accounting discipline as consisting of

1. *Accounting activities:* These represent selected points in the flow of socioeconomic activities such as transactions and other identifiable points in the flow of activities for which accounting has been made.
2. *Accounting entitites:* This includes any organizational unit such as business enterprises, government units, nations, or individuals.
3. *Accounting methods:* This includes such techniques as the computer, statistical analysis, and a variety of other measurement and communication methods.

THE PRIMARY CATEGORIES OF ACCOUNTING

Financial Accounting

[Financial accounting is] the accounting for revenues, expenses, assets, and liabilities that is commonly carried on in the general offices of a business.[10]

This is also referred to as general accounting.

Management Accounting

[Management accounting is] accounting designed for or adapted to the needs of information and control at the various administrative levels. The term has no precise coverage but is used generally to refer to the extensions of internal reporting for the design and submission of which a corporation controller is responsible.[11]

Social Accounting

[Social accounting is] the application of double-entry bookkeeping to socioeconomic analysis; it is concerned with the construction, estimation, and analysis of national or international (a) income, (b) balance sheets, and (c) design of the system of component accounts.[12]

Tax Accounting

The activity of tax accounting is concerned with the preparation of the various returns and reports required for compliance with tax laws and regulations, especially the federal income tax code. Also it includes the planning for the control of taxes in the administration and management of organization and for individuals, estates, and trusts.[13]

International Accounting

International accounting concerns itself with identifying differences in accounting theory in different countries and in the preparation and presentation of financial statements. Both are done in an effort to harmonize financial accounting standards based on criteria issued by authoritative bodies in different countries.

BASIC FEATURES OF FINANCIAL ACCOUNTING

The forensic accountant must have a broad level of education and experience in the area of the basic features of financial accounting. Accounting Policies Board (APB) *Statement No. 4* states that "the basic features of financial accounting are determined by the characteristics of the environment in which financial accounting operates." These features may be considered concepts, postulates, principles, or assumptions, depending on their individual perspective. This is the result of there being no general agreement as to the definitions of those terms. The features stated in *APB No. 4* are

1. Accounting entity.
2. Going concern.
3. Measurement of economic resources and obligations.
4. Time periods.
5. Measurements in terms of money.
6. Accrual.
7. Exchange price.
8. Approximation.
9. Judgment.
10. General-purpose financial information.
11. Fundamentally related financial statements.
12. Substance over form.
13. Materiality.

Some accountants feel the preceding should be supplemented with the following:

1. Realization.
2. Consistency.
3. Conservatism.
4. Disclosure.
5. Reliability.

Forensic accountants should fully understand the preceding features. They should have the education and experience necessary to evaluate each feature and determine if the relative information is or is not being handled properly, as to recordation, and presented properly, as to the primary and secondary accounting records (e.g., general and subsidiary ledgers) and financial reports. By effectively using these skills, forensic accountants are able, in their consultancy and examination work, to identify any situations of noncompliance with generally accepted criteria and focus on determining if that represents negligence, mismanagement, or fraud. The conceptual framework for financial accounting and reporting, as undertaken by the FASB, can be summarized in Figure 12–1.

FIGURE 12–1
Conceptual Framework for Financial Accounting and Reporting

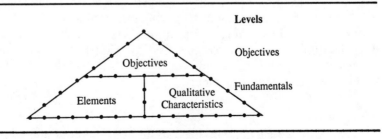

FINANCIAL STATEMENTS: FORM AND CONTENT

Characteristics of Financial Statements

Basic Financial Statements

The following statements should be prepared in accordance with generally accepted accounting principles (GAAP):

1. Balance Sheet.
2. Statement of Income.
3. Statement of Changes in Financial Position.
4. Statement of Changes in Stockholders' Equity.

As appropriate, these statements should be supplemented by descriptions of accounting policies and notes to them. An analysis of changes in retained earnings is sometimes presented separately from the Statement of Changes in Stockholders' Equity. When prepared, it is often as an extension of the Statement of Income.

General Purpose Financial Statements

General purpose financial statements have evolved over the years. The objective is for them to meet the needs of many users. They have been standardized, as appropriate, as to the form, content, and methods of preparation (GAAP). Both nonaccountants and accountants better understand them if standardized usage is followed.

"The term *differential disclosure* refers to the idea that complete general purpose financial statements are too complex for the 'average' user, and simplified versions should be provided in addition to the complete disclosure intended for 'sophisticated users.'"[14] The forensic accountant must, by education and experience, be a sophisticated user!

Special Purpose Financial Statements

There is usually an underlying reason why nonstandard or special purpose financial statements are prepared. It may include dissemination of internal management information, provision of information to various parties (e.g., creditors or potential creditors or potential equity investors) of an agreement or contract or other matters of interest to them, or statements unique to an industry. An example of a unique statement can be found in the garment industry. They use interim certified statements prepared on a break-even basis. The auditors review everything except all aspects of inventory. They then draw financial statements from the books of account and make an adjustment increasing or decreasing inventory and cost of goods sold to reflect break-even for the period covered by the statements.

Materiality

The financial statements only need to disclose material matters. Insignificant items do not need to be stated separately. However, insignificant items expected to become significant in the future often are stated in the financial statements, specifically for the purpose of providing the basis for later comparison. Generally, such items are lumped with the most nearly similar item in the financial statements. An example of this would be to include such things as accrued liabilities under the accounts payable caption. "No firm guidelines as to what constitutes materiality have been agreed on, except for the very general rule that items are material that would be of interest to a 'prudent investor.' "[15]

Comparative Financial Statements

It is now general pratice, when preparing financial statements as of a given date or for a specific period, to show comparable figures for the like prior date or for the like prior period. "The AICPA prefers comparative financial statements for most purposes for which financial statements are used [AICPA *Accounting Research Bulletin No. 43* (AC 2041)], but when there is good reason to do so, there is no objection to statements that show figures for the current year only."[16]

Limitations of Financial Statements

The basic financial statements have very definite limitations. First off, they are historical. Also, they are stated in the base currency of the company. This is a measure that fluctuates continually against other base currencies of the world and must be related to inflation and the prime interest rate.

Even as of a specific date or at the end of a specific period, they are essentially interim reports on the subject environment on which they report. While many estimates and judgments can be based on them, the correctness of such decisions can often not be determined until the future.

In addition, even though financial statements are postulated on the concept of the "going concern," hidden problems may be identified later that have an impact on the conclusions reached at any point in time.

Finally, since they are based on GAAP, which often provides several options, they reflect a considerable lack of uniformity. GAAP also restrict matters portrayed to a set of agreed-on conventions.

Notes to financial statements try to explain what they actually mean.

Basic Financial Statements

The Notes to Financial Statements are critical to the proper understanding of the financial statement. Most financial statements affirm this by including a statement something like the following: "The accompanying notes are an integral part of this statement."

Balance Sheet

The balance sheet is also called the statement of financial position or statement of financial condition. It shows the financial position of an entity as of a specific point in time. It shows three account groupings: assets, liabilities, and net worth (also called stockholders' equity). The accountant's equation is

$$\text{Assets} - \text{Liabilities} = \text{Net worth}$$

Income Statement

This statement shows all income and expense accounts. The income statement has two forms:

1. *Single-step form:* All items of revenue are presented and totaled, and all items of cost and expense are totaled. Income tax can be included under cost and expense or shown separately.
2. *Multiple-step form:* Accounts are broken into intermediate groupings (e.g., salaries, wages, and benefits; sales and marketing expenses; administrative and operating expenses) rather than as described under #1.

Whichever format is used, certain items are always shown separately (e.g., Extraordinary Items; Disposal of a Business Segment; and Cumulative Effect of Changes in Accounting Principles).

Net income per share is always shown as the last section of the income statement (except for wholly owned subsidiaries and nonpublic enterprises) as required by *APB Opinion No. 15* (AC 2011).[17]

Statement of Changes in Stockholders' Equity

This statement reflects all changes in every stockholder's equity account. There is considerable variation in the format of presenting such information.

Statement of Changes in Financial Position

The statement title and format are dictated by *APB Opinion No. 19* (AC 2021). However, the statement format is flexible. Working capital, cash provided, and cash used in operations must be disclosed. Extraordinary items, including net changes in the elements of working capital, should be shown.

FINANCIAL ANALYSIS

Objective

The *underlying objective of financial analysis* is the comparative measurement of *risk* and *return* in order to make investment and credit decisions. These decisions are based on some estimates of the future, be it a month, a year, or a decade. General-purpose financial statements, which describe the past, provide one basis for projecting future cash flows.[18]

The forensic accountant can use financial analysis as a useful tool in an effort to identify irregularities and/or fraud.

The Cause-and-Effect Ratios

While there are numerous ratios that can be used in analyzing financial statements, I have found the 15 cause-and-effect ratios an excellent beginning point.

Causal Ratios

The Ratio of Fixed Assets to Net Worth.   This measures the extent
to which invested capital or net worth is tied up in nonliquid, permanent,
depreciable assets. Indirectly, it measures the amount of capital that remains
relative to more fluid assets. It is calculated by dividing the depreciated value
of fixed assets by net worth.

$$\frac{\text{Fixed assets } - \text{ Depreciation}}{\text{Net worth}} = \text{Ratio}$$

A question arises as to whether, for this ratio, leased assets should be
considered as fixed assets. It should be recognized that some industries have
heavy investments in fixed assets relative to their total assets (e.g., metal
manufacturing, railroads, and airlines). Other industries have relatively low
investments in fixed assets (e.g., retailing). What is normal for the subject
business environment needs to be understood to put the ratio results into proper
perspective. Excessive fixed assets can adversely affect and distort the following
five effect ratios:

- Current ratio.
- Net sales to working capital.
- Inventory to working capital.
- Trade receivables to working capital.
- Long-term debt to working capital.

Collection Period.   This ratio is used as a tool in the analysis of a
company's trade receivables. The ratio uses total credit sales and all trade
receivables (e.g., accounts receivable, notes receivable, trade acceptances payable) arising from merchandise transactions.
  Two calculations are made:

1. Credit sales per day.

$$\frac{\text{Total credit sales}}{365 \text{ days}} = \text{Credit sales per day}$$

2. Collection period:

$$\frac{\text{All trade receivables}}{\text{Credit sales per day}} = \text{Number of days receivables outstanding}$$

These calculations are designed to measure the internal credit-and-
collection efficiency of the company, determine the probability of bad-debt
write-offs in the receivables (e.g., past due of three months or more), and

measure the company's receivables position relative to the accomplishments of that specific industry.

Information developed can impact on the following ratios:

- Net profit to net sales.
- Net profit to net worth.
- Net sales to net worth.
- Net sales to working capital.
- Fixed assets to net worth.
- Inventory to working capital.
- Long-term debt to working capital.
- Miscellaneous assets to net worth.

Net Sales to Inventory.   This ratio serves as an indicator of the inventory turnover and merchandising efficiency of a company.

$$\frac{\text{Net sales}}{\text{Inventory}} = \text{Inventory turnover}$$

This ratio impacts on the following ratios:

- Net profit to net sales.
- Net profit to net worth.
- Net sales to net worth.
- Net sales to working capital.
- Fixed assets to net worth.
- Trade receivables to working capital.
- Long-term debt to working capital.
- Miscellaneous assets to net worth.

Net Sales to Net Worth.   This ratio is commonly known as the trading ratio. It identifies the extent to which a company's sales volume is supported by invested capital.

$$\frac{\text{Annual sales}}{\text{Net worth}} = \text{Turnover}$$

Information can affect the following ratios:

- Current assets to current liabilities.
- Fixed assets to net worth.
- Current liabilities to net worth.
- Total liabilities to net worth.
- Inventory to working capital.
- Trade receivables to working capital.
- Long-term liabilities to working capital.
- Net profit to net worth.
- Net sales to fixed assets.
- Net sales to working capital.
- Miscellaneous assets to net worth.

Net Profit to Net Sales.   This ratio measures the success of a company with regard to its realization to profit from each dollar's worth of merchandise it sells.

$$\frac{\text{Annual net profit after taxes}}{\text{Net sales}} = \text{Ratio}$$

Robert Morris Associates changes this ratio by using pretax profit rather than net after-tax profit. While both have specific values, I prefer the ratio shown. This ratio affects all of the other 14 ratios in our base.

Miscellaneous Assets to Net Worth.   *Miscellaneous assets* includes all assets that are not current assets, fixed assets, and intangible assets and would include such assets as

- Due from officers, directors, or employees (representing loans or advances).
- Investments in or advances to subsidiaries.
- Loans or advances to affiliated companies.
- Investment in other than readily marketable securities.
- Any long-term receivables, such as a mortgage receivable.
- Inventory of supplies (where segregated, for general ledger purposes, from regular inventory).
- Cash value of life insurance.

It should be recognized that miscellaneous assets are quite vulnerable to write-off or markdown from book figures.

$$\frac{\text{Total miscellaneous assets}}{\text{Net worth}} = \text{Ratio}$$

Summary.   The six causal ratios are considered the most important ratios. With this foundation, the forensic accountant or analyst can easily relate to the effect ratios. Together, they provide the forensic accountant or analyst with the ability to examine any financial statement and, within minutes, identify the precise nature of any questionable balance relations reflected therein. Obviously, as and where needed, the forensic accountant or analyst can add additional ratios to the total of 15 cause-and-effect ratios. My experience indicates that there is a real danger of getting lost in too much detail when following the 100-ratio approach many analysts prefer. I am convinced that the more focused approach of starting with cause-and-effect ratios reduces the possibility of wasting time on incidental factors when analyzing financial statements. I consider the 15 ratios as being a unified system of analysis. Now, let us consider the 9 effect ratios.

Effect Ratios

Current Ratio.   This ratio provides a general picture of the adequacy of a company's working capital. That, in turn, indicates its ability to meet its day-to-day payment obligations. It also measures the margin of safety provided in meeting its payment obligations should it be found necessary to reduce the value of one or more current asset ratios. This is not a stand-alone ratio. The story it tells is conditioned by the quality of the major component parts of current assets. The current ratio is generally recognized as the patriarch among ratios. The current ratio is computed as follows:

$$\frac{\text{Current asset}}{\text{Current liabilities}} = \text{Current ratio}$$

Working capital is calculated as follows:

$$\frac{\text{Current}}{\text{assets}} - \frac{\text{Current}}{\text{liabilities}} = \frac{\text{Working}}{\text{capital}}$$

The acid-test ratio measures "quick" assets against current liabilities:

$$\frac{\text{Cash} + \text{Accounts receivable}}{\text{Current liabilities}} = \text{Percentage or amount}$$

The current ratio provides a quick picture as to the adequacy of the working-capital position of any company. For it to be truly meaningful, it is necessary to test receivables to be satisfied with their collectability and to test inventory to be sure it is not damaged or obsolete and is truly marketable.

Current Liabilities to Net Worth and Total Liabilities to Net Worth. The company with a lower-then-average ratio of debt to net worth denotes a strong ownership interest or position. Conversely, if the debt ratios are higher than the industry norm, management must be more apprehensive and may be forced by creditors to a course of action that restricts the degree of initiative and innovation by management. For either ratio to be put into proper perspective, compare the company results with overall industry results.

$$\frac{\text{Current liabilities}}{\text{Net worth}} = \text{Ratio}$$

$$\frac{\text{Total liabilities}}{\text{Net worth}} = \text{Ratio}$$

While both ratios are useful, it should be recognized that a preponderance of current debt carries with it more potential problems for a company's operating freedom. Why? Because of its early maturity and impact on working capital. Therefore, the current liabilities to net worth ratio should be considered the more critical of the two. On the other hand, long-term debt creates its own peril in that it is generally more exactly fixed as to maturity and repayment requirements. Further, as a general statement, repayment of long-term obligations is usually more enforceable because such debt is often backed by the pledge of specific collateral (e.g., hypothecation of fixed assets, or a mortgage or other lien on the specific long-term obligation).

Inventory to Working Capital.   The calculation of working capital assumes that all noncash current assets can be expected to be converted into cash within one calendar year. When current debts exceed current assets, a working-capital deficit occurs. Therefore, it could be said that working capital represents the margin of protection a company has to assure it can pay current debts. A write-down of receivables and/or a write-down of inventory, as not marketable, obsolete, or scrap are risks in that calculation. Such write-down would, of course, affect working capital of the firm. Historically, inventory has been the asset that most often results in business losses or even failure. This ratio, inventory to working capital, provides the measurement of that asset category. To compute this ratio, first calculate working capital assuming all current assets are convertible to cash at net book value.

$$\text{Current assets} - \text{Current liabilities} = \text{Working capital}$$

Second, calculate book inventory to working capital.

$$\frac{\text{(Book) Inventory}}{\text{Working capital}} = \text{Ratio}$$

Third, calculate all adjustments that should be made to reduce that book inventory value, such as style change, obsolescence, damaged materials/goods, physical deterioration, scrap, or lack of marketability. Such write-downs should also include identified pilferage and theft. This may be the result of a one-time full inventory; the accumulated results of an ongoing perpetual inventory, with net findings closed to the inventory account at specific intervals (e.g., calendar quarterly basis); or the use of historical write-down shrinkage percentage averages for the two most recent like prior periods. Fourth, recalculate the formula using the adjusted book value of the firm's inventory.

$$\frac{\text{(Adjusted book) Inventory}}{\text{Working capital}} = \text{Ratio}$$

Finally, compare the firm's percentage of inventory to working capital based on adjusted book inventory. Where available, compare that calculation to industry average figures. As an illustration, assume

1. Inventory: $500,000
2. Working capital: $1,000,000
3. Inventory to working capital: 50 percent
4. Industry average for inventory to working capital ratio:
   - 50 percent: Company right in line.
   - 70 percent: A bit heavy but, if valid reasons for overstock exist (e.g., expected strike), then it is acceptable.
   - 150 percent: Serious overstock position.

Now, assume a 50 percent write-down of inventory book value. The implications on working capital should be apparent.

Trade Receivables to Working Capital.   This has the same objective as did the inventory to working capital ratio. Here, however, the current asset category is trade receivables, which consists of all accounts receivable, notes receivable, and trade acceptances resulting from the normal activities of the business. This total should not include such things as special or unusual receivables, for example, the amount due from sale of a piece of surplus furniture, fixtures, or equipment; and receivables due from officers, directors, or employees.

This ratio interfaces with the collection period ratio, covered earlier under causal ratios.

The approach taken is the same as that used for the inventory to working capital ratio. First, calculate net book receivables for indicated categories and divide that by working capital.

$$\frac{\text{(Net book) Receivables}}{\text{Working capital}} = \text{Ratio}$$

Obviously, gross receivables would be adjusted downward based on the reserve for possible loan losses. To evaluate the adequacy of that reserve, develop some calculation on the receivables along the following lines. For example, you may rate two- and three-month past-due receivables at 95 percent, four- and five-month past-due receivables at 85 percent, and those more than five months past due at 60 percent. The reserve for possible loan losses should be approximately equal to the projected total net of the receivables not converted into cash. If an additional reserve provision is needed, calculate it and reduce the book receivables accordingly. Such adjustment will reduce working capital dollar for dollar.

$$\frac{\text{(Adjusted net book) Receivables}}{\text{Working capital}} = \text{Ratio}$$

Make the same comparison of the net result for the company against industry data, if available, in the same manner as done for the inventory to working capital ratio.

Here are some special considerations when making these calculations:

1. How many days' sales are outstanding at the calculation date?
2. How does the figure under #1 compare to the industry average, if such data are available?
3. What are the respective sales terms for the company?
4. How does the figure under #3 compare to the industry average, if such data are available?
5. What are the terms for purchases, on average, for the company?
6. How does the figure under #5 compare to the industry average, if such data are available?
7. Are any accounts receivable financed by sale of same (e.g., factoring)? If so, has this amount been considered in above calculations? It should be!
8. Is a seasonal element involved in the current receivables portfolio of accounts?

Failure to calculate real cash value of receivables can seriously impact working capital. This category ranks second only to inventory as a potential problem area. In recent years, an increasing number of firms have ended up in bankruptcy courts, either voluntarily or involuntarily, due to their inability to convert receivables into cash to meet working capital needs.

Robert Morris Associates and Dun & Bradstreet should be able to provide you necessary industry data.

Long-Term Liabilities to Working Capital.   Businesses generally use long-term borrowing to increase working capital. The objective is to generate profit and restore overall financial balance. This ratio measures three specific aspects of the debt structure of a business concern. First, it indicates if long-term borrowing was used to replenish working capital. If the ratio exceeds 100 percent, funds from long-term borrowing were probably diverted into fixed assets, with payment of unwarranted dividends hiding operating losses through creative bookkeeping.

Second, this ratio indicates whether there is room for further long-term borrowing. A top-heavy percentage indicates the company may be near the limit of such borrowing. If such borrowing is light or nonexistent, and the company has assets to support such borrowing, then such financing approach may be warranted to meet current or future working-capital needs.

Finally, it focuses the analyst's attention to the existance of long-term debt as such and the debt ratios already discussed. This helps to keep a proper perspective between long-term and short-term credit.

Long-term debt consists of any indebtedness payable more than one year from the date of the statement and includes intermediate financing, such as two-, three-, or four-year term loans or chattel mortgages, as well as real estate mortgages. Keep in mind that any part of such debt due to be repaid within one year must be classified as current, not long term.

The formula calculation is

$$\frac{\text{Long-term liabilities}}{\text{Working capital}} = \text{Ratio}$$

If desired, the company's ratio for this calculation can be compared to industry data.

Net Profit to Net Worth.   This ratio measures the profit return on investment (ROI), which is the reward for accepting ownership risk. The ratio is calculated as follows:

$$\frac{\text{Net profit (after taxes)}}{\text{(Tangible) Net worth}} = \text{Ratio}$$

Tangible net worth is the net of assets over liabilities after deducting intangibles. Obviously, if the business has a net loss (after taxes), this can threaten its going concern prospect. The ratio can be stated as a percentage:

(Tangible) Net worth	$200,000
Net profit (after taxes)	30,000
Net profit to net worth	15%

The above information can be compared to industry data to determine how well or how poorly the firm is doing against its competitors.

For smaller firms the ratio should serve a dual purpose: to measure the adequacy of profit ROI and to provide a secondary test of both profit and net worth.

Net Sales to Fixed Assets. This ratio is intended to measure the efficiency with which the company is utilizing its investment in fixed assets, such as land, plant, equipment, furniture, fixtures, and so on. Its secondary value is as a test of the adequacy of sales volume against assets employed in the business. It is indispensable in gaining a total understanding of a company's financial statement. Without this test, the adequacy of fixed assets would be based solely on the causal ratio of fixed assets to net worth. The calculation formula is as follows:

$$\frac{\text{Net sales}}{\text{Fixed assets}} = \text{Ratio}$$

Keep in mind that fixed assets are required to further sales by increasing production and service or reducing costs, or both.

Where industry information is available, the figure calculated for the company can be compared to those data.

Net Sales to Working Capital. This ratio indicates the demands made on working capital in supporting the sales volume of any business concern. The principle that a firm's sales volume requires a certain amount of working capital has been proven to be sound: The higher the level of sales to working capital, the greater the strain a company encounters in satisfying trade and bank creditors while meeting all obligations of the firm. Where the ratio appears disproportionately high, it serves to point out working-capital deficiencies. The ratio is calculated as follows:

$$\frac{\text{Net sales}}{\text{Working capital}} = \text{Ratio}$$

Again, if data are available, the company's ratio can be compared to the industry figure.

Red Flags

Proper use of the 15 cause-and-effect ratios will often provide the forensic accountant with red flags of possible wrongdoing. These can range from human error or deliberate incorrect entry to hide deficiencies of fraud.

If deemed appropriate, additional ratios can be added to supplement those set forth in the text. Such extra effort is generally not required unless the initial analytical reviews indicate areas of concern.

On-Book Frauds

The text in this chapter focuses on the efforts of the forensic accountant in their reviews of the transactions, accounting records, or financial reports of any individual, governmental, or business unit. Forensic accountants must be aware that these reviews are limited, in fact, to only on-book transactions, as reflected in the records and reports being examined. They must constantly be aware of the possibility of off-book transactions when they are reviewing on-book records and reports. They do this by looking for procedural or internal control deficiencies that could make it possible for off-book transactions to occur. The on-book reviews are *primary*. The follow-up reviews to identify off-book transactions are *secondary*.

The subject of off-book transactions is covered elsewhere in this book. That text focuses on how to identify such transactions and how to use various documents (e.g., bank statements, evidence of asset purchases made in cash, and so on) to develop the equivalent of a Statement of Source and Application of Funds. That statement, a modification of the Statement of Changes in Financial Position, will often become the primary financial statement for any environment where there are off-book transactions. Such statement is often incomplete but, even so, may effectively present enough of the facts developed to accomplish its end objectives either before a court or in out-of-court negotiations.

NOTES

1. American Institute of Certified Public Accountants, *Accounting Terminology Bulletin No. 1* (AICPA, 1944).

2. American Accounting Association, *A Statement of Basic Accounting Theory* (AAA, 1966), p. 1.

3. Ibid., p. 68.

4. Ibid.

5. Financial Accounting Standards Board, *Financial Accounting Concepts No. 1*, para. 7.

6. Financial Accounting Standards Board, *Statement of Financial Accounting Concepts No. 1*, para. 9.

7. American Institute of Certified Public Accountants, Special Committee on Research Program, *Journal of Accountancy* 106, p. 63.

8. American Institute of Certified Public Accountants. *Objectives of Financial Statements* (AICPA), p. 15.

9. AICPA, *Statement of Basic Accounting Theory*, p. 69.

10. Eric L. Kohler, *A Dictionary for Accountants*, 4th ed. (Englewood Cliffs, NJ: Prentice Hall, 1970), p. 188.

11. Ibid., p. 275.

12. Ibid., p. 391.

13. Lee J. Seidler and D. R. Carmichael, eds., *Accountant's Handbook,* 6th ed., Vol. i (New York: The Ronald Press, 1981), p. 1–8. Copyright © 1981 by The Ronald Press. Reprinted by permission of John Wiley & Sons, Inc.

14. Ibid., p. 4–4.

15. Ibid., p. 4–5.

16. Ibid.

17. Ibid., p. 4–17.

18. Ibid., p. 6–4.

CHAPTER 13

EVALUATING ORGANIZATION
AND INTERNAL CONTROLS

Sound organization is the "keystone" and effective internal controls are the "pillars" on which a strong firm is built.

George Beard

ORGANIZATION

Perspective

By reviewing and evaluating the organization of any governmental or business environment, forensic accountants can learn a great deal about possible strengths and weaknesses as to delegation of authority and responsibility, lines of communication, specific or general level of competency, and overall or specific internal controls in the procedures and processes in the subject environment. Related to such review, the job descriptions of the key management, supervisory, and control personnel must be reviewed and evaluated. Too often, auditors in a routine audit environment tend to limit their reviews of an organization to only determining who has what authority and responsibility and reviewing the lines of communication. Only by such broadened review can the forensic accountant determine the risks, threats, and vulnerabilities resulting from deficiencies in the overall organizational environment.

Definition of Organization
An organization is a developed process of administration involving people and functions.

Organizational Development (OD)
Organizational development deals with organizational aspects of the behavioral sciences and may also be known as human resources development.

General Organizational Structural Specifications[1]

Clarity of Purpose.   Since organizations traditionally have multiple rather than single goals, it is important that all such goals are understood by all management members.

Adaptability.   It is recognized that change is pervasive and affects all organizations. The degree of planned change must be understood by management.

Flexibility.   Any organizational structure must be sufficiently flexible to change as and when needed. If it is, it will avoid rigidity that can lead to internal pressures.

Efficiency.   This is accomplished through economy of effort to meet organizational economic and social objectives.

Stability.   The fundamental principle of stability of the organization as a whole recognizes that it must adopt mechanisms that are not vulnerable to disruption due to ongoing change. Stability represents a condition to be met by adaptability.

Organization Renewal.   This is the ability of an organization to change structurally to permit survival and future growth.

Organization Types

The organizational structure can change materially from company to company, even within the same industry. The five traditional types are line; line and staff; line and functional staff; line, functional staff, and committee; and matrix organizations.

The first four organizational approaches are in the traditional pyramid format (see Figure 13–1). They will vary as to being broad (e.g., fewer levels but more positions on any level) or high (e.g., more levels with fewer positions on any level).

Line Organization
The line organization is the simplest form of structure. It assumes a direct line of responsibility and control from the chief executive officer (CEO) or general manager to intermediate line executives to foremen to workers.

Line and Staff Organization
Line and staff organizations developed in industry in recognition of the need of line executives in large and complex organizations to have assistants who could handle specific advisory responsibilities in connection with such functions

FIGURE 13-1
Pyramid Organization

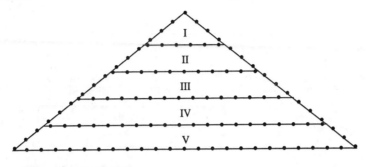

I. Executive management.
II. Intermediate management.
III. Junior management.
IV. Supervisors and foreman
V. Workers.

as research, planning, distribution, public relations, and the like. Over time, their activities and duties were increased to help them make a contribution. This eventually evolved into staff departments supplementing the line organization.

Line and Functional Staff Organization
This combined the advantages of the line and staff organization, and the functional organization. Under this form of organization, the staff departments are given authority over specialized activities, such as inspection, process engineering procedures, employment, purchasing, and so on. The staff function directs its activities in the operating units. If disagreement arises, the matter is taken up with the administrative head over both production and staff units.

Line, Functional Staff, and Committee Organization
This is the same as the line and functional staff organization except it adds committees, usually in large organizations, to facilitate coordination and cooperation.

Matrix Organization
The matrix organization structure focuses on providing a sense of flexibility, capabilities, work, and communication relationships and can involve multiple and simultaneous undertakings in any organization. In contrast to the traditional pyramid, it has an executive reporting to different people at different levels. Figure 13–2 shows a hypothetical matrix format involving five departments and three matrix groups.

Some of the problems in this organizational approach are

1. There may be a conflict in authority between formal roles and those assumed in the particular matrix model.

FIGURE 13-2
Matrix Organization

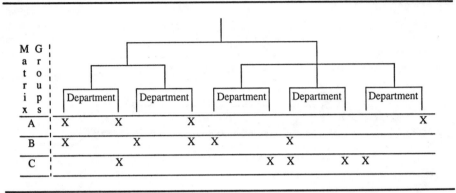

2. Leadership may not be accepted by group members.
3. Flexibility and, in some instances, transient composition may be difficult for some to accept.
4. Matrix design may create problems between peers.
5. Participation may be considered as assuming added duties or responsibilities.
6. If proven successful, people may be reluctant to revert back to a pyramid format if that is deemed to be desirable at some future time.

Urwick's 10 Principles of Organization

The following principles are part of Col. Urwick's "Notes on the Theory of Organization," prepared originally in connection with an address he made to the American Management Association (AMA).

Principle of the Objective. Every organization and every part of every organization must be an expression of the purpose of the undertaking concerned or it is meaningless and, therefore, redundant. You cannot organize in a vacuum; you must organize for something.

Principle of Specialization. The activities of every member of any organized group should be confined, as far as possible, to the performance of a single function.

Principle of Coordination. The purpose of organizing per se, as distinguished from the purpose of the undertaking, is to facilitate coordination, that is, unity of effort.

Principle of Authority.   In every organized group, the supreme authority must rest somewhere. There should be a clear line of authority from the supreme authority to every individual in the group.

Principle of Responsibility.   The responsibility of the superior for the acts of his subordinate is absolute.

Principle of Definition.   The content of each position should be reviewed for the duties involved, the authority and responsibility assigned, and the relationships with other positions. Such positions should be defined in writing and published to all concerned.

Principle of Correspondence.   In every position, the responsibility and the authority should correspond.

The Span of Control.   To the degree possible, the number of persons reporting directly to an individual should be limited to five or six. As a result of downsizing and the elimination of levels of middle management, it may not be possible to achieve or maintain that objective during a period of organizational transition (e.g., modifying from the traditional pyramid to an hourglass with reduced staffing at the middle management level). (Note: This is the author's modification of Urwick's original eighth principle).

Principle of Balance.   It is essential that the various units of an organization be kept in balance.

Principle of Continuity.   Reorganization is a continuous process. In every undertaking, specific provision should be made for it.

Organizational Purpose

1. An organization establishes a repetition of desired actions. Through the establishment of procedures, rules, and reporting relationships, the organization simplifies the processing of information and ensures that all necessary actions occur automatically. This enables management, at any level, to focus on issues that are new or nonrepetitive.

2. An organization ensures actions by organizational members will be coordinated. By having desired actions fit together in a systematic way, an efficient and effective pattern of overall effort will be ensured.

3. An organization makes behavior predictable. Members of the organization should act with reasonable assurance that other members will act in the same manner. This precludes anyone having to act on the basis of the unpredictable actions of others.

4. An organization stores information. Organizations learn in the course of their existence, and the information gained is added to their knowledge base.

5. An organization establishes an identity independent of the people within it. The organization becomes more or less free of members who could have been considered indispensable because back-up replacement people are available. Therefore, it ensures its existence in spite of personnel who may leave.

6. An organization allocates rewards to contributors and claimants. An effective organization contains a series of complex systems of arrangements between itself and the people or groups who contribute to it, including those having claims upon it. This enables mutually satisfactory rewards for different kinds of work or levels of performance.

Twelve Building Blocks of Internal Control/Check

The objective is to keep the 12 building blocks (see Figure 13–3) in proper alignment. If any block is out of alignment with other blocks, appropriate action(s) should be taken to bring it back into alignment. Any out-of-alignment situation creates risks, threats, and vulnerabilities that can be minimized by reestablishing the desired alignment. For example, a company moves one section of eight people from one division to another. What is affected? Answer:

1. *Block 2:* The budget for the two divisions must be changed to reflect the realignment. The subject unit may be either a profit or cost center. The change will result in one division being affected in one direction (e.g., reducing costs or increasing net income) and the other division in the opposite direction (e.g., increasing costs or reducing net income).
2. *Block 3:* The assignment may result in lost controls in one division and create a need for new controls in the other division.
3. *Block 4:* The job descriptions may change, with fewer persons in the section but with higher job classifications because of increased use of computers (e.g., adoption of paperless transaction trials and a higher level of computer skills required by all persons in the section).
4. *Block 5:* The reassignment of the subject section may necessitate rewrite of certain procedures, practices, standards, and systems to improve efficiency, effectiveness, and economy, and related internal controls/ checks.
5. *Block 6:* Refer to comments for Block 4. In addition, there may be a need to change or enhance the programs, systems, and related controls due to the increase in automation and computers in the revised work environment.
6. *Block 8:* Refer again to comments for Block 4. Because fewer but more qualified persons are used in functions, the job descriptions have to be changed to reflect such facts. In the example used, the grade levels probably have to be raised to reflect the revised job criteria.

So the simple organizational realignment of moving one section from one division to another affects a number of the 12 building blocks. Appropriate action(s)

FIGURE 13-3
Twelve Building Blocks of Internal Control/Check

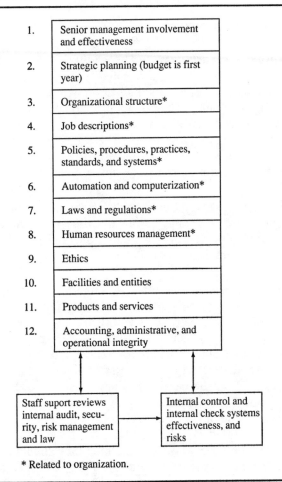

1.	Senior management involvement and effectiveness
2.	Strategic planning (budget is first year)
3.	Organizational structure*
4.	Job descriptions*
5.	Policies, procedures, practices, standards, and systems*
6.	Automation and computerization*
7.	Laws and regulations*
8.	Human resources management*
9.	Ethics
10.	Facilities and entities
11.	Products and services
12.	Accounting, administrative, and operational integrity

Staff suport reviews internal audit, security, risk management and law

Internal control and internal check systems effectiveness, and risks

* Related to organization.

must be taken, relative to each, to bring them back into alignment with the other building blocks.

Fraud in an Organization

Personal References/Background Checks

It has been projected that approximately 30 percent of fraud perpetrated by insiders (e.g., white-collar crime) was done so by personnel who had previous records of improper conduct, including fraud. It has also been projected that, in virtually all of these instances, a more diligent background check into their professional and educational credentials and performance would have revealed a record of improper conduct, including fraud, or antisocial behavior that, on its own, could be a red flag of potential problems.

Weak Organizational Structure

Out of Balance—Authority and Responsibility. This is a situation where one person has most of the responsibility, the authority is shared relatively equally with another. This puts the person with more responsibility than authority in a position of being afraid to act properly and/or promptly because, if anything goes wrong, he or she will get most of the blame. On the other hand, the person with more authority than responsibility can be a risk-taker, recognizing that if he or she is wrong, most of the blame will go to the other party involved, the one with more responsibility than authority.

Poor Job Descriptions. Such job descriptions are often out of date, as the job requirements have changed from the time when they were written. Further, almost none of them properly identify the internal control and internal check requirements of the job.

Inadequate Training. Too often, in large organizations, more time is spent in learning about the firm's ethics and benefit programs than the details of one's specific jobs. This is particularly critical for a new hire and somewhat less critical for a person who transfers into the position or is promoted into the position. Ironically, all will tend to rely on some helpful person working in the same area or in a similar job (e.g., data entry, and so on). Unfortunately, that helpful person can set up the person in a new position to do something they should not do or not do something that they should do.

In 1977, the Institute of Internal Auditors, Inc., published a book authored by Harold F. Russell titled *Foozles and Frauds*. It was enlightening!

A "foozler" is someone who did something they should not have done or did not do something they should have done. Their improper action(s) or lack of action(s) permits a fraud to be perpetrated although they are not aware of it nor do they benefit from it.

How many people in your organization are potential "foozlers"? It is possible that there are more than you imagine!

Fraud Cases

These are two actual fraud cases on which I was involved that relate to the potential deficiency in personal references/background checks.

The Case of the Computer Room Operator

I was called in to an insurance company in a major city to review the computer environment and set up the duties and responsibilities of an information security officer (ISO). MIS management and the general auditor had previously determined that this function should be established. Part of this assignment was to identify the total staffing and levels of the personnel to be assigned to the function. In addition, I was to write the job descriptions for each person in the function.

While reviewing the situation, I uncovered an ongoing fraud. With assistance of the EDP auditors, we identified the nature of the fraud, how long it had been in existence, and, finally, the fraud perpetrator. At the request of the general auditor, I interrogated the fraud perpetator and was able to obtain a full confession from him on audiotape. The confession was transcribed and the now-confessed fraud perpetrator signed it. The amount involved was $175,000 and the fraud had been going on for nearly six months.

To my surprise, about one hour after I had obtained the confession, the general auditor handed me a check covering my fees, expenses, and a five-figure bonus, and informed me that ''my services were no longer required.'' I knew right then that the company was not going to take any legal action against the computer room operator, who was the fraud perpetrator. They would make him resign and he would walk. Keep in mind that only one in five discovered computer frauds is ever reported outside the company where the fraud occurred.

Three days later, I received a discrete telephone call from a member of that insurance company's security staff. He told me that not only did they let him walk, but they gave him a three-month consulting contract at full-pay and a guarantee that his personnel file would not contain any mention of the fraud situation. In summary, it was a deal between the fraud perpetrator and the company that they wouldn't talk if he didn't talk.

Six months later, I was on a similar assignment in another city, also for an insurance company. I was sitting in the office of the head of MIS. It had a large picture window to the hallway and across the hall there was the main computer room. The head of MIS received a telephone call and, while he was talking on the phone, I noticed the faud perpetrator from the previously described fraud walk by. When the head of MIS had to meet with an executive officer ''for a few minutes,'' I took the opportunity to telephone my attorney back in Chicago. I described the situation without identifying either company or the cities where they were located. I asked him what I could tell the head of MIS where I was now working. He asked me to write down what he told me. I did. He spelled it out: ''N.O.T.H.I.N.G.''! I followed orders. Several weeks later as I was finishing up my assignment, I asked to check out the application program controls on the specific application where I had caught the fraud perpetrator in the first city. Guess what? I caught the same computer room operator perpetrating the same fraud. He had only been with his new employer a month when the same fraud scheme he had used in the first city where I had caught him was activated again. This time the fraud amount was only $85,000. Again, I was asked to interrogate him and obtained a confession. I was pleased when the general auditor, head of security and head of MIS all recommended to the president of the firm that the fraud be reported.

Remember, I could not mention anything about the first fraud. I did suggest to the head of security that he should go through security at his former employer. He did so and found that firm had not done any background check on him, ''because he had tested out so well'' when being interviewed for hire. On that basis, the second firm's human resources department, which had checked with its counterpart at the first firm and learned nothing derrogatory about the now-confessed fraud perpetrator, went back to the employer prior to that one. There they learned the subject, who was a computer room operator, had been caught in a fraud. It was exactly the same scheme I had caught him in twice. That company had reported the situation to the law-enforcement authorities and the subject had done three years in the state prison.

Had the second employer done a proper background check with the first employer, they would have learned about his fraudulent activities and the fact that he had served three years in prison for computer fraud. The third employer now had a much stronger case by reporting that the current fraud was not a first offense. To my knowledge, the third employer never knew officially about the fraud at the second employer. In fact, I think they knew off the record because security people do communicate information on wrongdoing for defensive reasons; that is, I will protect you now and you can repay the favor later. Based on the fraud at the third employer, the fraud perpetrator received another sentence of three years in prison. This was much more satisfying to me than the bonus received from his second employer.

The Case of the Rich Leasing Officer

This case occurred in London, England. For simplicity in presentation, I will write up the case as though I was the auditor in charge of an audit team reviewing the branch, merchant bank, leasing subsidiary office, and regional headquarters of a major U.S. banking organization.

One Saturday, when going from my hotel to the branch office to catch up on the workpaper review, I got off the "tube" at Bank Street, across from the Bank of England. Walking to the branch, I deliberately went by the Rolex dealer so I could check my watch to his outdoor clock. There was no one else on the street and no vehicles in sight. Then, in front of me, I saw a Rolls-Royce Silver Cloud, a car built many years earlier. When stopping to admire it, I was surprised to note that a vice president of the bank's leasing subsidiary was driving it. I waved to him but he did not respond.

In early afternoon, when taking a break, I wondered to myself how a vice president could afford a car worth several hundred thousand dollars, assuming he owned it because, were it mine, no one else would ever drive it.

I telephoned my administrative assistant at his home and directed that he check with the human resources department to determine how extensive a background check had been done on the subject (e.g., education, professional experience, personal references) and that he personally contact the president of a major leasing firm, mention my name, and ask for any information he could provide on the subject. The president had been on the board of directors of a Fortune 100 company where I had previously been an officer. He knew me well and would provide information that firm's human resources department would not give out.

He was to give the assignment top priority. By Monday evening, he was able to inform me that "no background check had been done on the subject because he had been recommended by the executive vice president, in charge of worldwide leasing." So the subject was hired in as a vice president with no background check. My assistant then informed the human resources department management that I wanted a thorough background check done on the subject. He agreed to do so and got it started immediately. My administrative assistant's telephone call to the president of the subject's former employer proved quite fruitful. He advised that the subject had only worked seven months for them and left under a "cloud of suspicion" of possible wrongdoing. It appeared that he was demanding and obtaining kickbacks from leasing customers to give them "preferred" rates.

His employment application indicated he had worked seven years for them. This was the entire time he had been professionally employed since completing his education. Follow-up identified he had worked for five other companies during that seven-year period. He had left two of them under a similar "cloud of suspicion" for the reason stated earlier.

Days later, the human resources department developed the following:

A. He claimed to have both a bachelor's and master's degree from a major university. In fact, he had only a backelor's degree and three credit hours towards his master's degree.

B. Two of his three personal references were actually deceased at the time he prepared the employment application. They were men of high reputation. It would appear he was gambling on no background check. If found earlier, he could, of course, have given replacement references.

Based on the initial information and before getting the information in #1 and #2, I initiated a full fraud audit of the leasing activities of the subject. The second ranking auditor on each phase of my ongoing audit work was pulled off to make up the team reviewing his leasing activities. The assignment given them was simple:

A. Check each lease on which the subject had been the leasing officer from the time the subsidiary office had been opened 14 months earlier.

B. Determine whether his immediate superior was a titular rather than actual head. He was the son of a neighbor of the chairman and, although he was a college graduate, he had no experience in leasing. I was concerned that the subject may be using him for a purpose as yet undetermined, possibly fraudulent, making him a "foozler."

It was found that he had negotiated a total of eight leasing deals. All eight were "sale and leaseback" arrangements. All involved shipping firms. All used the same appraiser. The total amount involved was $244 million. In each case, it was determined that it was a "brokered" deal. That meant the lead came from a broker. For providing the lead, the broker received a commission. This was acceptable practice in the United Kingdom. In all cases, the commission was 5 percent of the face amount of the lease. That meant that the commission paid came to $12.2 million.

As the audit progressed, it was identified that, in all eight leases, the broker on each lease was the corporate treasurer of the shipping company. That was clearly a conflict of interest under U.S. law. Ironically, it was not illegal under U.K. laws. My immdeiate thought was that the subject had made those arrangements. I did not believe that all eight treasurers would have initiated the same deals, all at the same brokerage percentage rate. Therefore, I arranged to meet with two of the treasurers to discuss the "sale and leaseback" leases.

About 15 minutes into each meeting, I casually inserted the brokerage arrangement into the conversation. Both treasurers indicated that the subject had proposed the arrangement, to encourage them to move forward with the proposed "sale and leaseback" arrangement. To receive the brokerage fee, however, they had to give 2 percent of the face amount of the lease, which was 40 percent of the brokerage fee, back to the subject. Based on those findings, other members of the audit team interviewed the other six treasurers and developed exactly the same information. This meant that the treasurers split $7.32 million between the eight of them while the subject received $4.88 million in kickbacks.

Since each phase of the audit was developing more negative information on the subject, I thought that it was probable the ship valuations were overstated. We then engaged an investigation firm to obtain background information on the appraiser who had been used on all eight of the lease transactions to place a value on the ships involved. It was found that his license had recently been suspended for a year. It was the second such offense. The third time he would lose his license forever.

After reviewing the report on the appraiser, I arranged to meet with him. During that meeting, he advised that the subject had given him $50,000 for each of the eight appraisals, which was double his usual fee. For that premium, he had valued the ships at 20 to 25 percent over what he perceived to have been their true values. He provided this information with no payment given or promised by me and no commitment for leniency for his wrongdoing should the subject be subsequently taken to trial. It was apparent that he was a bitter man and striking out at anyone who had bribed him for a false appraisal.

My last step was to determine how he got the managing director of the subsidiary, his immediate superior, to sign and accept all eight leasing transactions. I interveiwed the managing director and quickly learned that he "totally relied" on the subject, who had booked more business than the other four contact/leasing officers together. He finally admitted that with his limited knowledge of leasing, anything placed in front of him by the subject for signature was signed without meaningful question. I asked him specifically if any illegal or irregular transactions had knowingly been approved. He claimed that, to his knowledge, all aspects of each lease were correct and proper. He indicated that nothing would have been signed by him that he knew was irregular and improper.

I now cleared the data developed with the general auditor. He approved my interrogating the subject and, based on that meeting, taking any legal actions deemed appropriate. When confronted with the facts, the subject tried to con me that "he was only following orders." I contradicted that statement and pressed with the other data developed. In approximately 30 minutes, he broke and confessed. On the basis of appropriate legal advice from the attornies representing the bank in the United Kingdom, we had the subject arrested.

With appropriate court order, the bank took possession of his primary assets (e.g., Rolls-Royce Silver Cloud, paintings, and antique furniture). This was turned over to an auction company for sale. The bank recovered $2.1 million for the sale of those assets at auction. Cash and investments, converted to cash, generated another $250,000.

The eight leases were sold to another financial institution. The value placed on them was as follows:

1. Sale and leaseback amounts plus brokerage	$256,200,000
2. Less: Overvaluation (22 percent)	(53,680,000)
	$202,520,000
3. Less: Brokerage (5 percent on #1):	(12,200,000)
	$190,300,000
4. Less: Percentage of lease payments made to time of sale (3 percent)	(732,000)
Net received from purchaser	$189,588,000

The total loss to the selling bank was $65,880,000; combination of #2 plus #3.

With that finalized, the subject was taken to trial in the United Kingdom and received a seven-year prison sentence. On the basis of an international agreement between the United Kingdom and the United States, at the request of the subject, he was sent back to the United States to serve his sentence.

The impact of this substantial loss was that the bank discontinued its international leasing operations and closed its U.K. operations, which was supposed to be the first of a worldwide network of similar facilities.

The managing director of the U.K. leasing subsidiary and the executive vice president in charge of leasing worldwide resigned.

Summary

There are many risks inherent in an organization. They begin with the duties and tasks assigned to anyone, then, proceed to the authority and responsibility assigned to them and how current and complete the job descriptions are for themselves and subordinates. The organization helps identify the specific duties and tasks, authority and responsibility, and with whom they interface elsewhere in the organization.

Next in importance is hiring qualified people for specific positions. How diligent is the background check on those people? If psychological testing is done for certain positions, is that information used properly for any hire? Are people properly trained in their new positions, whether new hires or persons transferred from another position in firm? Is there an ethics policy, and are new hires indoctrinated in it?

Do policies and procedures exist in writing? Are they current? Do they contain adequate requirements for internal controls/checks? Do staff personnel (e.g., internal audit, loan reivew, and so on) periodically review, monitor, and test every work environment? Does the organizational structure change to meet the changing needs of the business?

There are no shortcuts to using the organization as an important managerial control vehicle. If it accomplishes what is intended, everyone in the organization will understand its goals and objectives, as well as the specific authority and responsibility assigned to them. It will also help to make the organization's ethics known. The job descriptions should not be limited to identifying authority and responsibility but should clearly identify the duties, work tasks, activities, and functions, and the level of internal control and check desired for each.

It is important to remember a statistic that I have heard over the years from various sources (but cannot name the original source) that indicates "30–35 percent of fraud perpetrators, within an organization, would not have been hired had thorough background checks been done before they were hired." The obvious indication is the individuals had something in their past that would have justified the firm not hiring them (e.g., drug, alcohol, or gambling problem; prior criminal record; prior record of fraudulent activity that was not prosecuted; or misrepresentation of education and/or experience in the job application).

Fortunately, there is a growing awareness of the importance of thoroughly checking the background of people being considered for employment in management or sensitive positions (e.g., computer programmers and analysts, computer operators, wire/money transfer specialists, foreign exchange traders, any position in the scientific and research areas, engineers, and so on). How far down the organizational ladder such checking is done is a difficult management call. Consider the following:

> Enough employers share [the] enthusiasm to make background checks of job applications a growth industry . . . Fueled by the litigation explosion and by the outlawing of lie-detector tests for job candidates, the searches have expanded to include a market basket of biographical data, from employment, credit history, and educational background to workers' compensation claims, driving violations and criminal records . . . The government has tried to limit abuse of this information through enforcement of the Fair Credit Reporting Act of 1978, and the enactment . . . [in 1992] of the Americans with Disabilities Act. Part of the statute of the act sharply limits the type and timing of health-related inquiries that employers can make about people [they] want to hire. But the controversy doesn't seem to have hurt the growth of the resume-checking industry . . . Employers of all sizes say they worry about a rising trend toward negligent-hiring suits, in which juries have faulted employers for not having looked thoroughly enough into the background of an employee who later commits a work-related crime.[2]

As a forensic accountant, the more information available on any suspect(s) in a fraud examination, either preventative (e.g., evaluating organization, procedures, practices, personnel, and controls) or investigatory (e.g., dealing with a possible, probable, or known fraud situation), the better for me to determine where to focus my attention. To put this into perspective, consider the *criminal equation* formula:

$$\text{Target} + \text{Motive} + \text{Access} + \text{Opportunity} = \frac{\text{Potentially successful fraud}}{\text{situation or criminal attack}}$$

- Target: The object of the possible or known fraud situation or criminal attack.
- Motive: Who and why some person(s) may, in the future, or have already attacked the target. Such action may be for gain, revenge, or malicious mischief.
- Access: Attempts to focus investigation on those with personal habits or historical conduct suggesting they would take advantage of ability to attack target.
- Opportunity: For the identified weakness to give rise to the opportunity for the possible or known wrongdoing. Background information may indicate a historical antisocial problem (e.g., having a criminal record; alcohol, drug, or gambling problem; petty thief; mischievous behavior; poor work record, and so on).

While the target would be designated by management for a preventative review and possibly relatively easy to identify if management calls in the forensic accountant only when there are known problems, the background check of all management personnel and those in sensitive positions would be helpful to enable focusing on the most probably troublemakers/fraud-perpetrators.

An awareness of the strengths and weaknesses in hiring practices, including background checks, and the organization are important to the forensic accountant regardless of whether it is a preventative or investigatory review.

INTERNAL CONTROLS

Definitions from the AICPA

The AICPA has a number of internal control–related definitions and descriptions in various subsections of *SAS No. 1* that are quoted here to set the stage for reviewing the subject from the perspective of the forensic accountant.

Internal Control

Internal control comprises the plan of organization and all of the coordinate methods and measures adopted within a business to safeguard its assets, check the accuracy and reliability of its accounting data, promote operational efficiency, and encourage adherence to prescribed managerial policies. This definition . . . recognizes that a "system of internal control extends beyond those matters which relate directly to the function of the accounting and finance departments."

Administrative Internal Controls

The plan of organization and the procedures and records that are concerned with the decision processes leading to management's authorization of transactions. Such authority is a management function directly associated with the responsibility for achieving the objectives of the organization and is the starting point for establishing accounting control of transactions.

You will note that both of the preceding definitions refer to "the plan of organization," reemphasizing the writer's position that organization and internal control should be reviewed as interrelated subjects.

Objectives of Internal Accounting Control

There are five general objectives of internal accounting control:

1. *Completeness:* All transactions that occur should be recorded in the accounting records.
2. *Validity:* All recorded transactions represent economic events that actually occurred and were executed in accordance with prescribed procedures.
3. *Accuracy:* Transactions are recorded at the correct amount, into the proper account, and on a timely basis at each stage of processing.
4. *Maintenance:* The accounting records, after the entry of transactions into them, are properly controlled so they continue to reflect accurately the operations of the business.
5. *Physical security:* Access to assets and the documents and records that control them is suitably restricted to authorized personnel.

All five together constitute what is known as the "concept of reasonable assurance." The AICPA defines that as follows:

The concept of reasonable assurance recognizes that the cost of internal control should not exceed the benefits expected to be derived. The benefits consist of reductions in the risk of failing to achieve the objective implicit in the definition of accounting control. Although the cost-benefit relationship is the primary conceptual criteria that should be considered in designing a system of accounting control, precise measurement of costs and benefits usually is not possible; accordingly, any evaluation of the cost-benefit relationship requires estimates and judgements by management.

The stated general rule of benefits exceeding costs for internal controls set in place can be modified for short periods when and if the circumstances warrant extraordinary control actions for a short period of time. This will be discussed further later in this chapter.

Limitations on the Effectiveness of Any System of Internal Control

There are three limitations on any system's internal control effectiveness:

1. Misunderstanding of instructions, mistakes of judgment, personal carelessness, distraction or fatigue on the part of the person responsible for performing the control procedure.

2. Collusion between responsible individuals, circumventing control procedures whose effectiveness depends on segregation of duties.
3. Errors or irregularities perpetrated by management with respect to transactions or to the estimates and judgments required in the preparation of financial statements.

Internal Control—Integrated Framework

More recently, the Committee of Sponsoring Organizations (COSO) of the Treadway Commission has indicated that "Internal Control means different things to different people. This causes confusion among businesspeople, legislators, regulators and others. Resulting miscommunication and different expectations cause problems within an enterprise. Problems are compounded when the term, if not clearly defined, is written into law, regulation or rule."[3]

The COSO defined internal control as follows:

> Internal control is broadly defined as a process, effected by an entity's board of directors, management and other personnel, designed to provide reasonable assurance regarding the achievement of objectives in the following categories:
>
> • Effectiveness and efficiency of operations
> • Reliability of financial reporting
> • Compliance with applicable laws and regulations.[4]

The first category relates to the business objectives of any organization (e.g., performance and profitability goals and safeguarding resources—assets and personnel). The second category relates to both the preparation and reliability of published financial statements and the financial data derived from them. The third category focuses on the risks for failure to comply with all laws and regulations affecting the specific organization.

It should be remembered that "while internal control is a process, its effectiveness is a state or condition of the process at one or more points in time."[5]

The COSO concludes that internal control consists of five interrelated components:

1. *Control environment:* This "sets the tone of an organization, including the control consciousness of its people. It is the foundation for all other components of internal control, providing discipline and structure."[6]
2. *Risk assessment:* This recognizes that "every entity faces a variety of risks from external and internal sources that must be assessed. A precondition of risk assessment is establishment of objectives, linked at different levels and internally consistent. Risk assessment is the identification and analysis of relevant risks to achievement of the objectives, forming a basis for determining how the risks should be managed."[7]
3. *Control activities:* These are identified as the "policies and procedures that help ensure management objectives are carried out. They help ensure that necessary actions are taken to address risks to achievement of the entity's objectives."[8]

4. *Information and communication:* "Pertinent information must be identified, captured and communicated in a form and timeframe that enables people to carry out their responsibilities. . . . Effective communication also must occur in a broader sense, flowing down, across and up the organization."[9]

5. *Monitoring:* "Internal control systems need to be monitored—a process that assesses the quality of the system's performance over time. This is accomplished through ongoing monitoring activities, separate evaluations or a combination of the two."[10]

There is synergy and linkage among these components, forming an integrated system that reacts dynamically to changing conditions. The internal control system is intertwined with the entity's operating activities and exists for fundamental business reasons. Internal control is most effective when controls are built into the entity's infrastructure and are a part of the essence of the enterprise.[11]

The COSO identifies what internal control can do:

Internal control can help an entity achieve its performance and profitability targets, and prevent loss of resources. It can help ensure reliable financial reporting. And it can help ensure that the enterprise complies with laws and regulations, avoid damage to its reputation and other consequences. In sum, it can help an entity get to where it wants to go, and avoid pitfalls and surprises along the way.[12]

The COSO also identifies what internal control cannot do:

- Even effective internal control can only help an entity achieve these objectives.[13]
- An internal control system, no matter how well conceived and operated, can provide only reasonable—not absolute—assurance to management and the board regarding achievement of an entity's objectives.[14]

For the full details of the conclusions of the COSO, there is a four-volume report. The first is an executive summary. The second deals with the framework and definition of internal control, the third deals with reporting to external parties, and the fourth deals with evaluation tools. It is available from any of the five organizations that participated in the study:

1. American Institute of Certified Public Accountants.
2. American Accounting Association.
3. The Institute of Internal Auditors.
4. Institute of Management Accountants.
5. Financial Executives Institute.

Internal Check

It is important to understand the importance of an internal check criterion being built into the procedures and practices of any accounting, administrative, or operational environment. I would define internal check as the design of transaction flows intended to provide effective organization and operational processing of any recordation process, whether accounting or administrative. It would also provide a degree of protection against fraud. A basic criterion is that organizational responsibility be assigned in such a manner that no single individual or group of individuals has exclusive control over any one transaction or type of transactions. The internal check criterion requires that each transaction be cross-checked or cross-controlled through the normal functional responsibilities of another individual or group. Properly established, internal check should be viewed as a deterrent to fraud. It should make it more difficult for a defrauder to abstract funds or other assets for which they are responsible and at the same time cover up those manipulations by entering corresponding amounts in the accounting records for such actions.

Perspective

While internal control has always been recognized as being important, it has received increased attention in the last two decades. Particular attention should be paid to the Treadway Commission, discussed earlier in this chapter, and the Foreign Corrupt Practices Act of 1977. This act restricts management from the direct or indirect (through agents) bribing of government or business officials to sell goods or services. It requires public companies to maintain adequate systems of internal controls.

While these are theoretically meaningful, do they really encourage better internal control and check requirements, with the specific objective of better identification of risks that may have or could result in fraud? Not in my opinion! Consider the following:

AICPA SAS No. 53, "The Auditor's Responsibility to Detect and Report Errors and Irregularities," explains the auditor's responsibility to detect and report irregularities in a clearer manner than previously. It focuses on red flags that identify a possible increase in the risk of material misstatements that should heighten the auditor's skepticism and describe how the auditor should respond when such conditions are encountered. The responsibility paragraph indicates that

> The auditor should assess the risk that errors and irregularities may cause the financial statements to contain a material misstatement. Based on that assessment, the auditor should design the audit to provide reasonable assurance on detecting errors and irregularities that are material to financial statement. (Supercedes SAS No. 16.)

According to the Institute of Internal Auditors, Standard 300.9 Investigation of Fraud:

> Investigation consists of performing extended procedures necessary to determine whether fraud, as suggested by the indicators, has occurred. It includes gathering sufficient evidential matter about the specific details of a discovered fraud. Internal auditors, lawyers, investigators, security personnel and other specialists from inside or outside the organization should conduct the fraud investigations.
>
> Internal auditors are not expected to have knowledge equivalent to that of a person whose primary responsibility is detecting and investigating fraud.

Internal auditing should assess the facts known relative to all fraud investigations in order to:

- Determine if controls need to be implemented or strengthened.
- Design audit tests to help disclose the existence of similar frauds in the future.
- Help meet the internal auditor's responsibility to maintain sufficient knowledge of fraud.

Figures 13–4 and 13–5 indicate the principles of how to determine the appropriate level of internal control required for any specific activity, function, work task, or duty.

Experience has shown that normally when procedures or practices are modified by line or staff management responsible for any activity, function, duties, or work tasks, they do so to improve the 3 Es. They focus on productivity. However, when they make any changes to procedures or practices, it is almost a certainty that internal control and check requirements will suffer. Sometimes such damage is minor. On other occasions, the changes to favor the 3 Es can literally eliminate any internal control and/or check requirements built into the original procedures or practices. Therefore, the original criteria and all revisions thereto need be known by the forensic accountant to properly evaluate internal controls.

Now look at Figure 13–5. Again, any changes to increase the 3 Es will, in all probability, result in reducing the effectiveness of the 2Cs. The result is that the actual risk environment in the subject activity, function, duty, or work task will be increased over the range of risks originally determined to be acceptable to management. Forensic accountants must understand the intent of the original controls so they can evaluate any variance from that objective in the actual, current functioning of the activity, function, duty, or work task.

Some years ago, The Institute of Internal Auditors published a book titled *Foozles & Frauds*. Consider the following:

> A dictionary defines a foozle as "an awkward, unskillful act; a bungle." It defines fraud as "intentional deception to cause a person to give up property or some lawful right." The intention to deceive is the important phrase; and in some situations, it is not necessary that the fraud be successful.[15]

> Frauds and foozles are usually so intermingled that it is difficult to separate them into cause and effect. Few frauds are designed from beginning to end. An error,

FIGURE 13–4
Balance Between 3 Es and 2 Cs

3Es:	2Cs:
– Efficiency	– (Internal) control
– Effectiveness	– (Internal) check
– Economy	

Risks

FIGURE 13–5
Hold Risks to an Acceptable Range of Risks

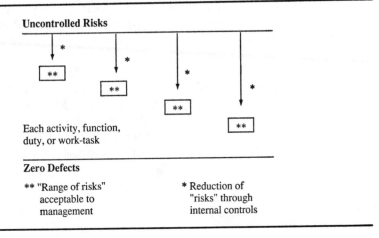

Uncontrolled Risks

Each activity, function,
duty, or work-task

Zero Defects

** "Range of risks"   * Reduction of
  acceptable to   "risks" through
  management   internal controls

or someone's bungle, can produce a monetary gain for a person who rationalizes that one such unlawful profit deserves another. He repeats the foozle. It now becomes an intentional fraud.[16]

From the preceding, we can then define a "foozler" as one who through his or her improper or ineffective action or lack of action enables a fraud to be perpetrated although he or she does not benefit from it nor is he or she aware of it.

Too often, sound procedures with adequate controls built into them are compromised as to the effectiveness of the controls and their end value by the actions or lack of actions of a foozler.

The 12 building blocks of internal control were illustrated earlier in the chapter in Figure 13–3. Any weakness in controls at any of the 12 phases indicated can leave an organization vulnerable to increased fraud risks. Determining the range of risks acceptable for any activity, function, duty, or work task is just the beginning. Systems, procedures, practices, and ethical standards of the firm should build in controls that are adequate to hold the relative exposures to an acceptable range of risks. Qualified, properly trained people who understand not only how to do a job right but also the controls built into the systems, procedures, and practices and the importance of assuring they are functioning as intended on an ongoing basis are the keystone of actually holding perceived risks to an acceptable range of risks.

It is important to establish sound internal controls to hold perceived risks to an acceptable range of risks for any activity, function, duty, or work task. It is important that changes to procedures and practices never be made without a full awareness of the effect to internal controls. It is important that all personnel involved in any activity, function, duty, or work task understand not only how to do their assigned responsibilities but also what the total procedural or practice objectives are as regards internal controls that have been built in. It is also important that personnel feel free to raise questions of their supervisors, or supervisors of their managers, relative to internal controls. If that communications capability is not available to them, then people who would like to question what they see or hear continue to keep potentially meaningful information to themselves and any wrongdoing, accidental or intentional, can continue without detection.

It must be understood that people perpetrate fraud. They misuse sound procedures or use weak procedures with ineffective internal controls to perpetrate fraud. It also must be recognized that people are the primary defense against fraud. But, for that to be so, they must understand what is proper procedure and practice and what constitutes improcedure procedure and practice for any accounting, administrative, or operational environment.

Summary

On-Book Fraud
Where the forensic accountant determines that a business is disciplined as to its organization, procedures, practices, and internal control requirements, the initial focus must be on the possibility of on-book fraud, actual or potential. That information is the beginning point to enable assessing specific risks, threats, and vulnerabilities within the organization. Review and evaluation of those factors may indicate that potential for off-book fraud, but that is an end conclusion or finding, not a beginning point.

Off-Book Fraud
Where the forensic accountant identifies that it is an undisciplined business (e.g., no formal organization or procedures), it must be recognized that off-book fraud is potentially as high a risk as on-book fraud.

Examples of Internal Control Manipulation

The Traveling Managing Director
The head of the merchant bank of a major U.S. bank headquartered in London, England, owned a 17-acre estate outside of Dublin, Ireland, complete with horses and permanent staff.

He decided to use his rank to bypass the procedural requirement that all travel for anyone employed by the merchant bank should be arranged through its travel desk. When he was scheduled for a trip to other parts of Europe or the United States,

1. He would have his secretary contact the travel desk and book the appropriate air and hotel accommodations for the trip. The arrangements would be approved by the managing director before final booking.
2. He would then telephone a travel agent and have them book the same trip, air only, on different flights on the same days. He would pick up the tickets on his own and have the merchant bank billed for the tickets.

3. He would then visit an airline office and book the same trip, air only, on different flights from either #1 or #2, on the same days or the preceding or following days. He would charge these tickets on his credit card.

He would then personally turn in the tickets under either #1 and #3 or #2 and #3 to the subject airline for the first leg of the trip and obtain monetary exchange orders (MCOs) enabling him to book travel on that specific airline any time over the next full year, paying for such travel by turning in the MCOs.

Before leaving on the trip, he would approve the invoice for the tickets arranged under #1. Upon his return, he would approve and pass along to his secretary one day apart the invoices for the tickets purchased under #2 and #3. The travel agent would be paid for the tickets under #2 and he would be reimbursed for the tickets under #3. While the secretary, travel desk clerk, and accounting department knew something was irregular, they did not want to challenge the managing director for fear of their jobs, proving again that "rank can intimidate." When it occurs, intended procedures and controls are neutralized.

The managing director used the MCOs to purchase air tickets for him and his wife to fly London/Dublin/London, enabling them to visit their estate in Ireland at the merchant bank's expense.

This on-book fraud was identified by an internal audit review of travel procedures and expenses. The review identified that travel expenses were being incurred that had not been booked by the travel desk, which was a procedural requirement. Further review identified the multiple tickets and charges for the same trip. Follow-up identified the fact that two of the three tickets booked were being turned in and converted into MCOs by the managing director. The final findings, with cooperation of the airline involved, was to identify how the MCOs were being used by the managing director.

The Foreign Exchange (FX) Deceit

A foreign exchange trader convinced the head of the Settlements Section of the Foreign Exchange Unit to charge two contract numbers to that business day at the end of the business day, although there were no deals yet booked to be recorded on them.

He convinced her that he had a "pending" contract about which he would know positively after the Settlements Section head had left for the day. If the deal went through, they would complete the contract the following day but backdate it to the current day. The second contract would only be used if an error was made in preparing the first contract form. If no deal went through, they would cancel both contracts. The contract control sheet would record them for that day, as was appropriate.

In fact, the trader had already made the deal with another institution. If the "spot" deal proved real profitable overnight, the trader would have his compatriate at the other institution consider the trade was with him personally. The deal would be booked between that other institution and his own trading company. He could set up such company simply by having 100 fanfold forms (multicopy forms) made up in his name. He would advise the Settlements Section head that "no deal was made." In that case, the two contracts set aside as part of the prior day's business would be canceled. Settlement would then be made by the other institution to the FX trader in the name of his FX trading company, usually at his home address.

If, however, the deal was only nominally profitable or resulted in a loss, the FX trader would tell the Settlements Section head that the deal was made. They would then have the contract clerk complete one of the two set-aside contracts, and the deal would be recorded between that FX unit and the other bank. Settlement would be made between the two institutions as when appropriate, depending on whether there was a profit or loss to the institution where the fraud scheme was set in place.

The Settlements Section head in this situation became a "foozler." By breaching the control procedures, she enabled a fraud to be perpetrated although she did not know of it or benefit from it.

NOTES

1. This section has been adapted from Peter F. Drucker, "New Templates for Today's Organizations," *Harvard Business Review* 52, no. 1 (January–February 1971), pp. 45–51.

2. Eugene Carlson, "Business of Background Checking Comes to the Fore—Despite Legal Constraints and Criticism, Screening Firms Thrive, Expand," *The Wall Street Journal,* August 31, 1993, p. B2. Reprinted by permission of The Wall Street Journal, © 1993 Dow Jones & Company, Inc. All Right Reserved Worldwide.

3. Treadway Commission, Committee of Sponsoring Organizations, *Internal Control—Integrated Framework* (Treadway Commission, 1992), p. 1.

4. Ibid.

5. Ibid., p. 2.

6. Ibid.

7. Ibid.

8. Ibid.

9. Ibid., pp. 2–3.

10. Ibid., p. 3.

11. Ibid.

12. Ibid.

13. Ibid.

14. Ibid.

15. From *Foozles & Frauds*, by Harold F. Russell, Copyright © 1977 by The Institute of Internal Auditors, Inc., 249 Maitland Avenue, Altamonte Springs, Florida 32701 U.S.A. Reprinted with permission.

16. Ibid., p. 3.

CHAPTER 14

CRIMINOLOGY

The antidote for crime should be administered in childhood, by the parents. The problem is not fundamentally that of the improper child so much as it is that of the improper home.

John W. Hill

INTRODUCTION

It is important for the forensic accountant to understand the factors that may impact on individuals, resulting in their becoming fraud perpetrators. This is important when one accepts the general principles that one out of every four persons will potentially steal every opportunity they get and two out of every four persons will potentially steal whenever they think they can get away with it, leaving one out of four persons able to resist all normal temptations and opportunities to steal.

For forensic accountants to effectively cope with fraud, they must recognize that, in general perspective, fraud is a crime. Therefore, fraud perpetrators are criminals.

With that as a foundation, it is necessary for us to understand the theories of crime that will help us answer such questions as

1. *Why* do people commit fraud?
2. *How* can fraud be reduced or prevented?
3. *What* happens to people who have been found to have committed a fraud?

OFFICIAL CRIME STATISTICS

Currently, the FBI compiles statistics in the Uniform Crime Report (UCR) that they collect from over 15,000 police departments. They track crime in two categories:

1. Part I: This includes murder, manslaughter, forcible rape, robbery, aggravated assault, burglary, larceny, arson, and auto theft.

2. Part II: This includes all other criminal offenses except traffic tickets.

In addition to statistics on the various offenses, the UCR provides information on arrestees and on police assaults. This information includes all known offenses, regardless of whether they have been resolved. The data are classified as

1. Crimes reported and arrests made.
2. Calculation of the percentage change of the crime categories from year to year.
3. Computation of the crime rates per 100,000 people.

The National Crime Survey (NCS) consists of a statistical study of 60,000 households and 136,000 individuals. Based on the findings of this survey, it is estimated that only about 45 percent of violent crimes, 24 percent of thefts, and 38 percent of household crimes are brought to the attention of the police. The survey does not accurately measure the extent of fraud and embezzlement.

A CRIME PERSPECTIVE

Computer Fraud

None of the statistics developed on criminal activity up to now provides much comfort regarding the level of computer fraud. It is now estimated that as little as 1 percent and no more than 15 percent of such fraud is being discovered. Of this, only one out of five discovered frauds is reported to law-enforcement agencies, and most of that is for federal interest computers. This is particularly meaningful in light of the fact that computer fraud is projected by the year 2010 to be the largest dollar area of fraud, including both white-collar crime and fraud by outsiders.

Crime Trends

Some 12 to 14 million crimes are being reported annually. Some interesting facts to consider: The majority of traditional criminal activities, as well as the victims involved, are between the ages of 18 and 25 years old. Crime in those areas seems to increase or decrease in nearly direct relationships to the size of this population segment to the total population.

On the other hand, white-collar crime has traditionally been committed by older individuals. As the population ages overall, it can be projected that crimes of this type will increase.

Based on the statistics, crime peaked in 1981. It dipped slightly and then started up again. In 1987, the police reported more than 13 million crimes, near the all-time record to that point in time. Bad economic times, drug use, and school dropouts are considered to be factors resulting in crime increases.

Crime other than white-collar crime is normally more prevalent in the summer months. To my knowledge, there is nothing to indicate patterns of when white-collar crime may increase. In recent years, the southern states have led the country in both overall crime and violent crime. Rural areas have much lower rates of crime overall than do cities. It would seem that the larger the city, the higher the general rate of crime. Approximately 10 million people are arrested annually for all categories of crime except traffic violation. Violent crimes are much more likely to lead to an arrest. Unfortunately, this would indicate that white-collar crime is less likely to be reported to law-enforcement authorities and result in an arrest and/or prosecution.

Crime Patterns

The general perception is that proportionately the greatest amount of crime occurs within the lower classes. This perception is based on the premise that people on the bottom of the social scale have more need or incentive to commit crime to acquire goods and services that, under normal conditions, would be beyond their economic reach. The general belief is also that those living in poverty areas commit the most expressive crimes (e.g., rape and assault), on the premise they are expressing their rage at society. While the crime rates in poverty environments are higher than elsewhere, criminologists have not, as yet, come up with a definite link (e.g., between poverty and crime). They do, however, acknowledge that there appears to be a connection, but it is not a certainty. There are many other factors to consider.

Age and Crime

Young males commit the greatest proportion of traditional crimes. Youths, age 15 to 18, make up only approximately 6 percent of the population, yet they account for nearly 25 percent of the index crime arrests and some 15 percent of total arrests. The peak for property crime is near 16 years of age, while the peak for violent crime is near 18 years of age.

There are a number of theories as to why young males account for so much crime. Research indicates the rate drops as the subjects get older, because, as they mature, they develop a broader, longer-term view of life. Accordingly, they are less likely to seek immediate gratification and, as a result, become less likely to perpetrate crimes. Ironically, some white-collar crimes, and hacker-type computer fraud, may not decline but may, in fact, increase as the subjects get older.

Gender and Crime

Males between 18 and 25 commit roughly 10 times as much crime as do women in the same age group. The statistics indicate women account for 25 percent of the arrests for property crime and only 10 percent of the arrests for violent crime. There are some theories indicating that as women progress economically, they will account for an increasing percentage of total crime, and, in my opinion, this will certainly be so in the area of white-collar crime. Others disagree with that theory on the basis that, at the current time, crime rates for women are remaining relatively stable as a percentage of all crime.

Race and Crime

Both the UCR and NCS agree that African-Americans commit a disportionate percentage of crime. While they make up approximately 12 percent of the population, they commit 46 percent of the violent crime and about 30 percent of property crime. Most theories explain this phenomenon on economic depravation, social disorganization, subculture adaptions, discrimination, and racism. Another theory is that they have an inability to identify with white society, white leaders, and institutional achievements.

Career Criminals

Researchers have found that criminal offenders can be broken into two groups: those who commit crime occasionally and chronic offenders. A study showed that 52 percent of the offenses studied were committed by 6 percent of the offenders. In violent crime, the same group accounted for between 70 and 80 percent of those crimes. Research has also shown that the more severe a sentence chronic offenders receive for wrongdoing, the greater the probability that they will repeat offenses.

Characteristics of Victims

Using the NCS, it can be found that the average victim has approximately the same characteristics as the criminal; that is, they are young, male, uneducated, and poor. The surprising conclusion from the study is that, regarding victims, as wealth increases, the likelihood of being a victim of violence or burglary decreases. On the other hand, as wealth increases, so does the likelihood of being a victim of personal thefts or larcenies.

Summary

It is interesting to note that crime patterns, as summarized herein, do not set out white-collar crime from other crime. Therefore, for our purposes, we have little to hold on that is meaningful to the effect and cause of white-collar crime.

CLASSICAL CRIMINOLOGY

Definitions

Criminology is "the scientific study of crime as a social phenomenon, of criminals, and of penal treatment."[1]

A criminal is "one who has committed a crime . . . A person who has been convicted of a crime."[2]

Overview of Concept

Criminology is rooted in a fundamental belief that man is a rational being. On that basis, it is assumed man can and will make rational choices. This concept consists of several basic elements:

1. Each person will have the option of choosing criminal versus noncriminal behavior.
2. Some persons will elect criminal behavior because that option may appear to be more attractive in the sense that it requires less work for a perceived payoff.
3. A specific person may choose not to commit criminal acts if he or she is controlled by fear of society's reaction to such actions.
4. The stronger the reactions against crime by society, the more likely it is to influence behavior.
5. There is no more effective crime-prevention device than punishment if it is strong enough to make crime unattractive.

The classic theory is that, under the proper set of circumstances, all persons have the potential to be criminals. They do not because of the expected sociological reactions to the wrongdoing and the fear of punishment.

Selected Principles of Criminology

General Deterrence
This refers to the inhibiting effect of sanctions on criminal activity. Partial deterrence does not intend for sanctions to eliminate a criminal act but to deter it. Absolute deterrence is to eliminate a particular criminal act.

Special Deterrance
This refers to the inhibiting effect that punishment of the convicted criminal is projected to have. The apparent failure of this approach in the United States is considered to be because punishment is inconsistent and there is a reluctance to deter criminals with punishments that may appear so brutal as to violate the constitutional provisions against cruel and unusual punishment.

Corporal Punishment
Corporal punishment is considered by some to be prohibited by the Constitution, yet the last whipping was in Delaware only decades ago. Some criminologists believe it is warranted in some form in today's U.S. society (e.g., electric shock, as quick and with no lasting effect).

Incapacitation
The intent of this concept is to seek out the career criminal, who are small in number yet who account for the greatest amount of crime and should be vigor-

ously sought out and incapacitated. To accomplish this, those supporting the indicated concept advocate the following measures to reduce crime:

1. Create uniform sentencing (Note: New federal sentencing guidelines were recently put into effect).
2. Make some incarceration mandatory for all but petty offenses.
3. When persons are incarcerated, make use of community-based programs for criminals to work and to receive treatment.
4. Adopt a format of progressively stiffer sentences for subsequent crimes committed by any specific individual.

The conclusions of researchers as to the value of incapacitation range from support to disagreement. One researcher contended that it would increase rather than decrease crime. Point #2, if adopted, would result in some incarceration for all but the most petty of white-collar crimes. Certainly the idea has potential merit.

Routine Activity Theory

This theory is based on the premise that both the motivation to commit crime and the supply of willing offenders are constant. The theory holds that as long as there are plentiful and valuable items to steal that are not directly guarded, thefts are likely to occur. Regarding violent crimes, the more the people put themselves in jeopardy, the more attacks can be projected to occur.

VARIOUS CRIMINOLOGY THEORIES

Biological Theories

Over the years, various qualified experts have come up with a number of theories to explain criminal behavior. Those who support the biological traits theories hold the view that criminal behavior is caused by physical characteristics rather than as a matter of choice.

The Born Criminal

One expert contended that physically retarded types constituted "born criminals." These were people destined by their deficient heredity to be criminals. In addition to them, he felt that more than half were either insane or criminaloids. This refers to individuals who by their physical and psychological constitutions were predisposed toward crime under certain circumstances.

Body Build Theories

Another expert advocated that three types of body build indicated the "born criminal" instincts: mesomorphs (e.g., those having well-developed muscles and an athletic appearance), endomorphs (e.g., heavy builds and slow moving), and ectomorphs (e.g., tall, thin, less social, and more intelligent). Most criminologists discount the notion of someone being able to discern any clues regarding tendencies towards criminal activity based on physical appearance.

Biocriminology

According to sociology, any type of crime can be explained as being a means of survival for people who perceive few other alternatives.

Some biologists and criminologists have contended that crime can, in part, be explained by diet and environmental conditions. It may surprise you to know that researchers have actually found a link between some vitamin deficiencies and crime.

Neurophysiology, the study of brain functions, has accounted for some criminal activity. Some brain functions have been linked to serious antisocial acts, including crime. They have accounted for periods of explosive rage and the related crimes (e.g., wife beating, child abuse, suicide, and homocide with no apparent motive).

Finally, researchers have actually tried to link crime with abnormal genetic coding. The typical person has 46 chromosomes, with males having an XY makeup and females an XX makeup. Some males have been found to have an extra X chromosome. The general opinion is that the extra chromosome has minimal impact on criminal activity.

Psychological Theories

This is the view, held by many psychologists, that early personality development and personality are the greatest single influence on criminality. Sigmund Freud believed that there was a three-part structure to the human personality:

> The *id*, present at birth, represents unconscious biological drives for sex, foods, and other life-sustaining activities. The *id* follows the pleasure principal—it requires gratification without the concern of others. The *ego* develops early in life and is the part of the personality which tempers the *id* through social learning conventions. The *ego* helps keep the *id* in check by learning that all pleasure demands cannot be immediately gratified. The *superego* develops when an individual assimilates community values. It is the moral aspect of people's personality, passing judgment on behavior. All three of these personality aspects operate in concert to produce behavior. Criminals are thought to have an unbalanced *id*.[3]

Social Learning Theories

Those supporting this theory think that people are not born with violent or criminal traits. These traits are thought to be learned through life experiences.

Psychobiological Theories

Supporters of these theories seek relationships among changes in brain cells, nervous system activities, and mental processes. They believe particular parts of the brain control many activities, including emotional behavior. We know that psychopaths are considered to be aggressive, dangerous, and antisocial persons who conduct themselves in an unknowing and callous manner. It is now believed that such mental condition is developed earlier in life due to inadequate nurturing.

Intelligence quotient (IQ) is thought to be a combination of genetics and environment. One published paper concluded that IQ has more to do with criminality than does race or social class. Would this explain hackers and white-collar crime involving computers? No research is known to help answer that question.

Personality is the patterns of behavior, including emotions, feelings, and thought, that distinguish one person from another. The influence of personality on crime is so far inconclusive.

Other researchers contend that crime may be a calculated choice based on the benefits of crime being instantaneous (e.g., sex, money, and so on) versus the benefits of noncrime being longer term (e.g., prestige, reputation, and happiness).

Social Process Theories

These theories hold that criminality is a function of individual socialization that people experience with other people, organizations, and institutions. Some of these theories are differential association, control theory, and strain theory.

Differential Association
The best known of all explanations to account for crime is developed by Edwin H. Sutherland in his book *Principles of Criminology*. It assures that criminal behavior is learned in interaction with other persons in a process of communication, particularly through participation within intimate personal groups. It suggests that the criminal learning process includes not only the techniques but also the shaping of motives, drives, rationalizations, and attitudes. It concludes that a person "becomes criminal because of an excess of definitions favorable to violation of the law over definitions unfavorable to violation of the law."[4]

Control Theory
This theory argues that the social system presses those with whom they are in contact into patterns of conformity. The theory rests on the thesis that when a person does not become attached to the controls of the social system, his chances of violating the law are increased.

Strain Theory
This theory stresses that individuals may become "strained" when they cannot achieve their financial goals and objectives through legal means. They then may elect to employ illegal means. The theory is deficient in that it does not explain why one person will turn to crime while another, in the same basic circumstances, will not.

WHITE-COLLAR AND ECONOMIC CRIME

It should be understood that white-collar and economic crime are not legal terms. They refer criminologically to a wide variety of offenses (e.g., antitrust violations, insider trading, and bribes; offering or accepting of same).

The common element of such improper behavior appears to be that they grow out of legitimate job-related efforts in the world of business, politics, and the professions. As a general rule, people do not seek jobs specifically with the intent to commit crime. The lawbreaking occurs when they are confronted with circumstances and conditions they feel cannot be resolved in other ways.

Economic crimes can be defined as "acts in violation of the criminal law and designed to bring financial rewards."[5] The data collected relative to such crimes indicate 30 million household or personal thefts occur annually. This is one for every eight or nine citizens.

White-collar crime is defined in *The Dictionary of Criminial Justice Data Terminology,* published by the Bureau of Justice Statistics, as

> Nonviolent crime for financial gain commited by means of deception by persons whose occupational status is enterpreneurial, professional, or semi-professional and utilizing their special occupational skills and opportunities; also non-violent crime for financial gain utilizing deception and committed by anyone having special technical and professional knowledge of business and government, irrespective of the person's occupation.

SUMMARY

To this point-in-time, there are many studies on various aspects of criminology trying to determine why some people perpetrate crimes while others do not. The unfortunate reality is that most of the studies in criminology deal with violent crime. While some forensic accountants have been involved in murders, most of us will never deal directly in situations involving violent crime. The remainder of the studies focus on economic crime. This, of course, is more meaningful to forensic accountants, who, in the course of their work, must identify Target + Motive + Access + Opportunity, which could result in an actual fraud or a potential fraud.

Unfortunately, to date, I have seen no really meaningful criminology study devoted exclusively or primarily to white-collar crime. Therefore, we must keep in mind that one out of every four persons will steal whenever they can and two out of four will steal whenever they think they can get away with it, leaving one out of four who are able to resist opportunities or access to steal. What is the explanation for white-collar crime? Quite honestly, I do not know! I do know that understanding selected theories of criminology, such as those selected for this text, helps me better understand people, from both a positive and negative perspective. This is helpful when involved in an actual or possible fraud situation.

NOTES

1. *Webster's Ninth New Collegiate Dictionary* (Springfield, MA: Merriam-Webster, 1986), p. 307.

2. Ibid.

3. Joseph T. Wells, *Fraud Examination: Investigative and Audit Procedures* (New York: Quorum Books, 1992), pp. 13–14. Reprinted with permission of Greenwood Publishing Group, Inc., Westport, CT. Copyright © 1992 by Greenwood Publishing Group, Inc.

4. Ibid., p. 16.

5. Ibid, p. 23

CHAPTER 15

LITIGATION SERVICES

The law does not generate justice, the law is nothing but a declaration and application of what is already just.

Pierre J. Proudhon

THE FORENSIC ACCOUNTANT IN LITIGATION SERVICES

The role of experts in the U.S. jurisprudence systems has been expanding rapidly, in recent decades. For many years, the courts allowed expert testimony only in those situations considered too complex for an average juror to understand. The Federal Rules of Evidence have changed the preception as to how expert witnesses can be used in the courts. Rule 702 covers "Testimony by Experts" and states:

> If scientific, technical, or other specialized knowledge will assist the trier of fact to understand the evidence or to determine a fact in issue, a witness qualified as an expert by knowledge, skill, experience, training, and education, may testify thereto in the form of opinion or otherwise.

One could place emphasis on the phrase "assist the trier of fact." The rules have also changed in that it is no longer required that the specific subject matter of the expert's testimony be beyond the ordinary person's understanding. The only real criterion is that such testimony help the trier of fact.

Rules 703 through 705 of the Federal Rules of Evidence also relate to testimony given by experts.

Rule 703. This allows an expert in reaching his opinion to rely somewhat on otherwise inadmissible facts or data. This is conditioned on the premise that they are "reasonably relied upon by experts in the particular field in forming opinions or inferences upon the subject." An example of this is where experts rely on hearsay evidence in certain circumstances. Ordinarily, hearsay evidence is not admissible in a court.

Rule 704. This permits experts to state opinions on the issue that is ultimately to be decided by the trier of fact. For example, an expert can state an opinion on issues such as liability or the amount of damages applicable in a given situation. The expert cannot give an opinion as to an alleged criminal's mental state.

Rule 705. This allows an expert witness to express an opinion without previously disclosing the facts or data on which such opinion is based. The rule only requires that such data be disclosed during cross-examination.

It can be seen from the preceding that the federal courts have now greatly liberalized the rules as to how an expert witness can be used. The result has been to encourage the use of experts in litigation.

ROLE OF THE FORENSIC ACCOUNTANT IN LITIGATION

Why a forensic accountant? For the same reason that lawyers would use certified public accountants; public accountants, in those states where this level of professional is licensed; or trained financial/accounting professionals with training and/or experiences as business advisors. In the rest of this text, they will be referred to as experts.

Lawyers need the best advice available when litigating, particularly in the areas of accounting, administration, cash management, compliance (e.g., with laws and regulations), computers—management and operations, credit management, data integrity and security, general management, internal controls, organization, planning (e.g., budgeting—capital and operational, and strategic planning), records retention (insurance), security, and taxes, unless they are trained in that specific area. The indicated experts can provide advice in any of the indicated areas as they do so routinely to companies with real problems. The indicated experts are qualified to provide advice on white-collar or economic crime in any of the stated areas of a business or governmental unit. Because those experts generally have sound quantitative skills, their services can be used in developing plans and performing reviews to develop evidence required in complex cases.

The indicated experts can be called upon to calculate the monetary loss incurred by the plaintiff (or cross-plaintiff) that has resulted from the defendant's (or cross-defendant's) legally wrongful acts. They are also qualified to address the business issues in cases involving legally wrongful acts. Where qualified, such experts can testify on subjects beyond their primary training, but only if they have suitable experience to do so. Some such areas are marketing, marketing research, sales, economics, quality assurance, and industrial engineering. The key is that the experts should never try to reach beyond their legitimate limits to avoid damage to their subsequent credibility.

Because of their expertise in planning and conducting data-gathering reviews, many lawyers will rely on the indicated experts to review large collections of documents, their objective being to identify key documents and extract, store, and analyze data relevant for discovery and trial.

The lawyer(s) representing a party involved in litigation will normally conduct the interview, select, and retain the expert(s) they will use on the case.

Such retention will normally occur after the complaint has been filed but, of course, before the trial. During the pretrial period, the expert will review documents, as requested; consult with the lawyer(s); and, if appropriate, conduct reviews of accounting and administrative procedures and records, evaluate internal controls, and evaluate operational practices. The expert(s) may assist in discovery primarily by educating the lawyer(s) as to the various types of business records that should be requested; drafting interrogatory and depository questions; indicating where it would be appropriate to conduct additional reviews to obtain needed evidentiary proof on any specific point/matter; and helping to identify key documents considered important to the case.

When data are developed through other than actual audit procedures (e.g., subpoena, warrant, and so on), the expert(s) can analyze them and evaluate their relevance. During discovery, the expert(s) may draw conclusions based on their analyses of the data and facts developed. If such opinions are considered by the lawyer(s) to be meaningful to the case, the expert(s) may be designated as expert witnesses and, in that capacity, may testify at trial as to their opinions.

When a lawyer designates an expert as an expert witness, the expert may have to appear and testify at a deposition, where the opposing party's lawyer will challenge and test their expertise to understand how they reached certain opinions, or, later, may testify as to those opinions in court, or both.

DESCRIPTION OF THE LEGAL PROCESS

Overview of a Lawsuit

The better the experts understand this structure, the more effectively they can fit their work into the process.

Legal Pleadings

Complaint.   This is the first pleading by the plaintiff in a civil case. It sets out the actions or inactions about which the plaintiff is complaining.

Demurrer.   This is where a defendant believes that the plaintiff has not fulfilled the legal standard of making a proper complaint, in which case he may file a demurrer. It disputes the sufficiency in law of the complaint or other pleading.

Answer.   This is the answer by the defendant to the complaint as filed by the plaintiff's complaint. As regards the allegations of the complaint, the defendant may agree with some and deny others. He or she may plead affirmative defenses that will preclude the plaintiff from prevailing, based on the facts pled in the complaint. The answer may also contain a cross-complaint in which the defendant will make claims on the plaintiff (cross-defendant). The plaintiff will have to answer and defend against the cross-complaint at trial. An answer is normally required to be filed within 20 to 30 days of receipt of the complaint, unless an extension is granted by the court.

Discovery

Discovery takes place in the time between the filing of the original pleadings and the trial. It is an attempt to determine the other parties' facts and theories. This is the period when the expert(s) is called on to perform most of his or her work. The expert(s) collects all available facts relative to the case, analyzes them, determines appropriate assumptions, and reaches his or her conclusions. Some of the legal tools used in discovery are discussed below.

Interrogatories

Interrogatories are written questions from one party requesting responses from the opposing party. The responses must be in writing and under oath. They are used to help obtain information from and about the opposing party when little is know about same. The expert's knowledge of business in a particular area or industry can be most helpful in formulating responses.

Requests for Production of Documents

Such request requires one party to provide documents it holds that are relevant to issues in the case. Such requests usually follow interrogatories and must be specific, or the opposing party will not produce the documents requested, even when it is clear what infomation is being sought. Therefore, any request needs to state exact titles of reports to force the requested documents to be produced.

The responding party does not usually copy the documents requested and send them to the requesting party. They will, instead, make the documents available at an agreed location, usually the responding party's business offices or his or her attorney's offices. The requesting party can then decide which documents are to be copied, at his or her expense.

The expert(s) can be asked to provide their expertise on accounting and financial reports to help the requesting party's attorney prepare the list requesting production of documents.

Requests for Admissions

A request for admission seeks the opposing party's verification of information as being factual. Such request must be relevant to the litigation. The fact of verifying the information as fact is usually adverse to the interest of the party making the admission.

Depositions

A deposition is merely the oral testimony of a witness questioned under oath by an attorney. It is transcribed by an official court reporter. That written record can be used in court. When an expert is employed, the opposition's attorney will usually take his deposition in order to better understand his background and his opinion relative to the case. In the opposite scenario, when the attorney for whom the expert is working prepares to ask questions of a person on the opposing side, including an expert they have engaged, the expert can assist, particularly in developing questions on the accounting or financial aspects of the case.

Subpoenas

These documents command a person to appear in court. A subpoena ad testificandum requires a person to both appear and testify as a witness. A subpoena duces tecum requires a person to produce documents in court that are then designated as evidence.

A subpoena is frequently the only method of obtaining information from third parties not related to the litigation. Any recipient of a subpoena who refuses to cooperate can be found in contempt of court and jailed. If a subpoena is objected to, a hearing on the relevance and propriety of materials demanded would be required.

The Trial

The following comments deal with various stages of the trial:

1. Opening statements.
2. Presentation of the plaintiff's case.
3. Direct examination.
4. Cross examination.
5. Redirect examination.
6. Presentation of the defendant's case.
7. Plaintiff's rebuttal case.
8. Defendant's surrebuttal case.
9. Closing arguements.
10. Post-trial briefs and findings of fact.
11. Verdict.

The verdict is the decision rendered by a jury or a judge in a bench trial. The verdict may be either general or special. In a general verdict, the decision is for either the plaintiff or defendant on all issues generally. In special verdicts, the jury decides only the facts of the case. The judge makes the decisions of the applications of law. The special verdict comes about when the jury is asked to make separate decisions as to different issues in the case. The normal routine is for this to be done through interrogatories to the jury.

A judgment is the official decision of the court. It covers the rights and claims of the litigants as decided by the jury. If the verdict of the jury is not accepted by the judge, he can make a judgment notwithstanding the verdict. It is the decision of the judge if he is the trier of fact. When he makes his judgment, the judge will often state the reasons for his decision as well as his understanding of the application of the relevant law. A directed verdict may be requested by the defendant at the close of the plaintiff's case when it is deemed that the plaintiff has not proven his case factually or as a matter of law.

In a jury trial, the jury decides the case and will render its verdict. Before such verdict is accepted by the court, the losing party may request, or, in some cases, the judge may volunteer, a decision that is contrary to the verdict that has been rendered by the jury. By not accepting the verdict of the jury and rendering an opposite decision, the judge renders what is known as a judgment non obstante verdicto (JNOV).

Appeal

The losing party in a trial who does not feel that the verdict was correct can appeal to a superior court to reverse the decision. It should be understood that the appeals court is not the forum for a new trial. What happens is that the appeals court will review the record of the original trial and determine if there was any legal error in the reasoning or record of the lower court. Since this is a defined legal process, it is geared to analysis of the law rather than the facts. As a result, the expert(s) can seldom make any contribution to assist the lawyer with whom he or she is working.

TYPICAL ROLES FOR THE FORENSIC ACCOUNTANT

Expert Witness

A lawyer would engage a forensic accountant to render an expert opinion at trial. Such expert opinion would usually relate to those areas of expertise of the forensic accountant. The intent is for the trier of fact to rely on the testimony of the expert witness as to any point or fact about which there is comment. If such reliance is accomplished, the trier of fact will base his final verdict in part on such testimony. It is not uncommon for the plaintiff and defendant to both have experts working on their side. Then the trier of fact must determine which one is more effective in presenting the points or facts they covered in their testimony.

Consultant

The expert engaged as a consultant is hired for the specific purpose of advising the attorney on the facts, issues, and strategy of the case. The expert is not engaged to testify at trial or to render an expert opinion. Typically, the work of the expert will generally be protected by the attorney work-product privilege, which simply means that the work is not discoverable by the opposing party. Both the plaintiff and defense may engage experts for the indicated purposes. In certain complicated accounting cases, the court (i.e., the judge) may also engage a consultant to clarify the information presented by the opposing sides.

Trier of Fact

The expert may be asked to decide certain facts in a dispute. The role is often described as one of a "special master." The appointment may be by the court or by agreement of the opposing parties. Under the "special master" concept, the expert will function as the judge and jury.

SERVICES TYPICALLY PERFORMED
BY FORENSIC ACCOUNTANT

Discovery Assistance

Since business seems to run on documents, business litigation will often depend on documents to prove or disprove an issue at trial. A qualified forensic accountant who understands the business environment involved can provide great assistant to the lawyer for whom he or she is working by identifying key documents for the matter being litigated.

Proof of Business Facts

Any position taken at trial must be supported by evidence dealing with the related facts. Usually, such information will be obtained from the business records of the companies involved. This information can be supplemented by data from industry and market sources.

Computation of Damages

Such calculation is a common task performed by the experts involved in commercial litigation. There are a number of types of damages (e.g., losses, lost profits) and methods to compute them.

Development of Strategy

Litigation consultants can suggest approaches to the business issues in the case. Most attorneys look to the expert to provide them guidance on how to approach a given accounting or financial problem.

GAAP/GAAS Rules and Compliance

Only CPAs are qualified to render opinions as to generally accepted accounting principles (GAAP) and generally accepted auditing standards (GAAS). Issues of this type arise when the accuracy of financial statements is questioned.

GAAP and GAAS are often factors when an accounting firm is being sued for violating them.

CONFLICT OF INTEREST

The expert must carefully investigate any and all possible conflicts of interest before accepting a litigation engagement. Prior relationships and current relationships with an opposing party are the highest risk concerns in conflicts of interest.

CHAPTER 16

WHERE IS FORENSIC ACCOUNTING GOING FROM HERE?

The future is not in the hands of fate but in ours.

Jules Jusserand

PERSPECTIVE

Forensic accounting is a profession that has, in recent years, gained broad acceptance by the legal profession as a meaningful and useful tool. As more and more lawyers become aware of the utility of this tool, it can be projected that the profession will grow. The number of qualified practitioners will have to increase substantially to keep up with the projected growth in the demands of the profession.

In recent years, some of the larger accounting firms have become quite active in setting up litigation support teams. In addition, some former partners and principals of those firms who are now in consulting practice for themselves have become active in soliciting business relative to litigation support and/or special reviews that, it can be anticipated, may at some future time result in the matter going to trial (e.g., bankruptcy actions, defaults on loans with foreclosure on properties required, and so on). It can be projected that other firms in both public accounting and independent consulting will begin offering these types of services, especially where the practitioner has some specific skill area (e.g., real estate fraud—land flips, straw men, and so on; inventory fraud—relative to violations of the False Claims Act and/or Anti-Kickback Act; and so on).

It is known that, in Canada, forensic accountants have been engaged to determine motives and evaluate books of account searching for possible wrong-doings in murder investigations. They are looking for the motive of a crime. We also know that, in both Canada and the United States, the forensic accountant is being used by lawyers, representing either the prosecution or defense, and, in some instances, by the court itself in an ever-increasing range of legal actions, both criminal and civil.

It should be understood that providing litigation support is not the exclusive area of practice of CPAs. There are some states that permit someone to sit for the CPA examination without experience. If they pass the exam, they can call themselves CPAs, although they have limited or no experience in auditing. Having not met the work requirements, they have not had the certificate issued to them. Further, in most firms, a CPA with five years of public accounting experience has probably not worked on more than five fraud cases, most of them involving stealing cash or inventory of nominal amount, and three complex accounting situations (e.g., bankruptcy, quasi-reorganization, taking title to properties by deed in lieu of foreclosure, and so on). Therefore, in my opinion, they do not qualify as forensic accountants.

There are other professionals who can match their experience in fraud reviews or complex accounting situations. Consider:

1. On average, certified fraud examiners (CFEs) have worked on over 50 fraud cases, some many more than that.
2. Certified internal auditors (CIAs) have probably worked on a broader range of simple frauds (e.g., cash and inventory) and probably have been involved in several larger frauds (e.g., purchasing, accounts payable, expense reporting, and so on).
3. Certified management accountants (CMAs) will probably have broad experience in complex accounting situations.
4. Computer-related certifications whose practitioners may be of value in litigation support involving those areas:
   a. Certified information systems auditor (CISA).
   b. Certificate in computer programming (CCP).
   c. Certified systems professional (CSP).

Therefore, the attorney looking for someone to provide litigation support or management looking for someone to deal with internal fraud, risk assessment, and/or internal control evaluation should seek out the person(s) with the specific skills relative to some general or specific scenario.

CONCLUSION

The only thing certain is that the profession of forensic accounting will grow, possibly more rapidly in the coming decade than in the immediate past decade. Lawyers and management will find a level of comfort and confidence with persons having recognized skills and experience in forensic accounting than with other persons without such credentials. As the profession gains broader recognition, this differential in acceptance and credibility can be expected to increase.

> No public man can be a little crooked. There is no such thing as a no-man's land between honesty and dishonesty.
>
> *Herbert Hoover*

INDEX

Other books of interest to you from Irwin Professional Publishing . . .

INNOVATIVE BILLING AND COLLECTION METHODS THAT WORK

Charles B. Larson

Shows accountants how to design and implement a streamlined billing and collection plan that will reduce the probability of late payments, increase revenue flow, and cut back on bureaucracy and paperwork.
ISBN: 1-55623-032-X

EVENT-DRIVEN BUSINESS SOLUTIONS

Today's Revolution in Business and Information Technology

Eric L. Denna, David P. Andros, J. Owen Cherrington, and Anita Sawyer Hollander

Revolutionizes traditional thinking about business functions, by encouraging companies to focus less on processes, and more on defining the impact of every business event.
ISBN: 1-55623-942-4

ACCOUNTING

In International Perspective

Gerhard G. Mueller, Helen Gernon, and Gary Meek

A nontechnical approach of international accounting covering key issues such as similarities and differences in accounting systems around the world, managerial accounting, and optimal forms of reporting.
ISBN: 0-7863-0007-8

MANAGING STRATEGIC AND CAPITAL INVESTMENT DECISIONS

Going Beyond the Numbers to Improve Decision Making

Thomas Klammer

Contains a collection of the ideas and experiences of the members of the work group and is based on several research projects sponsored by the CMS Program as well as providing a summary of the major findings of these research studies.
ISBN: 0-7863-0112-0

IMPLEMENTING ACTIVITY-BASED COST MANAGEMENT
Moving From Analysis to Action

Robert S. Kaplan and Robin Cooper

This research study documents key implementation issues and results, based on real-life.

ISBN: 0-86641-206-9

Available at fine bookstores and libraries everywhere.